Principles and Parameters
of Syntactic Saturation

OXFORD STUDIES IN COMPARATIVE SYNTAX
Richard Kayne, General Editor

Principles and Parameters of Syntactic Saturation
Gert Webelhuth

PRINCIPLES AND PARAMETERS OF SYNTACTIC SATURATION

Gert Webelhuth

New York   Oxford
OXFORD UNIVERSITY PRESS
1992

Oxford University Press

Oxford   New York   Toronto
Delhi   Bombay   Calcutta   Madras   Karachi
Kuala Lumpur   Singapore   Hong Kong   Tokyo
Nairobi   Dar es Salaam   Cape Town
Melbourne   Auckland

and associated companies in
Berlin   Ibadan

Published by Oxford University Press, Inc.
200 Madison Avenue, New York, New York 10016

Oxford is a registered trademark of Oxford University Press

Library of Congress Cataloging-in-Publication Data
Webelhuth, Gert.
Principles and parameters of syntactic saturation /
Gert Webelhuth.
p.   cm. — (Oxford studies in comparative syntax)
Revision of the author's thesis (Ph.D.)
—University of Massachusetts at Amherst, 1989.
Includes bibliographical references and index.
ISBN 0-19-507040-2.
—ISBN 0-19-507041-0 (pbk.)
1. Grammar, Comparative and general—Syntax.
2. Language and languages—Variation.
3. Generative grammar.   4. Germanic languages—Syntax.
I. Title.   II. Series.
P291.W42   1992   415—dc20   91-2617

2 4 6 8 9 7 5 3 1

Printed in the United States of America
on acid-free paper

*This book is dedicated to
my mother,
Ria Webelhuth,
and the memory of my father,
Hans Webelhuth,
for love, encouragement, and support
all these years*

Acknowledgments

This book is a revised version of my 1989 Ph.D. dissertation accepted by the University of Massachusetts at Amherst. I would like to thank Richie Kayne, the editor of the series, and the professionals at Oxford University Press for their kind and encouraging support in publishing the book; my thanks also extend to an anonymous reviewer for helpful comments and to Randy Hendrick with the whole Department of Linguistics at the University of North Carolina at Chapel Hill for providing me with the time and opportunity to prepare the revised draft. Peter Johnson did a wonderful job helping me proofread the book. Finally, I gratefully acknowledge a personal communication from Anders Holmberg which led to a significant revision of Chapter 3 below.

I felt that the acknowledgments from the dissertation would lose their freshness and originality if I tried to rewrite them. Even today, they forcefully bring back the relief I sensed when that chapter of my life was completed. Moreover, friends have told me that they authentically mirror me, good and bad. In honor of all those friends, here they are again, unchanged.

I have been looking forward to writing these acknowledgments for several years. There does not seem to be any other opportunity in academia to formally thank the people to whom one owes so much academically and personally. So I am going to enjoy this.

There are four people who have shaped my linguistic thinking most: Emmon Bach, Hans den Besten, Noam Chomsky, and Richard Kayne.

Emmon was the best possible dissertation chair I could have imagined. His own work on Categorial Grammars was an important inspiration, although, in his typical modesty, he never tried to impress his views on me with anything but the sheer force of his insights. Emmon was also always there when needed privately, and his experience allowed him to put up with canceled

viii ACKNOWLEDGMENTS

appointments, appointments that should have been canceled, and times when I simply didn't want any more. Thank you!

Few people have had the privilege to be introduced to Germanic syntax by Hans den Besten. The wealth of facts that he commands, the thoroughness of his approach, and his skepticism towards overly simple solutions will always be an unreachable ideal for me. Thanks also for the invitation to a great semester at the University of Amsterdam, and for your friendship.

Noam Chomsky's influence can be felt on every page that follows, although only indirectly after I kept refusing to show him my uncompleted work when a first version of my theory of free word order was discarded with lousy arguments. At the outset of this project I was skeptical about some parts of the GB-system, but I admit without shame that the more deeply I got entrenched into Germanic syntax, the more I became attracted to Chomsky's solutions. I consider it an honor to perhaps contribute one little piece to the gigantic intellectual mosaic this man has built so far.

Richard Kayne is an intellectual giant for me as well. In all these years I have not seen this "data machine" make one single descriptive mistake. It sometimes got to the point that I had trouble keeping up with his knowledge of the German facts. What impressed me most, however, was Richie's unshakable conceptual optimism. More than once I've heard him say "Don't give up so easily!" and "You can do better than that!" And he was right. With respect to whatever I have worked on, I have found that there is an explanation for almost everything. And if there is no explanation, then there is at least an explanation for why there is none.

Next I would like to thank the members of my committee. Jim Cathey strongly influenced the exposition and kept me honest with respect to Scandinavian. Roger Higgins contributed his legendary encyclopedic knowledge about language(s) and theories; he was always a safe bet when a datum or a reference was needed. Angelika Kratzer has been a witness to my career since my second semester as an undergraduate in Berlin. She advised me to go to Amherst, and has held her hand over me during my graduate years. Finally, David Pesetsky has helped in every domain. From buying a computer, giving job talks, and living that mysterious American way of life, to understanding the NIC and reading the appendix to OB. David is a perfect teacher, and the hours he put into advising us graduate students were far more than one could ask for.

My gratitude extends to the other faculty members of U Mass. I have gained from every course, from every conversation I had. It is especially Barbara Partee's influence that makes U Mass one of the leading research institutes in the field, leading also in humanness. Thanks for everything, Barbara; thanks for everything, Emmon and Barbara!

Back in Germany, where it all began, I owe almost everything to Gisa Rauh. Looking back, I realize how shamelessly I have exploited her commitment to the training of her students. There were more times than I can count when I didn't know which direction to go, and a phone call to Gisa provided me with exactly the right piece of advice. Without her expertise and support not only would this dissertation not exist, but I would not have been the author of anything. Thank you so much!

So many friends from the European GLOW community have helped. I received an intensive course in German syntax from Thilo Tappe on a 25-hour train ride to Venice two years ago. Günther Grewendorf and Sascha Felix have always put in a good word for me. Hero Janssen, Martin Prinzhorn, and Wolfgang Sternefeld are special friends whose work, comradeship, and unselfish cooperation I have appreciated and cannot but admire.

Hubert Haider is to be credited alone for leading Generative German syntax out of the malaise of the 1970s. He commanded the new theory, has an infallible sense for theoretically important data, and taught both to us youngsters. Discussing syntax with him over a glass of wine was a lecture in both modesty and good will. Although he wouldn't want it, for me he remains someone to look up to.

I would like to take this opportunity to send greetings to my consultants, who were in fact more than that. Hans den Besten, Christer Platzack, Kirsti Koch Christensen, Lars Hellan, Sten Vikner, Michael Herslund, and Kjartan Ottosson each spent hours not just giving me data and judgments but also their expertise built on many years of research and experience. A thousand thanks also for putting me up in Holland and Scandinavia, or for making the trips financially possible in the first place. Other informants were Sigridur Sigurjonsdottir, Arild Hestvik, and Fred Landman. A special hello goes to the native speakers at the switchboards of the Dutch, Norwegian, Danish, and Swedish embassies/consulates in Los Angeles and Washington, D.C., although they are not likely to ever read this. State-run institutions are good for something after all.

Thank you to Jan Koster for his teaching and encouragement; Joan Maling for the same and for allowing me to sit in on a seminar of hers on Germanic syntax at Brandeis; Thomas Gardner and Günther Grewendorf for always welcoming me at the Universities of Göttingen and Frankfurt; the Departments of Linguistics at Brandeis, Amsterdam, and MIT for letting me hang out for a semester; my students at UCLA and the University of Maryland who had to suffer through first drafts of my dissertation; Robert Stockwell, Robin Clark, Norbert Hornstein, and Amy Weinberg for the same and for strongly encouraging me to go ahead anyway; Alan Munn for doing a beautiful job in proofreading the dissertation and in printing the final copy; Lynne Ballard and Kathy Adamczyk for being the greatest secretaries in the world; all the members of the Department of Linguistics at the University of Maryland, especially Norbert Hornstein, Amy Weinberg, Alan Munn, and David Lebeaux, for doing all kinds of worldly things for me when I was preparing the final copy.

What would I have done without my fellow students and visitors in Berlin, Wuppertal, Amherst, Brandeis, Cambridge, and Amsterdam? Thank you to Janet Banger, Jim Blevins, Steve Berman, John Boyd, Toni Borowsky, Liesbeth Koenen, Anja Koperberg, Dirk Laszig, David Lebeaux, Anne Lobeck, Roland Noske, Sylvie Robidoux, Bozena Rozwadowska and family, Jean Rutten, Roger Schwarzschild, Mauro Scorretti, Rik Smits, Ray Turner, Jill Turner, Anne Vainikka, and Sandro Zucchi.

A few stand out. Joyce McDonough, Virginia Brennan, Sabine Iatridou, and Karina Wilkinson have shared so much. They are true everyday friends without whom I could not have existed. They all have a place in my heart.

As important is my friendship with Fred Landman. I will always remember our litany on those scorching summer afternoons in Massachusetts when we would go for French fries with me cursing how "[expletive] hot" it was and him saying that it was great. I paid too much attention to Fred's views on linguistics to remember whether we finally decided that McDonald's ketchup was better than Burger King's or vice versa. Be that as it may, we always agreed that it was high time for another cigarette. Thanks so much, Fred, both academically and personally!

Scott Myers should have been mentioned at the beginning among the people who have shaped my thinking, but I thought he would prefer to have his place here. One of the finest linguists I know, Scott is the one person who I have continually talked linguistics to for several years. Many hundreds of hours. Although he works in a different area, his expertise has been invaluable to me. I tested theories, job talks, and dissertation chapters on him, and more often than not sat up the whole night rewriting everything on his advice. Somehow he knows better than me what I am trying to say, and his good linguistic taste is simply out of this world. But it doesn't stop there. Scott has also been looking after me as a personal friend which, I realize, is not exactly an enviable task. Thank you, Scott, for what I do not have the verbal power to express.

From the first minute we met in Amherst, Gautam and Mahasweta Sengupta have been the most loyal friends I have ever had. For them, I was part of the family, and indeed, if it had not been for them, I doubt that I would have come through. Separated from my own nephews by geographical distance, I enjoyed seeing their son Gaurab grow up as much as they did. For me as a non-believer they were the equivalent of angels, and a list of what I owe to them would easily outgrow these acknowledgments.

Another "angel" came into my life in Los Angeles. Barbara Levergood has made my life richer than it has ever been through her love and happiness. She was the person I had been waiting for, and she told me so right away. Everything else I'll tell her in private.

Last but not least, there is my family. They are in the worst position, since they always only see the ugly side of what I do, the financial problems, jet lags, and long absences from home. This dissertation is as much theirs as it is mine. Thank you so much to my sister Ellen and her husband Volker, to my brother Wolfgang, his wife Gabi, and their sons Niko, Magnus, and Tim. Thank you above all to my parents Ria and Hans Webelhuth for the loving protection and life-long support that has made my education possible.

Chapel Hill   G. W.
April 1991

[Fall 1991]

Contents

Selected List of Definitions, Diagrams, and Overview Tables

Principles and Parameters
of Syntactic Saturation

Introduction

One of the challenges in writing a book that makes a detailed comparison of certain areas in seven different languages is the efficient organization of the wealth of empirical data. There is every reason to believe that all readers except those most interested in the subject would put a book aside that did not present the data in portions manageable to someone with an average attention span. Therefore I have made every effort to bring the material presented below into a reader-friendly format. I was helped in this endeavor by the supportive comments and suggestions of several readers and reviewers of pre-final drafts.

With the goal in mind to allow the reader to spend time on *evaluating* the data and the arguments rather than wasting it on *understanding* them in the first place, I followed a number of conventions throughout the book that I believe have made its exposition clearer and more consistent than it would otherwise have been.

All linguistic paradigms involving the Germanic languages will be given in a fixed form concerning the order of example sentences. The first sentence is always from German, the final one from English. Second, each example sentence is prefixed with an abbreviation identifying the language that it is taken from. The prefix is part of the numbering system. For instance, if the forty-third example sentence in some chapter is from Danish, then the example is numbered (43Da). Below I give all the abbreviations used for this purpose in the order in which all example sentences of a paradigm appear.

(1)　G = German
　　Du = Dutch

$$S = \text{Swedish}$$
$$Da = \text{Danish}$$
$$N = \text{Norwegian}$$
$$I = \text{Icelandic}$$
$$E = \text{English}$$

Sometimes I have had occasion to bring other languages into play. I then extend the coding system in obvious ways to keep the languages apart.

Third, each example sentence will be glossed, even if it has appeared earlier. To save space, translations will not always be added, however, since the reader will be able to infer the meaning of the non-English sentences from their glosses and the English sentence of the paradigm.

I have made a special effort, foremost in long chapters, to include summary tables displaying in one place the generalizations found in the preceding exposition. This should make the readers' first pass through the book much less confusing and, if used with the subject index, should also allow them to refer back to material already read in case that necessity arises.

Further, to cut the chapters into small sections with a particular theme, I have made judicious use of subsections.

Another problem one has to face in writing a book in linguistics today is formalism and notation. It seems to me that each obvious alternative has a number of advantages and disadvantages, and I have consequently wavered back and forth between them. Formalizing the book's content may make it more precise, which is certainly a property one would like a linguistic theory to have. Nevertheless, it is unfortunately the case that in formalizing a theory one not only gets those aspects of a general mathematical structure that one desires but also the undesirable ones, so that one has to deal with additional problems created by the choice of mathematical structures which may be completely independent of the leading ideas of the linguistic theory.

For these reasons I have tried to combine the desiderata of precision and readability. Except some adopted abbreviatory conventions of the field (e.g. the symbols representing the syntactic categories and relations), the book does not contain any formalism or notation that could obscure the content of its leading ideas. I believe that this will make these ideas much more easily accessible than an exposition where their core can only be obtained by peeling away those parts of the formalism that have to be added to make the formal theory consistent. The price for a formalism- and notation-free exposition is that the principles and generalizations now have to be stated in ordinary English; since we strive to keep the content of the book precise, even if not formal, this will at times lead to rather stilted statements. I trust that most readers will accept this in exchange for otherwise improved readability. Those not willing or able to make such a compromise may be referred to Chapters 2 and 7 of Webelhuth (1989) out of which this book developed; there an attempt is made to formalize some of the leading ideas and concepts contained herein, with all the detriments to readability that have been avoided in the chapters that we now finally turn to.   98812

1

A Restrictive Theory of the Concept "Possible Parameter of Natural Language"

1.1 The Tension between Descriptive and Explanatory Adequacy

Probably everybody who has had the opportunity to study a number of natural languages is struck by two apparently opposing features, how diverse they are on the one hand and how similar they are on the other. The following quotation from the nineteenth-century philosopher, linguist, and Prussian statesman, Wilhelm v. Humboldt is characteristic of this ambivalence:[1]

1. It is notoriously difficult to understand exactly, let alone to translate, Humboldt's writings. The reader should consider all translations as approximations. Here is the original:

> Wiewohl alle Sprachen im Ganzen ungefähr denselben Bau haben, und gleichen Gesetzen folgen, so giebt es doch schwerlich eine, die sich nicht noch durch irgend eine besondre Eigenthümlichkeit von den anderen unterschiede. ... Allein alle einzelne Sprachen finden sich zusammen, alle noch so entgegengesetzte Eigenthümlichkeiten vereinigen sich in dem Sprachvermögen des Menschen. Dieses Vermögen ist der Mittelpunkt des Sprachstudiums ... Wir haben daher darin ein Gebiet, das, neben der allgemeinen Gleichförmigkeit, innerhalb seiner Gränzen eine ganz unbestimmbare, und ewig unerschöpfliche Mannigfaltigkeit bewahrt. Doch auch dies Gebiet ist scharf begränzt einmal durch die Natur der Sprachen, als Werkzeuge, die aus einer bestimmten Zahl von Lauten bestehen, und nur eine bestimmte Anzahl von Verbindungen dieser zulassen; dann durch die Natur des Menschen, die Beschaffenheit seiner Organe, und den möglichen Umfang seiner Fähigkeit wahrzunehmen, zu denken, und zu empfinden; ferner durch die unabänderlichen Gesetze der allgemeinen Ideen. ... (v. Humboldt, 1904, Vol. IV, 243f)

Although as a whole all languages have approximately the same structure and follow the same principles, there is hardly one which doesn't differ from the others in some particular property. . . . Still, all individual languages, all peculiarities, however incompatible they may be, unite in the language faculty of mankind. This faculty forms the center of linguistic research. . . . We therefore have an area here which, apart from general uniformity, maintains within its boundaries a completely indeterminate and by far inexhaustible diversity. But also this area is strongly constrained, first of all by the nature of the languages, as tools which consist of a determinate number of sounds and which allow only a certain number of combinations of these; and also by man's nature, the structure of his organs and the possible extension of his capacity to perceive, to think and to feel; further, by the unchangeable laws of the general ideas. . . .

To discover those "same principles" that all languages follow, Humboldt proposed a research program that often is viewed as marking the beginning of the science of general linguistics:[2]

A nearly complete comparative linguistic theory would study the different manners of realizing grammar and its form in the individual grammatical constructions. . . . then in every individual language within the context of all its structures. Finally, this twofold work should be used to design a survey of human language considered as something general, its limits, the necessity of its principles and postulates, and the boundaries of its variation.

In the second half of the twentieth century, Humboldt's program, having lain dormant for over a century, was revived by Noam Chomsky within the framework of Generative Grammar. Approaching language from the viewpoint of individual psychology,[3] he also arrived at the conclusion that languages are very similar and yet at the same time very different (cf. Chomsky 1965, 27f). In light of the remarkable homogeneity of natural language (e.g.

2. The translation is extremely free. Below is the original from v. Humboldt (1973, 21):

Dächte man sich das vergleichende Sprachstudium in einiger Vollendung, so müßte die verschiedene Art, wie die Grammatik und ihre Formen in den Sprachen genommen werden, an den einzelnen grammatischen Formen . . . , dann an den einzelnen Sprachen, in jeder im Zusammenhange erforscht, und endlich diese doppelte Arbeit dazu benutzt werden, einen Abriß der menschlichen Sprache, als ein Allgemeines gedacht, in ihrem Umfange, der Notwendigkeit ihrer Gesetze und Annahmen, und der Möglichkeit ihrer Zulassungen zu entwerfen.

3. Chomsky (1982a, 32) casts this approach into the following succinct formulation:

The study of language is guided by a number of fundamental questions, among them the following:

(1) a. What constitutes knowledge of a language?
   b. How does such knowledge develop?
   c. How is such knowledge put to use?

Tomlin (1986) arrives at the result that in more than 90% of the world's languages the subject of the sentence precedes all objects in the basic word order), and the absence of any obvious plausible external cause for this uniformity, Chomsky (1965, 58) concludes that human language learners have to be strongly biased toward the linguistic structures they expect to encounter in their linguistic environment:

> A consideration of the character of the grammar that is acquired, the degenerate quality and narrowly limited extent of the available data, the striking uniformity of the resulting grammars, and their independence of intelligence, motivation and emotional state, over wide ranges of variation, leave little hope that much of the structure of the language can be learned by an organism initially uninformed as to its general character.

According to Chomsky, the simultaneous diversity and homogeneity of natural language is thus to be thought of as a reflection of the species-specific human language faculty, which, following an old tradition, he refers to as "Universal Grammar" (UG):

> The theory of UG must meet two obvious conditions. On the one hand, it must be compatible with the diversity of existing (indeed, possible) grammars. At the same time, UG must be sufficiently constrained and restrictive in the options it permits, so as to account for the fact that each of these grammars develops in the mind on the basis of quite limited evidence. (Chomsky 1981, 3)

Within recent years a particularly successful conception of Universal Grammar, or as Humboldt called it "the genetic predisposition for language,"[4] has emerged, the "Principles and Parameters" framework, which arose out of earlier work of Chomsky and others on the properties of language-particular grammars. Unlike these earlier proposals, the Principles and Parameters model denies that all linguistic rules for a language have to be learned. Rather, it offers the postulate that there are universal principles of grammar that are, without exception, invariant across languages. The content and the operation of these principles of grammar ensure the similarity of all natural languages. The principles of UG are supported by a set of parameters (options) provided by UG along a certain dimension, from which individual grammars may select, possibly subject to relative conditions of accessibility and markedness. In addition to language-particular options of parameter setting, it is assumed that each individual grammar contains a specific lexicon with a format for lexical rules, both again subject to universally defined well-formedness conditions. All language-particular options—the choice of parameter values and the composition of lexical entries—are thought to be fixable by the language

---

4. "die Naturanalage zur Sprache," (cf. v. Humboldt, 1973, 200).

learners only on the basis of positive evidence from their primary data. The sum of the universal principles, the fixed parameters, and the internalized lexicon are referred to as the *core grammar* of the natural language to which the learner has been exposed.

Beyond the issue of whether all rules of a grammar are learned, the Principles and Parameters approach to the analysis of linguistic form constitutes a major shift away from earlier conceptions of Generative Grammar in another respect. It opens the door to the possibility that the limitations on the complexity of natural language grammars can be explained in terms of the dense network of relationships that the universal principles of grammar impose on each well-formed phrase marker. Thus, rather than having an axiomatic status as part of a syntax of rules, these limitations may have no status at all in the grammar itself but rather are a consequence of the observation that a grammar whose phrase markers satisfy all the substantive constraints imposed by the principles cannot exceed a certain level of complexity.

This prospect would mark significant progress in our understanding of natural language, given that the mentioned limitations would then simply be another symptom of the fundamental properties of grammar that collectively leave their unmistakable mark on each construction of natural language; they would not have to be stated as irreducible properties of natural language (in addition to the principles capturing the significant generalizations) with no import for the substantive relations holding between the constituents in a phrase marker.

It is the goal of the present work to take some small steps in this direction, i.e. to detect a number of fundamental principles operative in the constructions of seven modern Germanic languages whose interaction entails strong limitations on the complexity of natural language grammars. If successful, the theory of grammar can be relieved of some or all of the independently stated limitations on rules that are known to grossly underdetermine the characteristic form of natural language outside of the still not precisely understood domain of grammatical complexity.

The approach to principles and parameters developed in this book breaks new ground in that it tries to derive the range of parametrization in part from the principles of grammar themselves. In other words, the *principles* of Universal Grammar are shown to affect not only the well-formedness of phrase-structure configurations but also the well-formedness of "possible parameters of natural language." More specifically, I argue that *there are general locality conditions on parameters analogous to the locality conditions on PS processes postulated by Ross* (1967), i.e. that the syntactic module of Universal Grammar can be stated in such a way that certain principles cannot be parametrized at all, and that certain statements cannot count as parameter values for those principles that are open to parametrization.

In this chapter I first present the major proposal of the book and then show how it can be arrived at and incorporated into a Principles and Parameters approach of the type described in Chomsky (1981).

Besides grammatical theory, our assumptions originate in the following ideas of the German philosopher and mathematician Gottlob Frege. In "Function and Concept" Frege writes:

> Statements . . . can be imagined to be split up into two parts; one complete in itself, and the other one in need of supplementation, or "unsaturated." Thus, e.g., we split up the sentence
>
> "Caesar conquered Gaul"
>
> into "Caesar" and "conquered Gaul." The second part is "unsaturated"—it contains an empty place; only when this place is filled up with a proper name, or with an expression that replaces a proper name, does a complete sense appear. Here too I give the name "function" to what is meant by this "unsaturated" part. In this case the argument is Caesar. (Frege 1984, 146f)

And the same idea about saturation occurs again in the following passage from "Concept and Object":

> . . . not all the parts of a thought can be complete; at least one must be "unsaturated," or predicative; otherwise they would not hold together. For example, the sense of the phrase "the number 2" does not hold together with that of the expression "the concept *prime number*" without a link. We apply such a link in the sentence "the number 2 falls under the concept *prime number*"; it is contained in the words "falls under," which need to be completed in two ways—by a subject and an accusative; and only because their sense is thus "unsaturated" are they capable of serving as a link. Only when they have been supplemented in this twofold respect do we get a complete sense, a thought. (Frege 1984, 193)

I will adopt Frege's idea that we conceptualize what we talk about in terms of objects and properties of objects or relations between them. Furthermore, I will assume with the work on categorial grammars that Universal Grammar grammaticalizes this division into objects and properties/relations by making available substantive universals that define each linguistic expression either as syntactically saturated or unsaturated. Syntactically unsaturated expressions would be all those that are marked for combining with a complement, but also all specifiers and modifiers, i.e. those elements marked for syntactically combining with a specifiable or modifiable expression. Avoiding all formalism, the informal statements in 1 would mark unsaturated expressions.

(1) a. [Category of Complement is YP]
    b. [Category of Specifiee is Y′]
    c. [Category of Modifiee is YP]

1a marks a head that combines with an expression of category YP in the complementation relation; 1b and 1c mark specifiers and modifiers, respectively.

Saturated expressions can also be represented in this system, namely as units that do not have any of the statements in 1 as part of their grammatical properties.

Next, we begin to impose strong conditions on the phrase-structural realization of the relations mentioned in 1, i.e. complementation, specification, and modification. Let us refer to these relations as the "forms" or "modes of saturation," because they each combine one incomplete expression with a constituent that saturates it. Then I will defend the claim made in 2.

(2) *The Saturation Condition, Part I*
   Universal Grammar allows one and only one phrase-structural realization of each of the modes of saturation. The incomplete expression and its saturator form a binary constituent.

The specific form that the realization of each grammatical relation takes is developed later in this chapter. In conjunction with the claim that every expression of natural language has to be either complete or incomplete, the Saturation Condition strongly limits the formal options of a sentence in any natural language. It predicts that each word is marked for zero or more of the features in 1, and that its role in phrase structure is completely determined by this property and the conditions on the realization of the grammatical relation it can enter. In this respect our theory differs from all other currently debated theories of syntax. Most versions of the Principles and Parameters approach, for instance, allow a complementation relation to be realized differently in configurational and nonconfigurational languages (cf. Chomsky 1981, Hale 1983).[5] The same is true for phrase-structure grammars and categorial grammar, where complementation is not associated with exactly one phrase-structural output, but rather is subject to language-particular phrase-structure rules (cf. Gazdar et al. 1985, Pollard/Sag 1987) or combination operations (cf. Bach 1988).

Apart from the binary branching requirement in 2, and the uniformity condition in 3, I try to defend an even stronger condition that cuts across all saturation phenomena.

---

5. This may be only partially true for the important proposals made in Kayne (1984). This theory is more closely related to ours, since it is the source of our binary branching requirement. As far as I am aware, however, Kayne's theory is relatively nonspecific concerning nonconfigurational languages, or whether there are universal requirements for the combination of a head and its complement that go beyond his binary branching condition. For some discussion cf. Kayne (1984, 228 fn 18).

(3) *The Saturation Condition, Part II*
    Every well-formedness condition on any mode of saturation makes
    reference only to the grammatical properties of the two expressions
    involved in the saturation process.

Part II of the Saturation Condition requires that every condition on the formation of a complex expression γ by combining two simpler expressions α
and β has to be a condition on α or β. Thus, to give an example, whether two
expressions can be projected to a phrase in the specification relation can only
depend on the feature structure of the two expressions themselves, not on the
feature structure of the newly created node or any node higher or lower in the
phrase marker than the two items to be combined.

In the remainder of this chapter I demonstrate that all the assumptions
made to this point strongly constrain the form of natural languages in that
every parametrized principle or parameter value that would violate the Saturation Condition is excluded from Universal Grammar. If that is correct,
then language-particular grammars are systematically prevented from
employing these parametric options, which, in turn, should leave a recogniz-
able mark on the form of the options that languages do make use of. Throughout this chapter I argue that the Saturation Condition systematically restricts
what should count as a possible pro-drop, WH-movement, and directionality
parameter. I demonstrate that all the parameter values proposed in the literature for specific languages satisfy the Saturation Condition; also, I show that,
for each parameter, the Saturation Condition rules out many imaginable values, and that indeed none of these values have been shown to be necessary
components of the description of an actually occurring natural language.

For future reference, I restate the two parts of the Saturation Condition as
in 4.

(4) *The Saturation Condition*
    a. Any well-formedness condition on saturation mentions only
       properties of the two elements of the saturation process.
    b. Any two elements in a saturation process form a constituent.

As already stated, the condition is not itself a part of Universal Grammar;
rather, it is a metacondition on the phrase-structure realization of saturation
phenomena. Every aspect of the grammar that deals with saturation (but not,
for instance, Binding) obeys the condition.[6]

6. I have elsewhere also applied the methodology of this work to binding phenomena, i.e. the
antecedent relation entering into the definition of chain and the binding theory of works like
Chomsky (1981, 1986a). The reader may consult Webelhuth (forthcoming). The present work
will ignore the parametric differences between individual languages with respect to binding theory, because they are independent of the saturation phenomena that we chose to concentrate on
here.

In the remainder of this chapter I seek to convince the reader that once the effects of the Saturation Condition are combined with the principles of a modular system of licensing, a theory of grammar emerges that is both powerful in its descriptive abilities and at the same time highly constrained in the grammatical configurations that its principles and parameters can license.

Having outlined the broad conceptual structure of a theory incorporating the Saturation Condition, Chapters 2–5 have as their purpose to put that theory to the test by studying "the different manners of realizing grammar and its form in the individual grammatical constructions" (Humboldt) of seven members of the Modern Germanic language family: the continental West Germanic languages German and Dutch, the insular West Germanic language English, and the Northern languages Icelandic, Norwegian, Swedish, and Danish. I hope that the comparison of some major grammatical constructions of these languages will shed some light on "human language considered as something general, its limits, the necessity of its principles and postulates and the boundaries of its variation" (Humboldt), in other words, on the form and content of Universal Grammar.

Of particular concern throughout this work is the question of whether the success of the Principles and Parameters approach can be furthered by carrying the fruitful methodology of constraining and eliminating language-particular rule systems from components like the phrase-structure rule system or binding rules into the domain of parameters themselves. To be more specific, the present work emphasizes the possibility that, just as the base component of Chomsky (1965) could be strongly constrained by a general theory of possible production rules (known as X-bar theory), so the parameter "component" of the current Principles and Parameters framework can be constrained by the development of a currently nonexistent theory of "possible parameters of natural language." The heart of this theory is the Saturation Condition in 4. The next section makes this idea more precise.

1.2 A Model of Explanation: X-bar Theory

As a basis for the analogy to be made later, what follows is a short review of the argument by Chomsky (1970) that the base component of the Standard Theory can be noticeably constrained once it is made to incorporate a number of generalizations over phrase-structure rules that the Standard Theory of Chomsky (1965) failed to express.

In the latter work it was assumed that deep structures are generated by a context-free phrase-structure grammar that might contain rules like those given in 5 for English.

(5) VP → V   AP → A   NP → N
     VP → V NP
     VP → V PP   AP → A PP   NP → N PP
     VP → V S   AP → A S   NP → N S
     VP → V NP PP
     VP → V NP S
     VP → V PP S   AP → A PP S   NP → N PP S

In Chomsky (1965) it was already noticed that the rules in 5 fail to express an important generalization, namely that each of the categories VP, AP, and NP expanded by the rules defines the domain of subcategorization for the verbs, adjectives, and nouns it contains. To remedy this situation, Chomsky added subcategorization rules to the grammar that are sensitive to the presence of the phrasal node. This was necessary, because (emphasis added)

> . . . in all cases, an important generalization would be missed if the relevant contexts were merely listed. The theory of grammar would fail to express the fact that a grammar is obviously more highly valued if subcategorization is determined by *a set of contexts that is syntactically definable.* (Chomsky 1965, 97)

Chomsky (1970) addresses the problem that there are a number of other generalizations concerning rule systems like that in 5 which were not captured by the model in *Aspects of the Theory of Syntax.* Consequently he proposes a revision of the base component that has since been referred to as "X-bar theory." This theory assumes that all phrase-structure configurations of natural language conform to the two schemas in 6.

(6) XP → YP X' ; [YP, XP] = $_{df}$ Specifier of X'
     X' → X ZP ; [ZP, X'] = $_{df}$ Complement of X

In words, the internal structure of phrases has to satisfy the conditions given in 7 (cf. Stowell 1981, 70).

(7) Every phrase is endocentric.
     Specifiers appear at the XP-level; subcategorized complements appear within X'.
     The head always appears adjacent to one boundary of X'.
     The head is one bar-level lower than the immediately dominating phrasal node.
     Only maximal projections may appear as non-head terms within a phrase.

Relocating these five generalizations from the language-particular rule system in 5 into Universal Grammar has a twofold explanatory advantage. First, it leads to a larger generalization over the English base component and hence to a more principled understanding of why English phrases have the shape they do. Second, by adding this positive discovery about English phrase structure to the theory of language, we can automatically rule out a number of potential phrase-structure configurations that were, in principle, available within the earlier rule-driven theory. Thus, take the three hypothetical rules presented in 8.

(8) $*VP \rightarrow A\ PP$
     $*VP \rightarrow V\ N$
     $*VP \rightarrow V\ V$

Although these are not found in English, this was as much an accident under the rule-driven theory lacking the constraints in 7 as the nonexistence of the rule $VP \rightarrow NP\ V$ in English. Within the new theory whose principles are based on the fact that all existing phrase-structure configurations in English have the properties in 7, the rules in 8 are unexpected on principled grounds. The first rule violates the constraint that all phrases are endocentric. The second one does not satisfy the requirement that non-head factors have to be maximal projections, and the last one violates the maximality requirement, as well as a plausible further constraint that each phrase have one unique head.

To sum up: the incorporation of X-bar theory has a twofold explanatory advantage. First, it makes it a theoretical necessity rather than an unexplained accident that the English phrase-structure system is so uniform, i.e. that heads of different categories and their complements and specifiers uniformly appear in similar configurations. Second, it makes available a principled explanation for why certain phrase-structure configurations are *not* found in English, specifically, those that lack some essential property of those configurations that are found. Because the new framework predicts, on principled grounds, the presence of certain properties and the absence of certain rules, whereas the earlier proposal has to take recourse to two unexplained and unrelated accidents, it makes more precise predictions about the shapes of the grammars of natural languages. Furthermore, because the framework does not fail empirically relative to the earlier one, it can be looked at as a prime example of a gain in explanatory adequacy.

This is but a preliminary discussion of X-bar theory. In section 1.4 we reinterpret the X-bar schema in 6 as a structure-building mechanism that allows us to eliminate the language-particular categorial components postulated within the rule-format oriented Standard Theory. The result is a principled theory of structure building.

1.3 The Bounds of Analytic Power

Having studied a prototypical example of a successful theoretical innovation in the previous section, we now pursue the possibility that an inquiry into the properties of parameters might reveal similar generalizations about their structure that are left unexpressed within current Principles and Parameters approaches. At the base of this possibility lies the realization that the parameter "component" of current Principles and Parameters approaches is as unstructured as, or even less structured than, the base component of the Standard Theory. To date, the literature contains two proposals of principled constraints on parameters, both extragrammatical.

Following Baker (1979 and later work) it is required, as already mentioned, that language-particular generalizations, including parameter values, be learnable on the basis of positive evidence alone. This means that the learners can decide, on the basis of the grammatical sentences they hear, whether a certain generalization is correct. They do not need any information that certain sentences are ungrammatical in their target language.

Although this may be an important requirement, it has to be noted that it is not sufficient to distinguish many reasonable hypotheses from unreasonable or even absurd ones. For example, in considering an inventory of hypothetical descriptive options from which individual grammars may choose, one of the choices from 9a can be found in many languages, whereas both options in 9b are absurd and do not characterize any grammar of natural language.

(9) a. Verbs precede or follow their complements.
    b. WH-words may occur in the sentences uttered before noon or after noon.

Suppose for both cases of 9 that the language learners operate on the assumption that they have been exposed to a representative sample of the language to be acquired. Thus, if they only hear sentences in which the verb precedes its complement, they will assume that this is the correct generalization for that language and that 9a qualifies as a possible parameter statement according to the only-positive-evidence requirement. Note, now, that this is also the case with 9b in a possible world in which Universal Grammar contains this parameter. Imagine that the hypothetical language learners in this world are only exposed to sentences containing WH-words in the afternoon. Again, under the assumption that they are exposed to a representative sample of the target language, the relevant parameter value would be learnable on the basis of positive evidence alone and hence would qualify as a possible parameter of natural language.

The foregoing example has demonstrated that our belief in 9b as an impossible parameter statement is not dependent on the only-positive-evidence requirement but on the empirical grammar-based fact that there simply are no languages that behave according to these generalizations. As a consequence, although the requirement may indeed rule out a number of unwanted parameter statements, it will at the same time allow statements like 9b to slip through whose absurdity can only be established on the basis of empirical linguistic evidence. We conclude that the only-positive-evidence requirement can at most be a necessary condition for what should count as a possible parameter of natural language, but all by itself it is not sufficient. Stronger constraints, in particular, grammar-internal ones, are needed.

A second proposal of a constraint on possible parameter values has recently been made by Wexler/Manzini (1987) and Manzini/Wexler (1987) on the basis of earlier similar proposals made by Gold (1967) and Berwick (1985). Called the "Subset Principle," the theory these authors propose states that, given any two values of some parameter, the language that is generated with one value is a subset of the language with the other value or vice versa. This constraint is also explicitly hypothesized to be extragrammatical; it is supposed to be part of a learning module.

The problem with this proposal is that it is demonstrably false or at least can be shown to fail for some reasonably established parameters. For instance, an investigation of the directionality parameter shows that its values do not satisfy the principle; a language that consistently takes the head-initial value will not have any sentences with transitive heads in phrase-final position. A language that consistently takes the opposite value will not have any sentences with transitive heads in phrase-initial position. Hence it is not the case that one language is a subset of the other.

The same situation obtains for the WH-movement parameter. We know that there are languages like English where in non-echo sentences with one single WH-phrase WH-movement is obligatory. In these languages there will not be any sentences with the WH-phrase occurring sentence-internally. In strict WH-in-situ languages, however, many WH-phrases will appear in sentences where they must be sentence-internal. Hence, it is again the case that neither of the two languages is a subset of the other.[7]

---

7. That the subset condition is satisfied in the one case that Wexler and Manzini deal with, namely the Binding Theory, is not surprising when one takes into account that under a strictly binary branching theory the domains defining governing categories have to be hierarchically ordered if there is more than one.

This observation may lead one to hypothesize that a different version of the subset principle is correct, namely one that says that *if* two parameter values lead to a subset situation, then the language learner will test the value leading to the smallest language first. Assuming a direct relation

In sum, we have to conclude that the subset principle either does not hold at all or, at the very least, that it has a rather restricted domain of application and like the only-positive-evidence requirement, will not allow us to formulate sufficient conditions for what should count as a possible parameter of natural language. Neither does it allow us to impose necessary conditions on this concept.[8]

1.3.1 Motivation for a Theory of Possible Parameters

The discussion in the previous section focused on the fact that current Principles and Parameters theory lacks grammar-internal conditions on what should count as a possible parameter of natural language and that this problem is not solved by the two proposed extragrammatical conditions on parameters just discussed.

The major goal of the current work is to overcome this imperfection by motivating an approach to the logical structure of Universal Grammar which imposes strong *grammatical* constraints on what is admissible as a possible parameter of natural language. Imposing grammar-internal conditions on parameters is, of course, compatible with the view that there are additional extragrammatical conditions, for instance the markedness hierarchy relating to a subset constellation (cf. footnote 7), the positive-evidence-only requirement, or requirements imposed by the parsing mechanism. The extragrammatical conditions could naturally be viewed as a further filtering mechanism operating on the set of parameters sanctioned by the grammatical module.

The principal motivation for a general grammatical theory of parameters comes again from the observations that natural languages are remarkably uniform and that natural language can be acquired so relatively easily given the conditions imposed on the language learner.

These observations suggest that learners acquiring a language do bring very strong and detailed hypotheses to the task of analyzing the primary data that form their linguistic experience, hypotheses that are based in particular on knowledge of the grammatical categories and relations sanctioned by Universal Grammar.

As a consequence, Universal Grammar should be formulated in such a way that language learners are forced to select from a maximally constrained set

---

between the markedness of an expression and the accessibility of a hypothesis about its governing category, this theory would predict that expressions with small governing categories are more frequent in the world's languages than long-distance elements. Judging from the literature, this prediction has a fair chance of being correct.

8. For earlier criticisms of the subset condition cf. Hyams (1987) and Safir (1987).

of hypotheses concerning the target language while still allowing them enough hypotheses to arrive at a correct grammar for any natural language they might be exposed to.

According to a reasonable evaluation metric those theories of Universal Grammar are rated as more desirable which eliminate unwanted hypotheses *on principled grounds* rather than by accidental exclusion from a list of available options. In this respect, hypothesized parameters do not differ from hypothesized phrase-structure rules. From the discussion in the previous section the reader will remember that X-bar theory was developed, among other reasons, to give a principled account of the nonavailability of rules like those given in 10.

(10) *VP → A PP
     *VP → V N
     *VP → V V

Each of the phrases generable with the rules in 10 violates at least one of the constraints on possible phrase-structure configurations in 7. Their nonavailability thus finds a principled and unified explanation, since together the requirements in 7 lay out parts of a specific conception of "possible natural language," and all the rules in 10 are incompatible with that conception.

We can compare this manner of excluding all three rules in 10 with an imaginable alternative. Suppose that instead of replacing the language-particular phrase-structure rules with an X-bar schema in order to rule out options like 10, we simply collect all the phrase-structure rules that we find in individual grammars and enter them as a set of parameters into Universal Grammar. If no individual grammar that we have investigated contains any of the rules in 10, then UG will not contain them. It is important to note, however, that although both versions of UG might exclude these rules, they do so for very different reasons. The "list" theory has only a negative motivation for excluding them, namely the fact that no actual language requires their postulation. But no independently motivated fundamental property of natural language is involved, and one's view of language would not change dramatically if it were found that one of the rules would have to be added after all. In other words, the threefold accident of excluding rules 10 from the list of parameters does not lead to any further insights into the nature of language and leaves us without specific expectations regarding the structure of languages against which the theory has not yet been tested.

The situation is very different in the theory based on the X-bar schema. Here, the exclusion of 10, first of all, is not a threefold accident but follows from a unified and strongly constrained theory of the phrase structure of natural language. Thus, given the assumptions about X-bar theory in 7, it would have nontrivial consequences to add one or more of the rules into the grammar, since the whole rule schema would have to be changed, with noticeable consequences elsewhere in the grammar.

More importantly, however, the X-bar theory-based UG differs from the "list" theory in that the negative conclusion about the rules in 10 is intimately tied to a positive generalization over the phrase structure of natural language. Thus, the "bad" rules are excluded because they all lack some property held in common by all the "good" rules. These positively motivated properties thus contribute to a structured definition of the concept "possible natural language," whereas the alternative theory offers only a randomly collected list of instantiated rules.

To sum up our argument so far: starting with Humboldt's observation that natural languages are very similar and very different at the same time, we have accepted Chomsky's view that this fact should be accounted for by attributing an innate language faculty to language learners. To be maximally general and explanatory Universal Grammar should exclude hypotheses more on the basis of positively motivated general properties of natural language than on the basis of accidental exclusion from a list that affords no further insights into the structure of language.

It is the major goal of this work to find *positive* grammatical generalizations among the parameters that have been proposed in the literature and thereby to replace the presently accidental exclusion of logically possible parameters with *principled* reasons for their nonexistence. If successful, this program will lead to a strengthening of the Principles and Parameters approach, given that the nonavailability of certain hypotheses to the language learner derives from their lack of at least one essential property common to all available hypotheses. In other words, it is the very integrity of the accessible parameters that makes the language learner disregard the inaccessible ones.

1.3.2 The Lower Bound of Analytic Power (Observational and Descriptive Adequacy)

In analogy with Chomsky's (1965) suggestion that there is a general domain characterizing subcategorization, it seems important to consider whether there is also an independently specifiable syntactic domain in which parameter statements are operative.

As a first step in our investigation, we may ask, what kinds of information must UG minimally allow particular grammars to refer to? (In a second step we will later ask what the upper bound on language-particular information should be.) To answer this question, it will be useful to look at a few examples.

Some interesting paradigms from Kayne (1984, Ch. 5) indicate that individual grammars must have the power to fix the syntactic category of an expression. Kayne compares the English morpheme *to* and the French morpheme *de*, which are both apparently meaningless elements and restricted in their distribution to nonfinite contexts. He notes that there are some systematic differences between them that can be accounted for in a unified manner, if the English element belongs to the category INFL while its French counterpart is a member of category COMP.[9] Thus, while English *to* as an INFL can occur in the IP-complement of a raising verb,

(11E) John seems [t **to** have left]

the absence of the French complementizer *de* in such complements follows from the nonavailability of a COMP node in these structures:

(12F) *John semble [t **d'**être   parti]
       John seems   to have left

(13F) John semble [t être   parti]
       John seems   have left

Second, if English *to* is an INFL, then it is not surprising that it can occur on either side of sentence adverbs, if the latter are assumed to occur IP-internally:

(14E) I told him [*not* **to** see anyone]

(15E) I told him [**to** *not* see anyone]

Assuming that French *de* is a complementizer, we would expect it to precede sentence adverbs obligatorily. The following sentences demonstrate that this prediction is correct:

(16F) *Je lui ai   dit [*ne* **de** voir personne]
        I   him have told not to see anyone

(17F) Je lui ai   dit [**de** *ne* voir personne]
        I   him have told to not see   anyone

Third, assuming that *to* is an INFL while *de* is a COMP we would expect that the English element does not interact with the availability of WH-words in the sentence, while the French word might show such an interaction, in the same way other complementizers demonstrably do. As the sentences below show, the English element is indeed oblivious to the occurrence of WH-words,

(18E) I told him [*where* **to** go]

---

9. In this work I will follow Chomsky (1986b) in assuming that complementizers and inflectional elements are functional heads in X-bar theory. This topic is discussed in more detail in the chapters to follow.

while the French word cannot co-occur with them:

(19F) *Je lui ai   dit [*où*   **d**'aller]
        I   him have told where to go

(20F) Je lui ai   dit [*où*   aller]
        I   him have told where go

Kayne presents more evidence for the conclusion that the English and French infinitive markers differ in categorization, but for our purposes the examples given are sufficient to establish that an elegant and unified account of their distribution can be given if Universal Grammar allows the individual grammars of English and French to contain the categorial statements given in 21 and 22.

(21) For any expression E $=$ *to:* E belongs to category [Infl, $-$fin].

(22) For any expression E $=$ *de:* E belongs to category [Comp, $-$fin].

A second grammatical property to which individual grammars must be able to refer is the grammatical relation into which an expression can enter and the syntactic category of the element to which it is related (i.e. its relator). As an illustration, note that although the two adverbs *probably* and *merely* can appear sentence-internally in English,

(23) a. John is *probably* being a fool

     b. John is *merely* being a fool

probably can also appear sentence-initially, whereas *merely* is banned from this position:

(24) a. *Probably* John is being a fool

     b. *Merely John is being a fool

Assuming for expository purposes that the adverbs in 23 modify a VP, it appears then from these examples that the grammar of English must be able to express the information that *merely* can only modify a VP while *probably* can modify both VP and IP. Since we are dealing with a lexical idiosyncrasy here, it is natural to encode this information in the lexical entries of these two morphemes, much as we entered the categories of *to* and *de* into their entries in 21 and 22. For *merely,* we could do this as shown in 25.

(25) For any expression E $=$ *merely:* E must modify VP.

The clause in 25 defines a part of the lexical entry of the adverb *merely.* It says that for all lexical entries, if X is the expression *merely,* then X can be used as a syntactic modifier of VP.

What we can keep in mind from this argument is that the grammar of English has to be able to refer to the grammatical relation that *merely* can enter, the category of its relator, and that this information can be represented as in 25.[10]

Having established that individual grammars must have access to (a) categorial and (b) relational information, we turn to a third paradigm to demonstrate that they also must be endowed with the option of fixing (c) the direction of combination for particular grammatical items. Note the following two paradigms comparing the word order of some English degree specifiers with their French counterparts:

(26) John is   Jean est

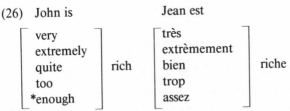

The generalization is that almost all specifiers of A′ precede the element they specify in English, with the exception of the morpheme *enough*. As we can

---

10. Grimshaw (1979), Pesetsky (1982), and Chomsky (1986a) argue that a number of selectional facts can be predicted by taking into account the meaning of the expressions to be combined. I am very sympathetic to this proposal and believe that it is as compatible with the version of the Principles and Parameters theory developed here as with previous ones.

What I am calling attention to, however, is that there remains a residue of c-selectional facts that cannot be reduced to s-selection, so that even if there are default cases of selection, individual items still can depart from defaults in the way described in the text. Among others, cases like the following have not been shown to be reducible to the relation between syntax and semantics:

(i) John hit Bill
(ii) John depends *(on) Bill

That *depends* categorially selects a prepositional phrase while *hit* is transitive is not obviously predictable from a semantic difference between these two verbs. In fact, so far, nobody has been able to identify a semantic feature distinguishing all transitive verbs from those c-selecting a preposition, or one that all and only verbs taking the preposition *on* have in common.

With other differences in categorial selection it is equally hard to see how they could arise from semantic differences. Thus take the following paradigm:

(iii) It is *likely* that John will leave
(iv)   It is *probable* that John will leave
(v)   John is *likely* to leave
(vi)   *John is *probable* to leave

In the absence of a semantic account of paradigms like (i)–(ii) and (iii)–(vi) and many similar ones it is necessary to maintain the position taken in the text, namely that even if a number of categorial facts are reflexes of semantic selection, individual grammars still need to be able to refer to relational and categorial information to be fully observationally adequate.

see in the right-hand column, the behavior of French degree adverbs is fully uniform in that all elements, including the translation of *enough,* precede their specifiee. We get the opposite pattern when we test which of the specifiers can follow their relator. From 27 we see that French again is more uniform than English.

(27)   John is rich   Jean est riche

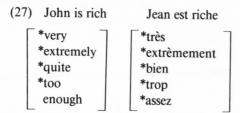

English allows one exception, as already mentioned. Clearly, every fully observationally adequate grammar of English will need a mechanism that expresses the idiosyncratic behavior of *enough* relative to the other specifiers. As in the two examples already discussed, the most economical solution is one that encodes this information in the lexical entry of *enough,* where we also find such (partially) unpredictable information as its underlying phonological representation and its meaning, among other characteristics. Using the so far unmotivated format for lexical entries that was introduced earlier, we can account for the behavior of *enough* with the formulation given in 28.[11]

11. Note that the argument in the text was chosen for expositional convenience and would not be entirely conclusive if *enough* could be shown not to be a specifier, but a modifier of some sort. However, the larger argument does not, of course, depend on this particular example. That the direction of combination has to be encodable into individual lexical entries is also shown by the behavior of adjectives in Romance languages and many other cases. In Italian, for instance, most adjectives appear to the right of the modified head, with a few idiosyncratic exceptions listed below:

   (i) *Adjectives Appearing Prenominally in Italian*
      bella (beautiful)
      brutta (ugly)
      buona (good)
      cattiva (bad)
      grande (big)
      piccola (small)
      brava (good)

It does not seem that the marked word order behavior of the adjectives in (i) correlates with any other of their properties. They also do not seem to fall into a semantic class that would distinguish them from all the adjectives that appear on the right. It thus is necessary to single them out one by one. This is exactly the argument made in the text.

   I am grateful to Marica de Vincenzi for compiling the list in (i) for me.

(28) For any expression E = *enough:*
    (a) E specifies A';
    (b) E specifies to the left.

To sum up: the preceding three arguments have led us to the following conclusion:

(29) *Every observationally adequate syntactic theory has to allow particular grammars to refer to at least the following information:*

    (a) the category of a morpheme;

    (b) selection in a grammatical relation;

    (c) the direction of combination.

1.3.3 The Upper Bound of Analytic Power (Explanatory Adequacy)

Having established that observationally adequate individual grammars should be able to refer to (a) categorial, (b) relational, and (c) directional features of an expression, we now turn to the question of what *constraints* UG should impose on language-particular grammars to ensure that the overall system of analysis a learner brings to the task of language acquisition is explanatorily adequate. In other words, which inviolable formal and substantive universals should we postulate as components of language learning? Recall from the discussion in section 1.2 that we intend to pursue the idea that positive generalizations over parameters automatically have the negative effect of excluding those logically possible parameters that do not fall under the generalization. To the extent that the excluded parameters are indeed inert, in that they need not be invoked in any empirical analysis, a theory of UG that expresses this positive generalization is clearly more desirable than one that does not.

In the following paragraphs I investigate a number of commonly postulated parameters and illustrate that these proposals do indeed all share a number of characteristics. On the basis of these identified characteristics I propose a "Parameter Theorem" that imposes strong constraints on what qualifies as a possible parameter of natural language. Furthermore, it will be shown that the Parameter Theorem is derivable in a theory of grammar that contains the Saturation Condition stated in 4.

We begin with an investigation of what the literature refers to as the "pro-drop" parameter. Example 30 gives a list containing a few types of languages and the environments in which they are subjectless:

(30) *Pro-Drop Languages*[12]

English:	no drop
Italian:	argument drop in finite clauses; expletive drop in participle constructions
German:	expletive drop (but not with weather verbs)
Hebrew:	only in past and future tense, but not in present tense
Finnish:	drop in first and second person; no drop in third person
Icelandic:	expletive drop (including weather verbs)

12. The list has been chosen quite arbitrarily and is, of course, incomplete. For instance, it does not distinguish between optional and obligatory pro-drop languages, although this distinction would have to be made in a complete survey. It also does not distinguish between languages that allow only subjects to drop and those that also allow objects to do so. If these language types were included, the list would become longer very quickly.

The information in the table is based on Rizzi (1982, Chapter 4 [Italian]), Borer (1986, 392 [Hebrew]), Platzack (1983 [Icelandic]), and a personal communication by Anne Vainikka (Finnish).

Traditional grammars have noted that there is a correlation between the richness of verbal morphology and the availability of pro-drop. This idea has been incorporated into the standard parameter theory in the form of a parametric choice given to individual grammars between "strong" and "weak" inflections (cf. Rizzi (1982) and Chomsky (1981)), where the former licenses pro-drop and the latter does not. This theory, whether in its traditional or modern form, is not flexible enough, however, to make enough required distinctions, since it is based on the two way contrast between "strong" and "weak" inflection. This can be seen from the entries in the table in the text. It shows that languages don't just differ in having pro-drop or lacking it altogether, but rather that a successful theory of pro-drop must be able to appeal to features such as FINITE or TENSE. In other words, a descriptively adequate theory of pro-drop must be capable of making finer distinctions than the standard theory has traditionally allowed.

Moreover, the relationship between pro-drop and spell out of inflection is no stronger than one of preference. There are obvious counterexamples to the claim that there is a rigidly deterministic dependence between the two:

(i) *Strength of inflection and pro-drop*

a. Italian

Sg	Pl
1 parlo	parliamo
2 parli	parlate
3 parla	parlano

b. Finnish

Sg	Pl
asun	asumme
asut	asutte
asuu	asuvat

c. Icelandic

Sg	Pl
1 tek	tókum
2 tekur	takið
3 tekur	taka

Looking at this list, we first find that a language is either pro-drop or it isn't. Second, upon careful examination of the environments in which pro-drop *can* occur, we observe that in all cases this environment can be defined in terms of a property of *pro* [referential, quasi-referential, or nonreferential in the sense of Chomsky (1981, Chapter 6)] or of the INFL′ that it specifies (finite vs. participial, present vs. future tense, first vs. third person). To demonstrate this, I will illustrate how a few of these cases could be analyzed.

We begin with English. For this language we may simply assume that it does not make use of a lexical morpheme *pro* at all. Because all complex phrase-structure configurations are projected from smaller expressions, and because English does not have an expression *pro,* it follows that it will also not have any bigger expressions containing this element, in particular no sentences.

In Finnish we only find *pro* as the specifier of a first or second person Infl. We may thus assume that this language has available a morpheme *pro* and that it is marked for first and second person but not for third. Its surface distribution will then follow.

We will also postulate a *pro* for Hebrew, but one that can only specify an I′ marked for [α Tense] and not [β Tense], where the two variables range over the tenses, allowing and disallowing pro-drop, respectively. In the format of the lexical entries used in the previous section, this could be expressed as shown in 31.

(31) For any expression E = *pro:* E specifies [I, α Tns].

The reader will have noticed that this statement is formally identical to 25 above (repeated in 32 for convenience), which determined the idiosyncratic behavior of the lexical morpheme *merely.*

(32) For any expression E = *merely:* E modifies VP.

Both statements identify a lexical morpheme and state that this morpheme has a certain relational property. And yet, despite their identity in form, the two statements have very different observable effects. The statement in 31 describes a highly visible property of sentence structure, since it affects the

---

The Italian and Finnish verb paradigms are isomorphic in the sense that each verb has six distinct forms in the present tense. Nevertheless, Italian allows pro-drop in all persons while Finnish licenses it only in the first and second person but disallows it in the third person. Icelandic still has five different forms for a verb in the present tense, only one less than Italian and Finnish, but allows no arguments to drop at all. Clearly a competence theory of pro-drop cannot be based on a correlation between pro-drop and inflectional morphology, since the correlation is empirically unreliable. Chung (1984) reaches this same conclusion with an interesting discussion of Chamorro pro-drop.

subject position, i.e. a position that is obligatorily present in each sentence of a natural language (cf. the Extended Projection Principle in Chomsky 1981). The statement in 32, however, will not have equally strong effects, since it determines the behavior of an optional modifier with a rather specialized meaning. Nevertheless, it is important to be aware that the quantitatively different effects of 31 and 32 are more of an epiphenomenon than a real one, since the two statements are identical in form and function.

We now turn to an analysis of the information that enters into the formulation of the WH-movement parameter.

In this domain we find the following options, among others:

(33) *WH-movement*
　　English:　movement obligatory at S-structure
　　Chinese:　movement prohibited at S-structure
　　French:　movement optional at S-structure
　　German:　movement obligatory, but restricted to finite clauses

What is noteworthy is that these four cases can also be distinguished solely by categorial and relational information. The first three cases could, for instance, be described by one version of the formulation given in 34.

(34) For any expression E = [+ WH]: E must/must not/can specify C′.

This statement says that every element that has the property of being a syntactic WH-operator also has or lacks the (obligatory/optional) property of specifying a C′, i.e. of appearing in the clausal operator position.

The German state of affairs is adequately captured in 35.

(35) For any expression E = [+ WH]: E must specify [C′, +fin].

35 says that every word used as a WH-operator in German has the property of specifying a finite C′, i.e. German is a WH-movement language but does not have infinitival questions. A comparison with the statement for *merely* in 25, once more repeated below,

(36) For any expression E = *merely:* E modifies VP.

will reveal that the WH-movement parameter can also be rendered as a statement of the form given in 37,

(37) For any expression E = P: E has property Q.

where P identifies a lexical entry or a natural class of lexical entries and Q is some (a) categorial, (b) relational, or (c) directional property of lexical entries. The difference between 35 and 36 is not one of quality, since they have exactly the same form and also identical functions; rather, it is one of quantity in that 36 singles out only one lexical entry and attributes an idiosyncratic property to it, while 35 assigns a grammatical property to a whole natural class of elements, i.e. all WH-operators. We would thus expect to find rules like 35, mentioning features contained in every individual grammar, much more often in natural languages than rules like 36, and in this case this is almost certainly correct.

With the conclusions that both pro-drop and WH-movement can be described in terms of the properties of lexical entries and only differ from statements encoding the idiosyncracies of lexical entries in mentioning more general or more visible features, we turn to an examination of a third parameter that is postulated frequently. We will test now whether the content of the Directionality Parameter is also amenable to such an analysis. To this end we ask whether the two directionality parameters in 38 for French and English can be recast as statements assigning properties to lexical items.

(38) French: Degree adverbs precede A′
English: Heads precede their complements

It is easy to see how these descriptive generalizations can be encoded. As shown in 39, the French case says nothing else but that every expression marked as a specifier of A′ can only be combined with an A′ by preceding it (the formulation makes use of some obvious abbreviatory conventions).

(39) For any expression E = [Spec, A′]: E specifies to the right.

The English generalization is also easy to express:

(40) For any expression E = [Compl: YP]: E precedes its complement.

If we compare 39, the reconstruction of one directionality parameter value in French, with 28, repeated below, the description of the exceptional directionality behavior of *enough,* we see that these two statements are qualitatively on a par and only differ in the number of expressions to which each applies.

(41) For any expression E = *enough:*
(a) E specifies A′;
(b) E specifies to the right.

So far our investigation has shown that three widely postulated parameters of natural language (pro-drop, WH-movement, and directionality) can be cast into a "normal form" for parameters, and that that form does not contain any information distinct from that which every observationally adequate grammar must have available anyway: (a) the category of an expression, (b) relational information, and (c) directionality of combination. We thus postulate 42 in analogy with 29.

(42) *The Correspondence Criterion*

Every explanatorily adequate syntactic theory refers to exactly the same information as every observationally adequate syntactic theory, namely:

(a) the categories of all morphemes;
(b) selection in a grammatical relation;
(c) the direction of combination.

The identity of the three types of information referred to in 29 and 42 implies that we are claiming that parameters of natural language are nothing but generalized versions of lexical statements. It was demonstrated above that all versions of the pro-drop parameter can be formulated as statements that assign either a categorial or a relational property to *pro* (cf. 31). In the preceding section it was shown that every observationally adequate grammar has to be able to encode such statements anyway, namely to fix the categories of such items as the English and French infinitive markers *to* and *de* (cf. 21 and 22) and the relations of such an item as *merely* (cf. 25). We also showed that all the information contained in the lexical statement of *merely* is sufficient to reconstruct all the versions of the WH-movement parameter (compare 35 with 36). Finally, we demonstrated that the directionality parameter was identical in form and function to a lexical statement determining that the specifier of A′ *enough* in English is idiosyncratic in following its specifiee (compare 39 with 41).

The insight in the Correspondence Criterion 42 leads us to formulate the generalization put forth in 43.

(43) If a parameter can refer to a feature F, then lexical entries can refer to F.

What 43 says is that the set of parametric properties is a subset of the set of lexical properties. This can be graphically represented as shown in 44.

(44)

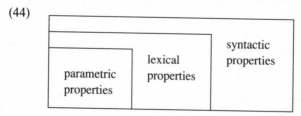

Thus, whatever is a parametric property is a lexical property and whatever is a lexical property is a syntactic property.

As a careful inspection of 44 reveals, the claim in 43 makes another interesting prediction about the relationship between lexical properties and parametric ones, namely that whatever is *not* a lexical property can also *not* be a parametric one. To prove this, imagine there is some nonlexical syntactic property P. It would be contained in the largest box in 44 but not in the box containing all the lexical properties. Hence, it could also not be in the smallest box representing the properties that a parameter can mention. It is this conclusion to which I intend to draw attention, because, as demonstrated in the next section, it can be shown to impose strong and apparently correct empirical constraints on the concept "possible parameter of natural language." I will conclude this section by formulating this result as the "Parameter Theorem":[13]

(45) *The Parameter Theorem*
      If no lexical entry can refer to feature F, then no parameter can refer to F.

In the next section I intend to show that by imposing strong constraints on the kind of information to which lexical entries can refer, we automatically also impose strong constraints on what kind of information parameters can contain. In this way, by formulating substantive *positive* generalizations over the structure of the lexicon, we will, as a by-product, be able to *eliminate in a principled manner* many parameter statements that are not made use of within the current Principles and Parameters model as a matter of accidental exclusion. This, I believe, leads to a significant increase in explanatory success of this framework, modeled on the elimination of arbitrary phrase-structure rules through the formulation of X-bar principles.

1.4 Locality Constraints on Lexical Information: The Variation Theorem

The importance of the Parameter Theorem lies in the fact that it ties the concept "possible parameter of natural language" to the structure of a component of the grammar (the lexicon) that is known to be subject to certain independently motivated restrictions. If it can be shown that these same restrictions figure decisively in an empirically satisfactory conception of parameters, then this would constitute an interesting argument for our view of parameters.

One important constraint on the lexicon that we will exploit prominently in our discussion throughout this work can be derived once the role of the lexicon in the building of syntactic structure is appreciated, i.e. its interaction with X-bar theory.

---

13. It will be obvious to the reader that the Parameter Theorem is logically equivalent to our generalization in 43.

Recall from our preliminary discussion of X-bar theory in Section 1.2 that Chomsky (1970) postulates the existence of the following two rule schemata:

(46) a. XP → YP X′ ; [YP, XP] = $_{df}$ Specifier of X′
     b. X′ → X ZP ; [ZP, X′] = $_{df}$ Complement of X.

In recent years, especially under the influence of Stowell (1981) and Chomsky (1981), these schemata have been interpreted as structure-building mechanisms themselves (i.e. as acceptance conditions) rather than as constraints over production rules. What this means is that both of the schemata in 46 represent a number of conditions that every phrase-structure configuration has to fulfill in order to count as a phrasal or as an X′ constituent. This is most easily illustrated with an example of the application of each schema.

Assume that the English lexicon contains the morpheme *hit* with the following informally stated properties and that the grammar has already determined that *Bill* is a noun phrase:

(47) *hit,* Category: $[+V, -N]$
     Category of Complement: $[-V, +N]$
     Verbs take their complements on the Right.

Assume further that the schema in 46b is an abbreviation of the following (informally stated) conditions on the combination of expressions to form X-bars:

(48) *Projection of the Complementation Relation*
     If a. α is a member of category X,
        b. β is a member of category YP,
        c. α takes members of YP as complements,
        d. α takes its complements on the right,
     then $[\alpha\ \beta]$ is a member of category X′.

(49)

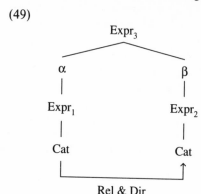

We can now show that the X-bar theoretic projection principle in 48, based on the lexical information about *hit* in 47 and the assumption that *Bill* is an NP, will accept the expression [hit Bill] as a member of category V'. For, take α in 48 to be *hit* and β to be *Bill*; *hit* is a member of category V, *Bill* is a member of category NP, *hit* takes complements of category NP and, like all verbs, takes its complements on the right. Thus, since both sub-expressions of [hit Bill] satisfy all the conditions imposed on them, the projection clause will license the whole expression as a V'.

Next, we give a short illustration of the application of the schema in 46a. Let us assume that the projection principle in 48 has projected the expressions *proud, of,* and *Mary* to the English expression *proud of Mary* of category A'. Let us also assume that the morpheme *very* is lexically represented as follows:[14]

(50) *very,* Category: [+Adv]
        Category to Specify: [+V, +N]
        Degree adverbs specify to the Right.

We will assume that all expressions composed of two elements standing in a specification relation are accepted by the following (informally stated) projection principle:

(51) *Projection of the Specification Relation*
       If a. α is a member of category YP,
          b. β is a member of category X',
          c. α takes members of X' as specifiees,
          d. α takes its specifiee on the right,
       then [a β] is a member of category XP.

Assume that we have already determined that *very* is a maximal projection of category AdvP. Then the projection principle in 51, based on the information contained in 50, will determine that [very proud of Mary] is a well-formed AP in English. The reason is that *very* is a member of category AdvP, *proud of Mary* is an A', *very* can specify adjectival expressions, and the specifier precedes the other element. Thus, since all the conditions in 51 are satisfied, nothing stands in the way of the newly produced expression counting as an adjective phrase.

We now return to the main purpose of this section, namely the demonstration that the interaction of X-bar theory and the lexicon imposes a strong condition on the form of lexical entries that can be carried into the domain of parameters.

14. It is inessential to the current argument what the feature structure of adverbs is. For expository purposes I have thus used a feature [+ ADV].

Close inspection of the two projection principles in 48 and 51 should convince us that no lexical entry can impose well-formedness constraints on its occurrence in complex constituents beyond the following ones:

(52) *Information That a Lexical Entry Can Bring to Syntactic Projection*
its own category
the grammatical relations that it enters
the categories of the elements it enters into grammatical relations with
the direction of combination in a grammatical relation.

What is important for us is what kinds of information the projection principles do *not* refer to. Since both of them obey the constraints in the Saturation Condition 4, they do not contain the following information:

(53) *Nonprojectible Information*
   a. the categories, relations, and directions of expressions that lie *outside* the new expression to be projected
   b. the categories, relations, and directions of expressions that lie *inside* any of the constituents to be combined.

Let us look at these two restrictions on lexical entries one by one. We can illustrate the effect of the first restriction by inspecting the following diagram:

(54)

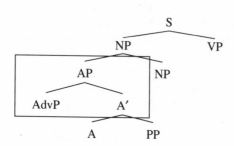

The AdvP and the A′ in 54 have to be projected to the AP by the projection principle in 51. What the Saturation Condition and 53a say is that the AdvP can impose categorial, relational, and directional restrictions at most on the expressions contained in the box in 54. In particular, the projection clause will prevent the AdvP from imposing restrictions on the NP, VP, and S-nodes, since the clause simply does not check the properties of these constituents when admitting the AdvP and the A′ as an AP. As a consequence, a theory of language incorporating only projection clauses like 48 and 51 predicts that AdvP may be subcategorized for a sister constituent, but they may *not* mention any information of the structure outside the adjective phrase. Thus, we find that 55 describes possible lexical entries in natural language, while 56 describes impossible ones:

(55) *Possible Lexical Entries*
   a. X is an Adv whose maximal projection specifies A′
   b. X is an A whose maximal projection specifies NPs
   c. X is a verb taking NP as a complement
   d. X is a word whose maximal projection specifies finite C′s.

(56) *Impossible Lexical Entries*
   a. X is an Adv specifying A′s if the sentence contains a doubly-filled Comp
   b. X is a verb taking NP-complements in nonfinite sentences and PP-complements in finite sentences
   c. X is an AP specifying nouns that occur in subordinate clauses but not in main clauses
   d. X is a preposition if it occurs in a sentence with subject–verb agreement and a postposition in a sentence without agreement.

The lexical entries in 56 are all impossible (or inert), since they contain restrictions on a context that is larger than that which the Saturation Condition allows any projection principle to take into account. In other words, the projection principles simply cannot "look up" the tree to check whether the subcategorization restriction imposed by the lexical items is fulfilled. Rather, they only check whether all the conditions on the local domain they mention are fulfilled and accept the local structure as well-formed, no matter whether the morpheme mentions additional information or not.

To sum up: the requirement in 53a imposes a strong locality condition on the information contained in lexical entries: lexical morphemes cannot influence any aspect of the structure that is outside the grammatical relation in which they are projected.

With this result, let us turn to requirement 53b. Whereas the earlier constraint said that the AdvP in 54 could not "look up" in the tree, i.e. to any position outside its AP-mother, the second constraint says that it also cannot "look down into its sister"; that is, it is blind to the internal structure of the A′ in 54. Thus, according to 53b, none of the following statements describe a possible lexical entry of any natural language:

(57) *Impossible Lexical Entries*
   a. X is an Adv whose maximal projection only specifies A′s headed by a denominal adjective

b. X is a V taking only those NPs as complements that contain a second person anaphor
c. X is a N taking only those sentences as complements that contain a stranded preposition
d. X is a complementizer that occurs only in those sentences which three sentences down contain a pseudo-passive structure.

The reason is the same as earlier. The Saturation Condition does not allow projection principles to refer to the information used in 57. (Of course, as a side effect of feature percolation, it *does* allow an expression to access indirectly some of the properties of its sister's head, because the features of its sister and that of its head are partially identical; however, no direct grammatical relation between the selector and the sister's head or any other constituent within the sister is involved.)

We are now in a position to import the restrictions on lexical entries in 53 into the domain of parameters. We begin by inspecting our major claim about the structure of parameters again, the Parameter Theorem from the preceding section.

(58) *The Parameter Theorem*
If no lexical entry can refer to feature F, then no parameter can refer to F.

The Saturation Condition and the present section have postulated two very strong independently motivated constraints on what kinds of features lexical entries can refer to: (a) they cannot refer to information higher up in the tree; and (b) they cannot refer to information lower than their sister constituents.

If the parameter theorem in 58 is correct, then parameters of natural language should fall under the same restrictions, because the information they can refer to is a subset of the information lexical entries can contain. The statement in 59 should therefore hold:

(59) *The Parameter Universal*
No parameter can assign a non-local property to a lexical item or a class of lexical items.

To test whether this is a plausible conclusion, we can compare a few statements that are possible and impossible parameters according to the present version of the Parameter Theorem in order to see whether the results square with the linguistic reality as far as it is known to us.

We begin with a number of a priori imaginable pro-drop parameters:

(60) a. The language allows pro-drop in sentences with a second person subject/the indicative mood/future tense.

b. * The language allows pro-drop in sentences with a stranded preposition/sentences with separable particles.

If the Saturation Condition and the Parameter Theorem are correct, then all of the statements in 60a should be typical of natural languages, whereas none of the statements in 60b should characterize a language. The reason is that the projection clause projecting *pro* as the specifier of an I' can check the constraints that this *pro* imposes on the I', e.g. that it be second person, indicative, or that it be marked for future tense. However, neither this projection clause nor any other one can check for the *pro* whether the I' it specifies contains a stranded preposition or a separable prefix, for the same reason that this clause will not be able to enact the co-occurrence restrictions of the lexical items in 56–57. We can put this as follows: *pro* cannot look out of its specification relation and therefore there should not be languages like 60b.

Looking back at the list of pro-drop languages presented earlier, we see that all the languages in this list can be characterized with parameter statements like those in 60a, and none requires a statement of the kind in 60b.

(61) *Pro-Drop Languages*

English:	no drop
Italian:	argument drop in finite clauses; expletive drop in participle constructions
German:	expletive drop (but not with weather verbs)
Hebrew:	only in past and future tense, but not in present tense
Finnish:	drop in first and second person; no drop in third person
Icelandic:	expletive drop (including weather verbs)

As a first result of our quest into the properties of parameters, we can list that the Parameter Theorem successfully rules out the statements in 60b as possible parameters of natural language. Since these statements are only excluded by accident in the current Principles and Parameters approach, our revision of this framework on the basis of lexical constraints on possible parameters thus leads to a first significant improvement of our understanding why languages do not make use of certain parametric options.[15]

15. David Pesetsky (personal communication) has made me aware that the theory of pro-drop in Rizzi (1982, Chapter IV) predicts that there is an implicational relation between argument pro-drop and expletive pro-drop that my theory fails to capture:

(i) If a language allows argument pro-drop, then it also allows expletive pro-drop.

The reverse does not hold; that is, there are languages that allow only expletives to drop but require argument pronouns to be overt (for instance, German and Icelandic).

In my parametric framework, (i) is not derivable directly as a theorem of the theory of pro-drop. I believe that there is a plausible explanation for (i) that is independent of the choice between

Next we examine two potential directionality parameters:

(62) a. The directionality of government of the verb depends on the category of its complement.

b. *The directionality of government of the verb depends on whether the sentence contains a doubly-filled Comp.

The first statement can be formulated in conformity with the Parameter Theorem, since all the information in the clause is contained within a lexical entry, i.e. a grammatical relation, the category of the relator and the direction of combination. In Chapter 3, I will present a word order paradigm in German that requires us to make use of such a parameter.

62b should not be a possible parameter statement in a Principles and Parameters theory based on the Saturation Condition, since it is not a local property of the lexical entries of verbs whether they can occur in sentences with or without doubly-filled Comps. And, indeed, to my knowledge, the literature does not contain a description of a language in terms of such a formulation. If no languages are found that require descriptions like 62b, then this is not an accident in our theory, since our assumptions about UG would not allow a speech community to adopt such a word-order convention.

Next, examine the following two potential bounding node parameters:

(63) a. IP is a bounding node in finite clauses, but not in infinitives.

b. *IP is a bounding node if it contains a verb in the double object construction (V NP NP) but not if it contains a V NP PP construction.

The parameter theorem makes us expect to find that the bounding node status of a maximal projection correlates with some local property of this node,

---

Rizzi's theory and mine. As is well known (cf. Montalbetti [1984]), pro-drop languages mostly allow the appearance of overt pronouns only with a focus interpretation. That means that a language violating (i) (i.e. an argument-drop language with an overt expletive) would have to allow this expletive pronoun to be focused. But this is impossible for semantic reasons; even non–pro-drop languages do not allow expletive pronouns to be focused, as the contrast between the following two English sentences demonstrates (phrases in capital letters are focused):

(ii) *IT_k John believes [t_k would rain]

(iii) HE_k John believes [t_k would change Mary's mind]

The sharp contrast between *Only HE left* and **Only IT rained* is more evidence that expletive pronouns, including even quasi-arguments, have to be unfocused in natural language.

I therefore conclude that (i) should indeed not be viewed as a consequence of the theory of pro-drop but rather should follow from a properly formulated theory of focusation. The implication then does not force a choice between Rizzi's theory of pro-drop and mine.

more specifically, with some property of one of its daughters. And, indeed, parameter values like 63a are very natural and have been invoked frequently (cf. Northern German). On the other hand, statements like 63b have so far not been found necessary to account for the bounding facts in any language. The Parameter Theorem makes this understandable: since it is not a local property of an IP-node whether it contains a verb in the double-object construction or in the NP PP construction, this is not formulable as a parameter of natural language.

We conclude our demonstration of the empirical fruitfulness of the Parameter Theorem by looking at a case of preposition stranding:

(64) a.   Prepositions can be stranded by pronouns but not by full NPs.
     b.   *Prepositions can be stranded in sentences with SU-V agreement, but not if there is no agreement.

64a is a possible parameter value according to our conception of parameters, since all of its information characterizes the local sisterhood configuration affected by the Saturation Condition. Students of the modern Germanic languages will recognize that German and Dutch fall under this parameter value. However, I know of no language where preposition stranding would alternate with subject–verb agreement, and there should not be such a language, since it is not a local property of a preposition to determine whether the subject of the sentence it is contained in agrees with the verb.

To sum up: we have found evidence that our attempt to tie parameters to the lexicon by requiring that they only make use of information available in lexical entries leads to an empirically justified theory of cross-linguistic variation which, once it is incorporated into the standard Principles and Parameters model, causes a marked improvement of its predictions. The most important of these predictions can be formulated as follows:

(65) *The "Variation Theorem"*
      With respect to saturation phenomena (i.e. constructions not involving chains or anaphoric binding), individual natural languages vary only in properties characterizing the following configuration:

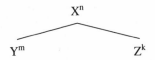

$$X^n$$
$$Y^m \qquad Z^k$$

1.5 A Theory of Possible Parameters: The Identical Projection Function Model

We are now prepared to develop the theory of grammar that will allow us to derive the Parameter Theorem and the Variation Theorem from the structure of Universal Grammar.

Before going into specific details, I want to devote a few paragraphs to the major idea underlying the building of syntactic structure in this model, the concept of *compositional projection.*

We can illustrate this idea with a comparison of how chemistry describes the formation of complex chemical elements. A chemistry textbook would typically contain a diagram like 66 as the description of the fact that the basic elements hydrogen and chlorine can react to form the complex element hydrogen chloride:

(66)

$$ H \cdot + \cdot \overset{\cdot\cdot}{\underset{\cdot\cdot}{Cl}} : \longrightarrow \quad H \overset{\cdot\cdot}{:} \overset{\cdot\cdot}{\underset{\cdot\cdot}{Cl}} : $$

A chemist would look at 66 as the description of a process that is possible only because hydrogen and chlorine each have certain basic properties no matter which reactions they enter. In particular, a chemist would postulate universal principles that will predict that an element with all the properties of hydrogen can react with an element like chlorine and will also predict what the outcome of this reaction must be (for instance, that the newly formed compound itself can react with NaOH to from NaCl and water). In other words, a natural scientist would expect that all the properties of the compound element can be predicted from the properties of the elements it contains and the laws of nature—kernel forces and electromagnetism, for example.

Returning to the question posed at the beginning of this section, I want to propose a theory of phrase structure that uncompromisingly adopts the idea of compositional projection within the domain of linguistic structure. To this end I formulate the following requirement on all structure building allowed by my model:

(67)   *The Compositionality Principle of Syntactic Projection*
The syntactic properties of a complex expression are completely determined by
a. the syntactic properties of its parts, and
b. the projection clauses.

It should be obvious that the compositionality principle by itself is not sufficient to derive the Parameter Universal and the Variation Theorem from the preceding section. The reason is this: all currently debated theories of syntax allow language-particular structure-building mechanisms. For rule-based systems this is obvious, since they associate the informal description of a language construction by construction with a list of language-particular rules. But also within the Principles and Parameters system it has been proposed frequently that languages can differ in what kind of structure-building system they make use of. Thus, Farmer (1980), Hale (1983), Haider (1981), Kiss (1987), and many other works propose that so-called configurational languages project an X-bar structure, while nonconfigurational languages choose a structure-building format leading to "flat" sentences, i.e. sentences without a verb phrase or even without any phrasal constituents at all.

Similar differences in structure building have been proposed on other grounds. Holmberg (1983) and Taraldsen (1984) have proposed that languages can differ in which constituent they take to be the head of the sentence (Infl or the verb), and Platzack (1986) proposes that they can differ in which structural relation a Comp-node bears to a sentence (sister or daughter).

It is clear that compositional projection could even be satisfied by such systems, since it would also be possible to predict all the properties of a complex expression from the properties of its parts and the properties of the structure-building process that the language happens to choose. However, the Parameter Theorem 45 that we are trying to derive makes a stronger claim, namely that no parameter shall have access to information not available to lexical entries. All the parameters just mentioned allow languages to differ in aspects that clearly go beyond the influence of a single lexical entry on grammatical structure. Thus, when we listed a number of impossible lexical entries according to the Parameter Theorem in the last section, we found the following examples:

(68) *Impossible Lexical Entries*
    a. X is an Adv specifying A's if the sentence contains a doubly-filled Comp.
    b. X is a verb taking NP-complements in nonfinite sentences and PP-complements in finite sentences.
    c. X is an AP specifying nouns that occur in subordinate clauses but not in main clauses.
    d. X is a preposition if it occurs in a sentence with subject–verb agreement and a postposition in a sentence without agreement.

Even in such languages as Warlpiri, German, and Japanese we do not find such lexical entries, though these languages have been argued to use structure-building mechanisms that are weaker than standard X-bar theory or that even suspend it completely.

If we intend to derive the Parameter Universal with all its demonstrated advantages in substantially constraining the way natural languages can differ from one another, we are led to the conclusion that the additional structure-building mechanisms proposed above are not licensed by Universal Grammar. If the power of parameters is supposed to be limited to that of lexical entries, then the structure-building mechanism that imposes the locality condition on lexical information must be universal. In other words, we are claiming that all structure building must obey the Saturation Condition without exception. We will refer to this model of grammar as the "Identical Projection Function Model":

(69) *The Identical Projection Function (IPF) Model*
Individual grammars consist of a lexicon and a projection function mapping sets of expressions from the lexicon into well-formed phrase markers: *the projection functions for all natural languages are identical and satisfy the Saturation Condition!*

In other words: the major claim of the present work is that there are no individual grammars of German or English or Warlpiri, but that there is only one single structure-building component, namely Universal Grammar itself, which projects the lexicons of these languages into phrase-structure configurations. The model thus essentially differs from all phrase-structure rule systems and modifies the Principles and Parameters theories by removing all nonlexical aspects affecting the nature of syntactic projection from the domain of parametrization. Thus, whereas in the Standard Parameter Model there are no constraints on which principles of the grammar can be parametrized, as can be seen from the list of proposed parametrized principles below,

(70) *Principles for Which Parameters Have Been Proposed*

X-bar Theory	Holmberg (1983)
Case Theory	Koopman (1983)
Government Theory	Chomsky (1986b)
Movement Theory	Engdahl (1980)
Theta Theory	Haider (1981)
Binding Theory	Koster (1987a)
Projection Principle	Hale (1983)

the framework proposed here does not allow any language-particular variation outside the domain of lexical specification, because of the effects of the Parameter Theorem and the Saturation Condition. The first constraint ensures that parameters have the same descriptive power as lexical entries, and the second one restricts this power to statements characterizing a phrase-structural sisterhood configuration.

The diagram in 71 makes the internal structure of the IPF-Model and, hence, the conception of natural language that it embodies more precise.

(71)

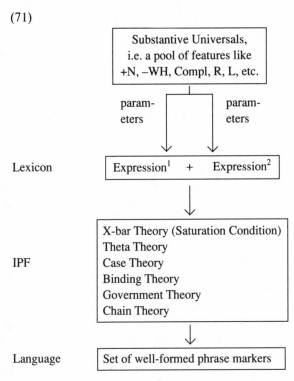

	Substantive Universals, i.e. a pool of features like +N, –WH, Compl, R, L, etc.
	parameters parameters
Lexicon	Expression^1 + Expression^2
IPF	X-bar Theory (Saturation Condition) Theta Theory Case Theory Binding Theory Government Theory Chain Theory
Language	Set of well-formed phrase markers

Universal Grammar defines a definite set of syntactic, semantic, and phonological features out of which all grammatical representations—phonological, morphological, semantic, and syntactic—are composed. These substantive universals are then compounded into possible lexical entries by parameters that are all of the form given in 72.

(72) *Preliminary   Definition   of   "Possible   Parameter   of   Natural Language"*

If P, Q are atomic or complex substantive universals, then only statements of the following form are possible parameters of natural language: for any expression E with property P: E has property Q.

In other words, parameters in the present model are taken to be the generators of the possible lexicons of natural language. Their function is to assign properties to lexical entries so that the latter can be interpreted by the Identical Projection Function and, combined with other items, form complex syntactic expressions. A parameter in this model can apply just to one lexical item (cf. 28, above, assigning a directionality property to *enough*), or it can affect a whole natural class of items, for instance, all adjectives, all WH-words, or all specifiers (cf. 39, fixing one directionality parameter in French).

Once the lexicon of a particular language (with all idiosyncratic, semi-regular, and fully regular properties) has been built, it has to be interpreted by the one structure-building mechanism that is available for all natural languages, namely the IPF. We assume (for the time being) the following (informally stated) universal projection clauses for complementation, specification, and modification structures:

(73) *Projection of the Complementation Relation*
   If a. α is a member of category X,
       b. β is a member of category YP,
       c. α takes members of YP as complements,
   then, if α takes its complements on the right,
           $[\alpha\ \beta]$ is a member of category X'; and
       if α takes its complements on the left,
           $[\beta\ \alpha]$ is a member of category X'.

(74) *Projection of the Specification Relation*
   If a. α is a member of category YP,
       b. β is a member of category X',
       c. α takes members of X' as specifiees,
   then, if α takes its specifiee on the right,
           $[\alpha\ \beta]$ is a member of category XP; and
       if α takes its specifiee on the left,
           $[\beta\ \alpha]$ is a member of category XP.

(75) *Projection of the Modification Relation*
   If a. α is a member of category YP,
       b. β is a member of category X^n,
       c. α takes members of X^n as modifiees,
   then, if α takes its modifiee on the right,
           $[\alpha\ \beta]$ is a member of category X^n; and
       if α takes its modifiee on the left,
           $[\beta\ \alpha]$ is a member of category X^n.

This theory of language derives the Parameter Theorem of section 1.3 and the Variation Theorem of section 1.4. The Parameter Theorem,

(76) *The Parameter Theorem*
   If no lexical entry can refer to feature F, then no parameter can refer to F.

holds because the function of parameters is restricted to building lexical entries or whole classes of lexical entries. Outside of the lexicon the grammars for all natural languages are identical, so that parameters cannot refer to any other than lexical information.

Second, the Variation Theorem,

(77) *The "Variation Theorem"*

With respect to saturation phenomena (i.e. not constructions involving chains or anaphoric binding), individual natural languages vary only in properties characterizing the following configuration:

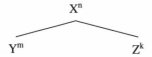

holds because the identical projection rules of X-bar theory for all natural languages obey the Saturation Condition. As a first formulation of these rules (a rule for external arguments will not be given here) in 73–75 shows, they all produce at most binary expressions as in 77, and they only allow individual items to differ in their categories and in the direction of combination. It follows that any syntactic difference between two arbitrarily chosen natural languages must be reduced to a difference obtaining in the local relation depicted in 77, or to a multitude of such local differences. But globally, all languages must have the same structure, since neither individual lexical items nor parameters are capable of weakening or suspending the effects of the Saturation Condition on the operation of the universal projection principles.

To conclude this section, we take a look back at how we arrived at our conception of possible parameters. On the first page of this chapter we quoted Humboldt as writing that

Although as a whole all languages have approximately the same structure and follow the same principles, there is hardly one which doesn't differ from the others in some particular property. . . .

We are now in a position to modify this statement slightly so that it does not read like a near-paradox:

Although as a whole all languages have the same *global* structure and follow the same principles, there is hardly one which doesn't differ from the others in some particular *local* property. . . .

The IPF-Model would indeed lead us to expect that all languages have approximately the same global structure, but that each language can have its own particular characteristics. The distinction in the organization of the grammar between the Universal Projection Function governed by the Saturation Condition and the language-particular lexicons has the effect that Humboldt describes.

Second, the IPF-Model is not only compatible with extragrammatical constraints on possible parameters but in addition imposes very strong *grammatical* restrictions on language variation and therefore satisfies our demand in section 1.3.1 that Universal Grammar itself should put limits on the form of cross-linguistic variation.

Third, the IPF-Model also satisfies the promise made earlier that the inventory of parameters can be restricted in a *principled* fashion rather than just by accidental exclusion. In the discussion of the explanatory advance brought about by X-bar theory, I wrote in section 1.3.1:

> More importantly, however, the X-bar theory-based UG differs from the "list" theory in that the negative conclusion about the rules in 10 is intimately tied to a positive generalization over the phrase structure of natural language. Thus, the "bad" rules are excluded because they all lack some property held in common by all the "good" rules. These positively motivated properties thus contribute to a structured definition of the concept "possible natural language," whereas the alternative theory offers only a randomly collected list of instantiated rules.

If the constraints on parameters that can be derived from the IPF-theory of language prove to be empirically viable beyond the parameters analyzed earlier (and that is what I will argue in the chapters ahead on the basis of a case study of seven modern Germanic languages) then the evaluation of X-bar theory as a *principled* means of capturing essential properties of natural languages which automatically exclude undesirable options carries over to the exclusion of undesirable parameters by the Saturation Condition. The feature constraint on possible parameters (the "Parameter Theorem") and the locality condition on possible parameters (the "Parameter Universal") are properties reflecting the conception of natural languages as being the product of lexicons projected into sets of phrase-structure configurations by a property of the human mind, the Identical Projection Function based on the Saturation Condition. The projection clauses defining this function only operate on lexical information and only project local trees. This positive generalization over structural descriptions automatically excludes in a principled manner all parametric variation that cannot be characterized in these terms. In this sense a theory based on the Saturation Condition—if empirically maintainable— is more highly valued than one that excludes the undesirable parameter options accidentally and would thus further improve the predictions of the current Principles and Parameters framework.

1.6 The Atomization Problem

In the preceding five sections we have developed a conception of saturation parameters that leads to the welcome result of reducing all cross-linguistic variation to a component of the grammar where languages are independently known to differ, the lexicon. This reduction also leads to a plausible theory of language acquisition as is stressed in Borer (1984, 3):[16]

> Insofar as [it] will account for a wide range of interlanguage variation, it is clearly a desirable system: it places the burden of learning on the grammatical component that is idiosyncratic and learned in every language: the vocabulary and its properties.

Thus, not only does Humboldt's observation that languages are both so similar and so diverse find a plausible explanation but also Chomsky's demand

16. Borer (1984) describes a very interesting conception of grammar, which she calls the "lexical learning model." She writes (page 2f):

> . . . there are *no* language-particular choices with respect to the realization of universal processes and principles. Rather, interlanguage variation would be restricted to the idiosyncratic properties of lexical items.

Although our theory is an instance of this general model, there are actually few similarities between Borer's framework and mine. In her system the child has to learn the "inflectional properties of different formatives and the inventory of inflectional rules operating in the input grammar" (p. 3). These latter rules allow languages to differ from each other in ways that are impossible in the system developed here. This becomes clear from the following description of the model from Borer (1984, 253; emphasis added):

> It should be borne in mind that the parametric model proposed in this study falls short of accounting for all interlanguage variation. The reader may recall that our parametric system concentrates on the mapping from level to level, a focus that stems from the nature of the inflectional system proposed in Chapter 1. It is entirely plausible that *additional parametric possibilities* would be offered by other subcomponents of the grammar. In particular, we have in mind the phrase structure component, in which one must include parameters connected with the order of elements and, possibly, the number of bars associated with different categories. Similarly, our system offers no explanation for a major parameter: that which distinguishes between configurational languages and non-configurational languages.

The present model does not have much to say about "the mapping from level to level," since it focuses on the realization of saturation phenomena in the phrase-structure component. More importantly, what distinguishes the two models is that mine is based on the Saturation Condition, whereas the parameters in Borer's model are not constrained in a similar way. Our model is thus precisely motivated by the intent to disallow the "additional parametric possibilities" that Borer mentions in the paragraph above. Its phrase-structure component does not allow languages to differ randomly with respect to the order of elements, let alone the number of bars associated with different categories. Finally, the Model does *not* countenance the existence of a configurationality parameter, since this would undermine its most essential claim, namely that all natural languages make use of one and the same projection mechanism for syntactic structure. Chapter 5 presents a theory of free word order that solves the relevant problems in Germanic without the use of such parameters.

is met, that UG "be sufficiently constrained and restrictive in the options it permits" (Chomsky, 1981, 3) for every possible grammar to develop in the mind on the basis of quite limited evidence.

However, despite the advantages of requiring that the application of parameters not lead to impossible words, it can be shown that the theory is not optimally constrained yet in that it still allows languages to differ from each other in undesirable ways. We illustrate this with the following parameter, which could be a part of English:

(78) For any expression $E = V$: E precedes its complement.

This parameter can be interpreted as a lexical redundancy rule that determines that every expression that is a verb precedes its complement in phrase structure. Although this type of parameter statement makes use only of lexical information and therefore is subject to the locality constraints on parameters, it is still too powerful, since no aspect of the theory prevents a language community from exchanging the two properties mentioned in 78, with the result in 79.

(79) For any expression $E = $ [precedes compl]: $E = V$.

78 and 79 make use of exactly the same information, but now the parameter reads: every expression that precedes its complement is a verb. Although the state of affairs expressed by the statement may indeed accidentally hold in some languages, we would still not like to allow a parameter of this sort, since it is typically the case that the directional behavior of a formative depends on its category and not vice versa. The category of an expression often depends on the denotation of the expression but is in general completely independent of its direction of combination. Crucially, the type of parameter that we have allowed so far does not discriminate between directions of property assignments, i.e. the system can assign both categorial properties to lexical items already marked for directions and directional properties to items already marked for a category. Our assumptions will thus have to be sharpened.

A second problem with a lexical approach to parameters can also be illustrated with a parameter statement like that in 78, repeated below for convenience:

(80) For any expression $E = V$: E precedes its complement.

Recall that one of our major motives for developing the lexical conception of parameters derived from the observation that a number of desirable parameters can be formulated precisely in terms of the type of information that can be referred to in lexical entries. Thus, in Section 1.3.3 we juxtaposed some parameter statements and a few statements assigning idiosyncratic properties to lexical morphemes, for example the property of specifying to the left to the adverb *enough*. Now, however beneficial this program can be shown to be, it also leads to an explanatory problem, namely the problem of "atomization" of generalizations. Thus, since our framework permits us to assign properties to individual lexical morphemes, it would also allow us to write a parameter statement for a hypothetical verb 'HYP,' as shown in 81.

(81) For any expression E = HYP: E precedes its complement.

Compare 81 with the desirable parameter in 28. The problem is that natural languages do not seem to differ from each other in that individual verbs can specify their direction of complementation. In this respect complementation structures behave fundamentally differently from specification and modification configurations, since both individual specifiers (we saw an example above: *enough*) and individual modifiers[17] can fix their directionality.[18] Although our parameters, as developed so far, would allow individual verbs to differ in their direction of complementation, this never happens in the languages that I know of; consequently, although our theory can describe that all verbs in one language show the same word-order behavior relative to their complements, its account is "atomistic" in the sense that it attributes this uniformity to the recurring coincidence that all verbs behave alike, even though they would not have to.[19]

In what follows I would like to propose an extension of the theory developed above, which at once solves both the direction-of-property-assignment problem and the atomization problem. In the next section I argue that the

17. For example, the VP-adverb *quickly*, which can both precede and follow its VP-modifiee, as opposed to *hard*, which must follow:

(i)   John *quickly* [opened the door]
(ii)   John [opened the door] *quickly*
(iii) *John *hard* [opened the door]
(iv)   John [opened the door] *hard*

For interesting observations concerning adverb and particle order, cf. Kayne (1985, 105f and fn. 11).

18. Note, however, that there is one exception to this generalization. Adpositions differ from the other complement takers in not having to govern uniformly. Thus, German has both prepositions and postpositions, and apparently this is true for other languages as well. We will ignore this for the present discussion and treat adpositions like the other complement takers. In Chapter 4 a theory of prepositions is developed from which this difference is derivable.

19. In general, atomization is a well-known problem of rule-driven theories. Thus, a Syntactic Structures type phrase-structure grammar also could not account in a principled manner for the fact that there appear to be no languages where transitive verbs differ from each other in direction of complementation.

Severe cases of atomization are found in virtually all systems of this kind.

proposed solution finds support from recent theories of morphology and leads to an overall theory of structure building in natural language that integrates morphology and syntax in an appealing way.

Let us attack the direction-of-property-assignment problem first. It is our intention to allow parameters to add directional information to lexical morphemes that are already specified for a category, but to rule out the opposite case. The obvious way to do this is to assume that lexical entries do not come into being holistically, but that they are built up in a step-by-step fashion from the features in the pool of substantive universals. Put differently, information cannot just be added to lexical morphemes randomly but has to come in a structured manner following the order shown in 82.

(82) 1. Phonological/semantic information
      2. Categorial Information
      3. Relational Information
      4. Directional Information

Thus, we suppose that at first a morpheme consists only of phonological and semantic information. Then the parameters start building up the syntactic aspects of the expression. First, a category parameter adds a syntactic category on which relational and directional properties are superimposed. This level-ordered fashion of building up lexical entries will make it impossible for information coming in early (e.g. category) to depend on information that must be added later (e.g. direction of combination). To the extent that no generalizations are found that contradict the order of attribute assignment in 82, the direction-of-property-assignment problem is solved.

With this we turn to the atomization problem. Remember that this problem is rooted in the fact that some properties of language are morpheme-specific while others can only be assigned to whole classes of morphemes (e.g. an individual *modifier* can contain a directionality statement, but an individual verb entering the *complementation* relation cannot) since all verbs of a language apparently have to behave alike in this respect.

The solution to this problem lies in an additional restriction on the manner in which parameters operate, i.e. the way lexical entries are constructed out of the features contained in the pool of substantive universals. What is in order is a slight modification of 82 so that the different types of information added to a lexical entry are not just *level-ordered* but also *goal-directed* in that for each parameter (each information type) Universal Grammar specifies a property of lexical entries with which the parametric information can be associated; i.e. we modify 82 so that *parameters do not apply directly to lexical entries but rather to their attributes.* For instance, according to the new proposal, to capture the fact that direction of combination can be fixed at the level of individual modifiers and specifiers but has to be specified for all verbs (more precisely, all heads), Universal Grammar decrees that relational information can be assigned to individual lexical entries, whereas direction of θ-marking is attributed to the *category of a morpheme*.[20] In this way, since the θ-directionality parameter does not have access to individual items, whereas the directionality parameter for relations not involving θ-marking does, the theory predicts the desired contrast between X^0-heads and other categories.

(83)
Input

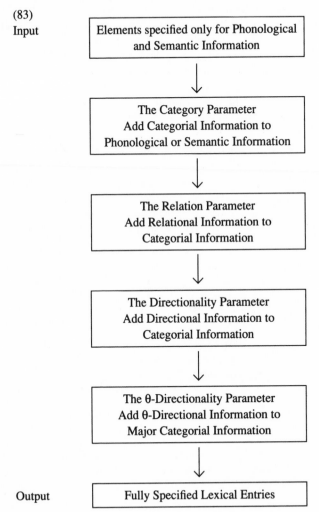

| Elements specified only for Phonological and Semantic Information |

| The Category Parameter
Add Categorial Information to
Phonological or Semantic Information |

| The Relation Parameter
Add Relational Information to
Categorial Information |

| The Directionality Parameter
Add Directional Information to
Categorial Information |

| The θ-Directionality Parameter
Add θ-Directional Information to
Major Categorial Information |

Output | Fully Specified Lexical Entries |

20. The idea of a "direction of θ-marking" was developed in Koopman (1984) and Travis (1984).

To implement this proposal, we need to offer a technical mechanism that will allow Universal Grammar to identify both individual morphemes and whole natural classes of morphemes. The latter can be accomplished easily through reference to major syntactic categories, e.g. features like $[+N]$, $[+N, -V]$ etc. and minor ones like $[+Tense]$, $[+Nominative, -Plural]$. To access individual lexical morphemes we may, for convenience, assume that Universal Grammar makes available a set of minor categorial features $[E_1, \ldots, E_n]$ (where "E" is mnemonic for "expression") that uniquely identify lexical entries. For instance, the English morphemes *bank* (edge of a river) and *bank* (financial institution) could be distinguished by referring to the first element as E_{14} and the second as E_{27}, thus allowing parameters to access them individually via the E-feature, where reference to syntactic category and underlying phonological representation would not suffice.[21]

The diagram in 83 puts the two proposals just developed together.

The set of assumptions presented in 83 have the following consequences: all syntactic parameters have the sole function of adding syntactic properties to lexical morphemes already specified for other properties.[22] The parameters have to apply in the order given and have to obey the restrictions imposed on them. For example, the first syntactic operation, the category parameter, will add categorial information to lexical entries, which at this point contain only phonological and semantic information. This system predicts that the categorial properties of a class of morphemes can depend on their semantic and/

21. This mechanism would also be employed in the c-selection of idiosyncratic prepositions. thus, in our system *hope* would be subcategorized for the E-feature of *for*, while *depend* would select the E-feature of *on*. Other applications involve idioms.

22. I assume that, both for the category parameter and the relation parameter, Universal Grammar contains default rules that apply in an Elsewhere fashion after all the language-particular parameters have operated. Thus, the rules of "Canonical Structural Realization" proposed in Grimshaw (1979) and Pesetsky (1982), and the "Realization Rules" from Williams (1981) would assign a default value to every lexical entry that has certain semantic information but did not get categorial or relational information by a parameter.

Such a system seems to be optimal. On the one hand, it allows languages to fix the properties of their lexical entries according to our constraints on parameters and the Saturation Condition. On the other hand, however, we do not lose the important insight that there are default realizations for semantic structures—for instance that an object-denoting element will typically be nominal.

The default rules will not be stated in this work, since our focus is on what kinds of lexical and syntactic structures are available at all. This is of primary interest, since the default rules are only a matter of markedness distinctions among the structures that the parameters make accessible. To rephrase this, our theory is a theory of absolute accessibility, whereas the study of the default rules deals with relative, or ranked, accessibility.

In a more comprehensive system the default rules would, of course, be stated, because they contribute substantially to the canonical patterns we find in the form of natural languages.

or phonological attributes but not, for example, on their directional behavior. This first prediction is confirmed, as the examples of semantico-categorial (84) and phono-categorial (85) correlations demonstrate.

> (84) *Categorial Features Dependent on Semantic Features*
>> a. all semantic WH-operators have the syntactic feature [+WH] in English;
>> b. all nouns denoting week days in German have the syntactic feature [+ masculine].
>
> (85) *Categorial Features Dependent on Phonological Features*
> Almost all basic nouns ending in schwa in German have the syntactic feature [+ feminine].[23]

The prediction that we wanted our system to make, namely that directional properties depend on categorial ones and not vice versa, follows from the asymmetric ordering imposed on the application of parameters.

The second syntactic parameter type that applies to lexical entries adds relational properties to categorial ones. Since there is no restriction on which categorial features may be affected, it is possible for a relational parameter to apply to one single lexical morpheme, i.e. by reference to the E-feature, which is defined as a minor categorial feature. Thus, both of the statements in 86 are possible parameters of natural language.

> (86) *Relational Parameters*
>> a. Assign [Category of Complement is PP] to E_{12} (= *live*);
>> b. Assign [Category of Modifiee is N'] to [+V, +N].

86a fixes the complementation frame of the English verb *live*, which the parameter formally refers to as expression "E_{12}." The parameter says that every lexical entry with the categorial property of being expression E_{12} has the relational property of combining with a PP in the complementation relation.[24] The second parameter is much more general in assigning a relational property to a major categorial property of lexical morphemes, in this particular case, the category "adjective". 86b is interpreted as follows: add the relational feature [Category of Modifiee is N'] to all lexical entries that have the categorial property [+V, +N].

Finally, we may give an illustration of the two directional parameters. The first one will add directions of modification and specification relations; the

---

23. Consult Mills (1984) for both statistical and language acquisition evidence.

24. The examples in this chapter have been chosen for purposes of illustration and therefore have been simplified for ease of exposition.

second one, directions of θ-marking. The former parameter applies to categorial properties irrespective of whether they are major or minor; consequently, both of the statements in 87 qualify as possible directionality parameters of natural language.

(87) *Directional Parameters*
    a. Assign [Direction of Specification of A′ is Left] to E_{77} (= *enough*);
    b. Assign [Direction of Specification of A′ is Right] to [+ Adv].

Our revised system predicts that directional properties may depend on categorial attributes (cf. 87b), since the latter are already available in lexical morphemes when the directionality parameters apply. Second, as predicted, the directions of modification and specification may be fixed for individual morphemes—e.g. *enough* in English—since the relevant parameters have access also to minor categorial features, including the E-features.

The statement in 87b would be appropriate for all English specifiers of A′ except *enough.* This parameter will allow all adverbial morphemes identified as specifiers of A′ to make use of the information that they specify to the right. We will assume that it does not have to be mentioned explicitly in the second parameter that it fails to apply to *enough;* rather, we will invoke Kiparsky's (1973) *Elsewhere Condition* to prevent a more general principle from applying to an item that is specified for a different value of a function by a more specific principle. In other words: since 87a particularly singles out the morpheme *enough,* 87b will not apply to this element, although it satisfies the description of the rule.

Finally, the statements in 88 are examples of possible and impossible direction of θ-marking parameters.

(88) *Direction of θ-Marking Parameters*
    a. Assign [Direction of θ-marking is Left] to $[+V, -N]$;
    *b. Assign [Direction of θ-marking is Right] to E_{79} (= *hit*).

The first parameter decrees that all verbs in some language θ-mark to the left; i.e. the resulting language would have a basic OV word order. Examples of such languages are German and Dutch, where verbs differ from all other categories of the language in θ-marking to the left. An elsewhere parameter would fix the direction of θ-marking for all other heads. 88b, however, is an impossible parameter; i.e. the present theory does *not* allow directions of θ-marking to be stated for individual heads, since to access an individual element rather than the whole class of heads, a minor feature has to be mentioned in the parameter (i.e. the E-feature). This is exactly what the informal formulation of the parameter schema for directions of θ-marking excludes (unlike the statements for modification and specification).[25]

To sum up this section: we noted at the beginning that although the IPF-Model as outlined in the previous sections imposes very strong locality conditions on the effect of parameters (feature associations), the earlier version did not constrain the direction of feature assignment; e.g. that direction typically depends on category rather than vice versa. Second, we were looking for a way to at least partially overcome the atomization problem inherent in today's syntactic theories. We proposed a theory that maintains the suggestion from the previous sections that parameters should be construed as operations building properties into lexical morphemes, so that the latter become projectible into phrase-structure configurations by the universal projection clauses obeying the Saturation Condition. However, the extended theory of the present section imposes further restrictions on the nature of parametric operations in that it (a) requires the parameters to apply in a fixed order, and (b) specifies an "address" for each parameter type; i.e. it allows some kinds of information to be associated only with natural class properties of morphemes rather than with individual lexical items. Furthermore, it was proposed that parameters are ordered by the Elsewhere Condition of Kiparsky (1973).

1.7 A General Theory of Structure Building: Morphology within the IPF-Model

Before giving a summary of the assumptions spelled out in this introductory chapter, I want to devote one section to the question of how the Principles and Parameters approach to syntax developed here can be made to interact with a theory of morphology that has been proposed in recent years. In particular, I will demonstrate that this theory can be incorporated very efficiently into the IPF-Model with two desirable consequences: (a) the morphology-enriched IPF-theory leads to a very natural characterization of morphological effects in the process of structure building, and (b) the empirical function of morphological, and in particular, affixational processes lends strong support

25. The reader will be aware that we have now built a slight redundancy into our system of directionality parameters. Complement takers are marked for two directions of combination, a directionality of complementation and a directionality of θ-marking. The former may be lexeme-specific but cannot be used, since it will always be overridden by the latter, which is categorially uniform.

In Chapter 4 we discuss the issue of uniformity of directionality again, when we examine the syntactic properties of adpositions.

to the overall thesis put forth in this book, namely that the interaction of the Saturation Condition and the Parameter Theorem construes parameters as lexical generalizations, i.e. operations producing lexical morphemes that can be projected to complex syntactic constituents by the Identical Projection Function.

Di Sciullo and Williams (1987, 22) give the following list of assumptions that have generally been agreed upon in the generative literature on morphological objects within the past decade: (a) words have heads, and suffixes are generally the heads of their words; (b) suffixes belong to lexical categories; (c) affixes have argument structures, as do lexical items; (d) there is no inflectional/derivational distinction in morphology; and (e) affixes cannot be assigned properties or be treated by rules different from stems, except that they must be bound.

In sum, the assumptions above mean nothing else than that the basic morphological building blocks are lexical entries, each specified for a set of grammatical properties that determine if two elements can be combined at all, and what the result of the combination will be.

In the following paragraphs I focus on the properties of affixes and pursue the consequences of the following conjecture:

(89) *The Affixation Conjecture*
      Like parameters, affixes have the function of assigning properties to linguistic expressions; *therefore, affixes can have parametric effects.*

I will argue on the basis of empirical examples that the affixation conjecture not only is correct but also allows us to see the function of affixation in grammatical structure building in an interesting new light.

As an illustration of the functional equivalence of parameters and affixes, we may examine the different means that English and German employ to equip adjectives with the information that their maximal projections can be used as modifiers of N′:

(90)

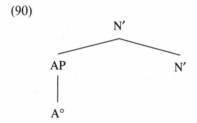

In English, there is no morphological distinction between predicative and attributive adjectives.

(91) a. the boy is *young*
      b. the *young* boy

Therefore, the general parameter given in 92, attributing the property of being a modifier of N′ to the category "adjective" will have the effect that every English adjective can project the AP in 90.[26]

(92) Assign [Category of Modifiee is N′] to [+N, +V].

Note that 92 is a well-formed parameter of natural language according to the theory of parameters developed in the previous sections; 92 assigns a relational property to a categorial property that is allowed by 83. The result of the operation named by the parameter is a set of lexical items whose maximal projections are now projectible by the Modification Clause of the Identical Projection Function. Before the lexical entries underwent the parameter, the IPF could not project them as modifiers, since they did not have the relevant relational feature.[27]

Let us now turn to German. The following examples illustrate that German uses a different strategy to allow APs to modify N′:

(93) a. der Knabe ist *jung* / * *junge*
          the boy   is young
      b. der * *jung* / *junge* Knabe
          the   young   boy

As the difference between 93a and 93b shows, German predicative adjectives differ from attributive adjectives in that the former are uninflected, whereas the latter must carry an inflectional ending. Thus, in German—unlike English—it is *not* the case that it is a property of basic adjectives that their maximal projection can be used as a modifier. Rather, German only allows *complex* adjectives to be inserted into the A⁰-slot in 90, i.e. adjectives that have been produced by affixation. Hence, the information [Category of Mod-

---

26. Because we decided in the previous section to view parameters as assignments of properties (features) of expressions to other properties of these expressions, we will formulate parameters as such operations from now on.

27. In other words, before *young* underwent the parametric operation in 92 the modification clause was undefined for it, because it can only project maximal projections as modifiers that are headed by an expression marked as [Category of Modifiee is X], for some X. After the parameter has applied, the lexical entry of *young* will contain [Category of Modifiee is N′] and will therefore now be projectible in a relation from which it was barred earlier.

ifiee is N′] (abbreviated below as [Mod: N′]) necessary to head the AP in 90 is not contained in any basic adjective in German but rather is contributed by the inflectional affix:

(94) German

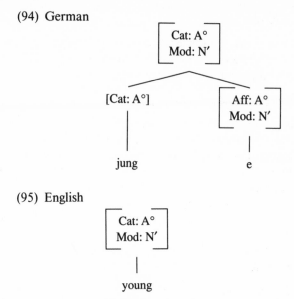

jung   e

(95) English

Cat: A°
Mod: N′

young

The analytical difference between English and German can be summed up as follows: both languages (ultimately) allow every adjective to head an AP modifying an N′, but the languages differ in the way they achieve this category-wide generalization: English uses a parameter assigning the relational property [Category of Modifiee is N′] to the categorial property [+N, +V] and derivatively to all adjectives of the language; German, however, assigns the property to one single lexical morpheme, namely an inflectional affix. Thus, the German rule is highly idiosyncratic compared to the English one, in fact, as idiosyncratic as the rule assigning the direction "Left" to the English specifier *enough*. However, this lexical idiosyncracy is transcended through another highly idiosyncratic decision, that of giving the inflectional affix under discussion the property of attaching to the whole class of adjectives (let E_{50} be the morphosyntactic E-feature of the affix):

(96) Assign [Category of Modifiee is N′] and [Category of Stem is A⁰] to E_{50}.

The previous examples illustrate nicely what has been emphasized throughout this chapter, namely, that idiosyncratic properties of lexical items can have widespread, i.e. parametric, effects on the surface appearance of a language (cf. the earlier analysis of pro-drop as the postulation of one lexical entry *pro* with certain relational properties). In the case under discussion, one language (German) achieves the same broad-scale effect with two highly idiosyncratic property assignments which another language (English) achieves with one general parameter affecting a whole natural class of elements, in this case the class of all adjectives.

Similar functional equivalences of affixes and parameters can be found in other domains, in fact even in the domain of classical choices like the WH-movement parameter. Thus, whereas all Germanic languages make use of a general parameter allowing all WH-operators in [Spec, C'], Finnish uses an affix to license WH-phrases to move to this position as the following examples 97 and 98 illustrate.[28]

(97) John antoi Marylle kirjan
      John gave Mary   book
      nom   allative acc
      'John gave a book to Mary'

(98) Kirjan*ko* John antoi Marylle?
      book-Q   John gave Mary
      'Was it a book that John gave to Mary'

Again, what one language does by feature assignment with parameters can be done with affixation in another language. The affix is the head of the complex phrase in 98 and allows it to undergo WH-movement. Schematically, the function of affixation can be represented as in 99.

(99)

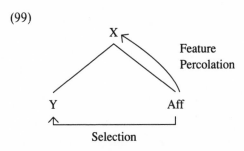

As depicted, an affix (a) selects a class of expressions to attach to, and (b) percolates its features to the complex constituent resulting from this attachment. Once one adopts the view of parameters in the Identical Projection Function Model, the role of affixation in structure building becomes obvious, since parameters in this model have exactly the same function, namely to build a

28. I am grateful to Marja-Leena Sorjonen for supplying the Finnish examples.

new class of expressions with well-defined grammatical properties. The theories of affixation developed in Lieber (1980), Williams (1981), Selkirk (1982), and Di Sciullo and Williams (1987) thus fit very naturally into the IPF-Model, because the concept of parameter and the treatment of affixation reinforce the overall assumptions the theory is built on: languages are sets of basic and derived expressions, where each expression is associated with a set of grammatical properties. The derived expressions are built compositionally from subexpressions by the application of projection principles, which impose sharp locality conditions on the information relevant to the production of new complex expressions. Underived expressions are listed in a lexicon and are produced by parametric operations accumulating grammatical properties into units. These operations, though open to language-particular manipulation, are also sharply constrained in the information they can refer to and the order in which they apply. Thus, both parameters and affixes answer the need of a language community to have at its disposal a number of expressions that (1) satisfy the need of the community to make conventions for certain communicative purposes, and (2) at the same time contain all and only that grammatical information needed by the projection clauses obeying the Saturation Condition to (recursively) combine expressions into larger ones.

In order to implement the idea that parameters and affixes are functionally equivalent, I will assume the following informally stated universal projection clause for affixation (for simplicity's sake we ignore the linear order of affixation in 100).

(100) *Projection of the Affixation Relation*
    If a. α is an affix,
         b. β is a non-affix with properties Y,
         c. α attaches to expressions with properties Z,
         d. Z is a subset of Y,
    then $\delta = [\alpha\ \beta]$ is an expression which has
         e. all the properties of α, and
         f. all the properties of β that α is not marked for.

Like the projection clauses for modification, specification, and complementation, the one that accepts expressions produced by affixation obeys the Saturation Condition; i.e. it is completely local in not allowing reference to information outside the newly created expression, or to information embedded in the expressions to be combined. The morphology-enriched IPF-Model thus correctly predicts that, just as the statements in 101 are impossible parameters of natural language, so also affixes like those in 102 cannot exist in any natural language.

(101) *Impossible Parameters*
  a. *Prepositions can be stranded in sentences with SU-V agreement, but not if there is no agreement.
  b. *The directionality of government of the verb depends on whether the sentence contains a doubly-filled Comp.
  c. *The language allows pro-drop in sentences with a stranded preposition/sentences with separable particles.

(102) *Impossible Affixes*
  a. *Affix X can be put onto prepositions only in sentences with no SU-V agreement.
  b. *Affix Y only attaches to verbs in subordinate clauses with doubly-filled Comps.
  c. *Affix Z only attaches to subjects of sentences containing a stranded preposition.

The function of affixes thus lends further support to the view that parameters derive well-formed lexical entries for the projection process.

But the benefit is not just in one direction. Combining the IPF-Model and the above theory of affixes also motivates certain assumptions in the theory of morphology. In particular, the functional equivalence of parameters and affixes leads to the expectation that one and the same language may put the two mechanisms to use in different scopes; i.e. where one construction makes use of a parameter to equip expressions with certain information, another one may use an affix. There is good empirical support for this conclusion as well. As a first illustration, observe the following structure of the inflectional paradigm of the noun *hand* in Turkish, which is often cited as a prototypical example of an agglutinative language:

(103)

	Sg	Pl
Nom	el	el-ler
Gen	el-in	el-ler-in
Dat	el-e	el-ler-e
Acc	el-i	el-ler-i
Loc	el-de	el-ler-de
Abl	el-den	el-ler-den

We find that the citation form, the nominative singular, is morphologically unmarked, whereas every other specification of the features CASE and NUMBER is expressed by one phonologically distinct affix; e.g. the genitive is marked with *-in,* the plural with *-ler,* etc. In other words, a speaker who knows the properties of the affixes appearing in 103 is able to predict a number of the properties of all the eleven complex forms (barring homophony);

e.g. that an expression ending in *lerde* is a noun, its CASE is locative, and its NUMBER is plural. The only expression whose properties are not recoverable in this way is the citation form, i.e. the one that is morphologically unmarked. A speaker who does not know the morpheme *el* will not be able to predict, for example, that it is a noun, etc. Thus, the properties of being a noun, of being nominative and singular are assigned to *el* not by affixation but rather by the only other grammatical means to provide morphemes with features, a parameter:

(104) Assign [Category is N], [Case is Nominative], and [Number is Singular] to E_{412}.

This system of fixing the properties of the base of a morphological paradigm through a parameter, and of completing the paradigm by affixation is highly efficient, since the speaker in this way can produce a fully specified paradigm by memorizing only the base of the paradigm and the affixes with their properties. The complex forms of the paradigm will receive their properties by application of the projection clause for affixation in 100. To give an example, the accusative plural of *el* is derived from *el, ler,* and *i* as follows:

(105)

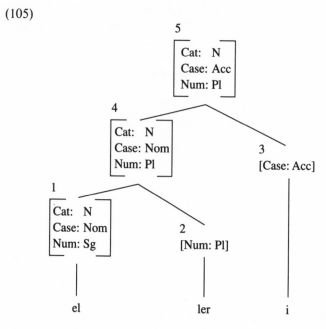

The properties of the basic morphemes in 1, 2, and 3 have been assigned by parameters unique to these three items. But their interaction to produce the members of the paradigm in 4 and 5 is due to the application of the projection clause for affixation. Consequently, although the basic form *el* is singular, the complex form *el-ler* is plural, since the feature value "Plural" of the affix overrides the feature value "Singular" of the non-head. In the same way, *i* percolates its accusative feature up to the complex word, with the result that *el-ler-i* has all the features of the two affixes plus the major categorial feature of the basic expression *el*.

The form of such a typical morphological paradigm can therefore be viewed as the result of the most economical interplay of the two feature-assigning operations within the IPF-Model: parameters compose the citation form of the paradigm and the affixes whose properties are completely unpredictable. The projection clause for affixes then constructs the rest of the paradigm compositionally on the basis of the smaller expressions. This enables a speaker to productively generate the whole paradigm with minimal means.

One final piece of evidence that I will present for the mutually supporting view of parameters and affixes taken here is the phenomenon of suppletion in morphological paradigms. Thus, examine the following subpart of the German verb paradigm:

(106)

	Affix	Parameter	Affix & Parameter
1	geh-**e**	bin	seh-**e**
2	geh-**st**	bist	sieh-**st**
3	geh-**t**	ist	sieh-**t**

The singular present forms of the verb *gehen* (to go) are completely predictable from its present stem *geh* and the properties of the boldface affixes. In contrast, as in English, the verb *sein* (to be) builds its paradigm completely through suppletion, e.g. there are no recurrent stems and affixes that will compose the first person form *bin*. This morpheme thus has to be listed as an independent lexical entry whose properties are assigned by a parameter. And, finally, we find verbs like *sehen* (to see) where parameters and affixes interact to produce the correct forms of the paradigm. Thus, whereas the first person singular is composed of the stem *seh* and the productive affix *e,* the second and third persons take the productive affixes *st* and *t,* but attach them to the suppletive stem *sieh.*

Like the Turkish noun paradigm in 103, the German verb paradigms display openly the functional equivalence of parameters and affixes postulated in the affixation conjecture 89: parameters and affixes are functionally equivalent in supplying grammatical expressions with the properties they need to be projected into phrase structure by the Identical Projection Function. The first verb in 106 builds its paradigm exclusively through affixation, the second one uses only parameters, and the third one, finally, makes parameters and affixes interact to complete its paradigm.

We sum up our section on morphology. We have not really added anything to the generative theory of morphology but have pointed out that the crucial aspects of this theory are compatible with our assumption that parameters attribute properties to lexical entries. Parameters and affixes are thus seen as two sides of the same coin. They build properties into expressions, which can then be referred to in the structure-building process. Empirical evidence for this functional symmetry was presented. We believe that our theory of parameters and the theory of morphology are mutually supportive in that each theory derives conceptual and empirical plausibility from the other. The lexical theory of parameters is strengthened in that the function of affixes shows that language-wide generalizations can be rooted in lexical idiosyncracies. The theory of morphology is supported conceptually and empirically in that the existence of affixation as an expression-building operation becomes natural when seen against the background of parameters with the same function, and in that the typical forms of morphological paradigms can be viewed as those which are economically representable with parameters and affixes.

1.8 Summary

In this chapter we have proposed a new interpretation of the Principles and Parameters approach to linguistic theory. In conformity with the programmatic supposition of Chomsky (1965) that a successful theory of grammar would inform the language learner optimally as to the general character of the structure of natural language, it was suggested that the language-acquisition device analyzes natural languages as potentially infinite sets of expressions composed of a finite stock of basic expressions by an Identical Projection Function that obeys the *Saturation Condition.* Viewed in this way, the task of the language learners is to detect all the basic expressions of their language and their properties, i.e. to learn the vocabulary of the language. In this respect, the present model contrasts with earlier proposals within Generative Grammar, where the child is forced to fix many of the properties of the structure-building operations as well.

By limiting all parametric variation to the presyntactic lexical component, the new theory imposes a locality condition on the effect of parameters, which apparently correctly predicts that there should be a strong empirical correlation between the concepts "possible lexical entry of natural language" and "possible parameter of natural language." To the extent that this prediction proves to be correct when confronted with further data, this unified approach to parameters would constitute an important improvement over standard practice, since the correlation noted would allow us to reduce the power of parameters to the independently necessary constraints on lexical material. In other words, the theory would lead to an authentic reduction of the power of one component without compensatory enrichment of any other grammatical module. In the light of the absence of *any* grammar-internal constraints on parameters in the current Principles and Parameters Theory, every such empirically motivated restriction is desirable.

According to the proposals made (the Saturation Condition and the Parameter Theorem), the class of parameters allowed in the present framework is highly constrained in that

(107) a. They all have the same form and function, namely to assign grammatical properties to other grammatical properties;
   b. the properties mentioned in each parameter have to be drawn from a closed pool of substantive universals;
   c. there are universal coocurrence restrictions on which properties may be mentioned in one parameter;
   d. the application of different parameters is ordered asymmetrically;
   e. each lexical entry produced by parametrization must satisfy the requirements of at least one of the universal projection clauses of the IPF to occur in complex expressions.

It was argued on the basis of empirical evidence from pro-drop, WH-movement, and directionality that these indeed are desirable properties for parameters.

Finally, we suggested that the view of parameters as generators of lexical expressions projectible by the IPF-Model is reinforced by recent assumptions about morphological, and in particular affixational, processes within the generative literature. Affixes there are viewed as lexical expressions in their own right, which can carry categorial, relational, and other syntactically relevant information. In support of this view, it was shown that affixes can attach to whole classes of expressions as heads and percolate their features to the newly created complex expression while suppressing the features of the non-head that the affix itself is marked for. Affixes take classes of "old" expressions and form new ones with additional properties. In this sense they perform the same function as parameters in the IPF-Model. The trade-off between the use of affixes and that of parameters was documented with examples from Finnish, Turkish, and German. Finally, it was claimed that the typical form of a morphological paradigm (one citation form and a number of affixes) was a reflex of the most economical interaction of parameters and affixes within our model.

The remainder of the book will concentrate on the effects of the Saturation Condition. It will be argued that this condition not only plays a role in restricting the parametric options of pro-drop, WH-movement, and directionality, but also plays a crucial role in the distribution of argument clauses, pied piping, and free word order constructions.

The epilogue, finally, will sum up all the evidence for the Saturation Condition and its effects on parameter theory.

2

Basic Word Order

2.1 Introduction

The remainder of the book will apply the theory of morphosyntax presented in Chapter 1 to selected problems in the analysis of the seven modern Germanic languages: German, Dutch, English, Norwegian, Swedish, Danish, and Icelandic. Its goal is to demonstrate that it is possible to give an insightful account of some of the major properties of these languages *without* resorting to any language-particular tools beyond those already proposed.

Emphasis is placed throughout on the questions of (1) whether it is possible to attribute those properties that all languages share to the theory of grammar (Universal Grammar) itself rather than to their individual grammars, and (2) whether it is possible to capture the idiosyncratic properties of an individual language purely with mechanisms satisfying the definition of possible Saturation Parameter argued for in Chapter 1.

2.2 Documenting Directionality in Modern Germanic

We begin our journey through Germanic syntax with an overview of the major word order generalizations in the different dialects of this language family. Together with the specifics of the Comp/Infl systems to be developed in the next chapter, we will then be able to account for a sizable amount of the syntax of these languages. The present chapter deals only with word orders that I hypothesize to be base-generated. Alternative word orders of a number of categories will be discussed in the following chapters.

The results of the following data overview will be collected later in this chapter. I discuss the word order patterns along the dimension of grammatical relations. We will first look at specifiers, then at complements, and finally at modifiers.

In those languages that allow specifiers to co-occur with overt complementizers,[1] the specifiers precede the complementizer in the string. We will assume that phonologically empty complementizers behave in the same way:[2]

(1G) Ich weiß nicht [**welches Buch** *e* er   lesen will]
      I   know not   which book C he   read wants

---

1. Throughout this book I assume the structure of the sentence proposed in Chomsky (1986b). Comp (= C) and Infl (= I) are fully integrated into X-bar theory. [Spec, I′] is the subject position and [Spec, C′] the clausal operator position which is the landing site of all Germanic question and relative clause operators that move at S-structure.

The idea that verbs move to an Aux/Infl-node was apparently first proposed in Klima and Bellugi (1966), Jackendoff (1972), and Emonds (1978). The claim that Infl is the head of the sentence stems from unpublished work of Ken Hale. Stowell (1981) postulates Infl′- and IP-nodes and Pesetsky (1982) argues for the existence of an Infl′. To my knowledge, Stowell (1981) is the first work to argue that Comp is the head of S-bar, and Chomsky (1986b) fully integrates Comp into the X-bar system by postulating C′ and CP-nodes.

Second, following Abney (1987), Hellan (1986), Bowers (1987), and many works since, I will adopt the "DP-Hypothesis" concerning the structure of nominals; that is, I assume that nominal phrases are headed by a (possibly phonologically empty) determiner (abbreviated "D") rather than a noun. The following schema illustrates the suggested structure of an English nominal like *the old house:*

(i)

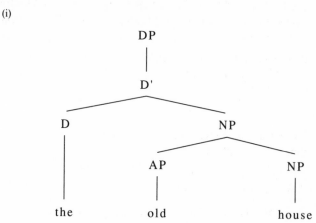

Possessive phrases like *John's* in *John's mother* are interpreted as specifiers of D′.

2. A number of Icelandic example sentences have been taken from Thráinsson (1979) and Zaenen (1980). Some examples have also been built in analogy to sentences in these works.

(2Du) Ik   weet niet [**welk   boek** *of* hij wil   lezen]
       I   know not   which book C he wants read

(3S)   Jag vet   inte [**vilken bok**   *som* hon ville   låna]
       I   know not   which book C   he   wanted borrow

(4Da) Jeg ved ikke [**hvilken bog** *e* hun ville   låne]
       I   know not which book C she wanted borrow

(5N)   Vi vet   [**hvem** *e* Marit snakker med]
       we know who C Marit talks   with

(6I)   Hann spurði [**hvern** *e* hún hefði talað   við]
       he   asked who   C she had   talked with

(7E)   I don't know [**which book** *e* he wants to read]

In accordance with the theory of directionality parameters developed in Chapter 1, the generalization noted above can be expressed by the following parameter:

(8) *Specifiers of Comp specify to the Right.*

We may interpret this statement as follows: if an expression already has the relational property [Category of Specifiee is Comp] in its lexical entry, then the directional property [Direction of Specification is Right] gets added.[3] As a consequence, the X-bar theoretic projection clause for specification will only be able to project two expressions to a CP if the specifier precedes its C'-sister.

Let us now turn to the specifier of I', the subject position. The following sentences document that all Germanic languages allow the subject to precede the constituent it specifies:

(9G)   daß [**Peter** *ein Buch lesen will*]
        that Peter a   book read will

(10Du) dat [**Jan** *een boek lezen kan*]
        that Jan a   book read can

(11S)   att [**Johan** *hade sett Eva*]
        that Johan had   seen Eva

(12Da) at [**du** *har mødt Eva*]
        that you have met Eva

(13N)   at [**Ola** *skal komme*]
        that Ola shall come

3. Later in this chapter we will see that it is disadvantageous to retain 8, since we can derive it as a special case of a larger generalization of Germanic word order.

(14I)   að [**Olafur** *hafi lofad*   *Maríu þessum hring*]
         that Olaf   has promised Maria this   ring

(15E)   that [**John** *has read a book*]

16 fixes the directionality parameter for specifiers of I'.

(16) *Specifiers of Infl specify to the Right.*

This brings us to the specifiers of A' and Adv'. In all languages the specifier precedes these categories:

(17G)   [**sehr** *alt*]
        very old

(18Du) [**heel** *oud*]
        very old

(19S)   [**mycket** *gammal*]
        very   old

(20Da) [**meget** *gammel*]
        very   old

(21N)   [**veldig** *gammel*]
        very   old

(22I)   [**mjög** *gamall*]
        very old

(23E)   [**very**   *old*]

(24G)   [**sehr** *schnell*] laufen
        very fast   run

(25Du) [**heel** *snel*] lopen
        very fast   run

(26S)   springa [**mycket** *snabbt*]
        run   very   fast

(27Da) løbe [**meget** *hurtigt*]
        run very   fast

(28N)   løp [**veldig** *fort*]
        run very   fast

(29I)   hlaupa [**mjög** *hratt*]
        run   very fast

(30E)   run [**very** *fast*]

The formulation of the parameters necessary for these cases is obvious.

As the following examples show, all languages except Icelandic allow a possessive phrase to precede its D′-specifiee; Icelandic shows the opposite order:

(31G)   [**Peters** *Mutter*]
        Peter's mother
(32Du) [**Jan's** *moeder*]
        Jan's mother
(33S)   [**Johans** *bok*]
        John's book
(34Da) [**Peters** *mor*]
        Peter's mother
(35N)   [**Jons**   *sko*]
        John's shoe
(36I)   [*Módir* **Jóns**]
        mother John's
(37E)   [**John's** *mother*]

Putting the data from these five paradigms together, we get the following picture:

(38)   *The Word Order of Specifiers in Germanic*[4]

	G	Du	S	Da	N	I	E
Spec, C′	R	R	R	R	R	R	R
Spec, I′	R	R	R	R	R	R	R
Spec, A′	R	R	R	R	R	R	R
Spec, Adv′	R	R	R	R	R	R	R
Spec, D′	R	R	R	R	R	Ⓛ	R

The parameter in 39, restricted to Icelandic, expresses that possessive phrases follow the D′ they specify:

(39)   *Specifiers of D′ specify to the Left.*

The remaining thirty-four entries are predicted by the following parameter:

(40)   *Specification is to the Right.*

40 fixes the directionality value for all specifiers in Germanic to "Right," with the exception of specifiers of D′ in Icelandic, whose value has been set to

4. The table is to be read as follows: if the value of the two categories listed on the left is "R," then the element mentioned first takes the other one to its right, otherwise to the left.

"Left" by the more idiosyncratic 39; the Elsewhere Condition will make 39 apply before 40 in Icelandic. In accordance with the operations associated with directionality parameters, 40 decrees that every lexical entry containing a statement

(41) [Category of Specifiee is X]

is changed to 42 as a result of the application of the parameter:

(42) [Category of Specifiee is X]
│
[Direction of Specification is Right]

This entails that all specifiers have to precede the X′-constituent they specify.

With this treatment of specifiers we turn to the word order behavior of complements. Here we have to consider two types of directionality statements, those that depend on the grammatical relation complementation, and those that refer to θ-marking and are assigned to major categories, since individual lexical heads never differ from each other in this respect.

We will therefore treat the functional heads C, I, and D first, and examine the θ-marking heads later.

Comp takes its complements on the right in all Germanic languages:

(43G)   Peter sagte [**daß** *Hans Maria geküßt hat*]
        Peter said   that Hans Maria kissed   had

(44Du) Piet zei [**dat** *Jan Komen zou*]
        Piet said that Jan come   would

(45S)   Vi kunde inte tro   [**att** *han var död*]
        we could not believe that he   was dead

(46Da) Hans siger [**at**   *Peter har mødt Eva*]
        Hans says   that Peter has met   Eva

(47N)   Jeg vet   [**at**   *Petter skal komme*]
        I   know   that Petter shall come

(48I)   Jón segir [**að**   *Olafur hafi séd Egil*]
        John says   that Olaf   has seen Egil

(49E)   Judy believes [**that** *she will leave tomorrow*]

We can fix the directionality of complementation for the functional head "Comp" as follows:

(50) *Complementizers take their complement on the Right.*

This parameter enters [Direction of Complementation is Right] under [Category of Complement is Infl] in the lexical entries of all complementizers, and thus expresses the generalization found in 43–49.

Next, we turn to Infl and its VP-complement. Here we see another split among the Germanic languages. Assuming that the auxiliary in the sentences below marks the position of Infl, we witness that in German and Dutch Infl follows the VP, while in all other languages it precedes:

(51G)   daß Peter [*ein Buch lesen* **will**]
        that Peter a   book read will

(52Du) dat Jan [*een boek lezen* **kan**]
        that Jan a   book read can

(53S)   att Johan [**hade** *sett Eva*]
        that Johan had seen Eva

(54Da) at du [**har** *mødt Eva*]
        that you have met Eva

(55N)   at Ola [**skal** *komme*]
        that Ola shall come

(56I)   að Olafur [**hafi** *lofad   Maríu þessum hring*]
        that Olaf   has promised Maria this   ring

(57E)   that John [**has** *read a book*]

The parameters are easy to state and we will not do this here. Instead, we turn to the word order behavior of determiners. In all Germanic languages a determiner head can take its NP-complement on the right:

(58G)   [**das** *Haus*]
        the house

(59Du) [**het** *huis*]
        the house

(60S)   [**den** *man*]
        the man

(61Da) [**disse** *konstruktioner*]
        these constructions

(62N)   [**disse** *konstruksjonene*]
        these constructions

(63I)   [þessi *hringur*]
        this   ring

(64E)   [**the** *house*]

Taking the three functional heads C, I, and D together, we get the picture shown in 65.

(65) *The Word Order Behavior of the Functional Heads in Germanic*

	G	Du	S	Da	N	I	E
C, Compl	R	R	R	R	R	R	R
I, Compl	Ⓛ	Ⓛ	R	R	R	R	R
D, Compl	R	R	R	R	R	R	R

Two parameters are sufficient to capture all these entries. German and Dutch are characterized as follows:

(66) *Infls take their complement on the Left.*   (G/Du)

This parameter has the following effect on the lexical entries of all Infls in German and Dutch:

(67) [Cat. of Compl. is V]   [Cat. of Compl. is V].
                    → |
                          [Direction of Complementation is Left]

Infls will thus be forced to take their VP-complements on the left.

However, all the remaining heads listed in 65, i.e. all Comps, determiners, and the Infls in the SVO languages, will fall under the parameter given in 68.

(68) *Complementation is to the Right.*   (Germanic)

Since parameter 66 mentions the category Infl while 68 mentions no particular categories at all, the latter parameter is more general and will therefore apply after 66 in German and Dutch. This predicts the correct word order of functional heads and their complements in all the Germanic languages.

With this we turn to the θ-marking heads. Beginning with verbs, we see that they show the same behavior as Infls, i.e. in German and Dutch verbs take their complements on the left, in the other languages the complement appears on the right:

(69G)   [*ein Buch* **lesen**]
        a   book read

(70Du) [*een boek* **lezen**]
        a   book read

(71S)   [**träffade** *flickan*]
        met   the girl

(72Da) [**kender** *en mand*]
        know   a   man

(73N)   [**vant** *løpet*]
        won the race

(74I)   [**drekkur** *vodka*]
        drink   vodka

(75E)   [**reads** *a book*]

This state of affairs is not difficult to capture. German and Dutch are characterized as follows:

(76)   *Verbs θ-mark to the Left.*

The other languages substitute "Right" for "Left" in 76.
Adjectives precede their complements in all dialects.[5]

(77G)   [**stolz**   *auf Maria*]
        proud of   Mary

(78Du) [**tevreden** *met hem*]
        satisfied with him

(79S)   [**tillgiven** *sin husse*]
        devoted his master

(80Da) [**stolt**   *af Eva*]
        proud of Eva

(81N)   [**stolt**   *av Eva*]
        proud of Eva

(82I)   [**montinn** *af Maríu*]
        proud   of Mary

(83E)   [**proud** *of his children*]

This leaves us with nouns and adpositions. They both govern to the right in all languages.

---

5. Some complements of adjectives can or must appear on the left. They are not discussed here because I assume them to be derived by movement rather than being base-generated. In Chapter 5 their properties are analyzed in detail and related to Case theory.

Nouns:

(84G) die [**Zerstörung** *der Stadt*]
      the destruction the city (gen)

(85Du) de [**verovering** *van de stad*]
      the conquest of the city

(86S) [**erövringen**   *av staden*]
      the conquest of the city

(87Da) [**erobringen** *af byen*]
      the conquest of the city

(88N) [**ødeleggelsen** *av byen*]
      destruction of the city

(89I) [**eyðilegging** *borgarinnar*]
      destruction the city

(90E) the [**destruction** *of the city*]

Prepositions:[6]

(91G) [**mit** *einem Hammer*]
      with a   hammer

(92Du) [**met** *Marie*]
      with Mary

(93S) [**med** *honom*]
      with him

(94Da) [**til** *sin sekretær*]
      to his secretary

(95N) [**med** *Ola*]
      with Ola

(96I) [**í** *Rússlandi*]
      in Russia

(97E) [**with** *Mary*]

---

6. At least German and Dutch also have some postpositions. I will come back to this issue in Section 4.3 of Chapter 4.

For a more detailed discussion in the literature, consult v. Riemsdijk (1978), Bennis (1986), den Besten/Webelhuth (1990).

The survey in 98 sums up the basic word order of heads and θ-marked complements.

(98) *The Word Order Behavior of the θ-marking Heads in Germanic*

	G	Du	S	Da	N	I	E
V, Compl	Ⓛ	Ⓛ	R	R	R	R	R
A, Compl	R	R	R	R	R	R	R
N, Compl	R	R	R	R	R	R	R
P, Compl	R	R	R	R	R	R	R

We see that the behavior of the θ-markers is similar to that of the functional heads in 65. The situation in 98 is easy to characterize with two directionality parameters, one that sets the θ-marking direction of verbs to "Left" in German and Dutch, and one that sets the θ-direction of all major categories to "Right":

(99)   *Verbs θ-mark to the Left.*   (G/Du)

(100) *θ-marking is to the Right.*   (Germanic)

After our examination of some modifiers, we will show that an even larger generalization is possible.

This leaves us with modifiers. I will only study a few examples here. Relative clauses adjoin to the right of their head in all Germanic languages:[7]

(101G) [*der Mann* **der   Maria liebt**]
        the man   who Maria loves

(102Du) [*de jongen* **die   daar zit**]
        the boy   who there sits

(103S) [*boken*   **som jag köpte**]
        the book that I   bought

(104Da) [*en mand* **som kan li′ dig**]
        a man   that likes you

(105N) [*den mannen* **som har skrevet denne boken**]
        the man   that has written this   book

7. There are different theories about the correct analysis of relative clauses. Partee (1973) argues on semantic grounds that they should combine with a common noun (an NP in our system), while Bach/Cooper (1978) show that the analysis we assume in the text is compatible with a compositional semantics.

(106I) [*madurinn* **sem ég talaði við**]
      the man   that I   talked with

(107E) [*the book* **that John bought**]

Modifiers of adjective phrases adjoin on the left.

(108G) [**drei Meter** *lang*]
      three meters long

(109Du) [**drie meter** *hoog*]
      three meters high

(110S) [**tre   meter** *lång*]
      three meters long

(111Da) [**tre   meter** *lang*]
      three meters long

(112N) [**tre   meter** *lang*]
      three meters long

(113I) [**þriggja metra** *langur*]
      three   meters long

(114E) [**three years** *old*]

And, finally, adjectival modifiers of NP also precede their relator.

(115G) das [**alte** *Haus*]
      the old house

(116Du) het [**oude** *huis*]
      the old   house

(117S) det [**gamla** *huset*]
      the old   house

(118Da) denne [**gamle** *mand*]
      this   old   man

(119N) denne [**gamle** *mannen*]
      this   old   man

(120I) þessi [**gamli** *madur*]
      this old   man

(121E) the [**old** *house*][8]

8. English also allows/requires the AP to occur on the right when it is heavy.

  (iE) We saw a [[**man**] *too old to walk*]

Putting all the data from the paradigms presented together, we get the over-view shown in 122 of the basic word order in Germanic.

(122) *Basic Word Order in Germanic*

	G	Du	S	Da	N	I	E
Spec, C′	R	R	R	R	R	R	R
Spec, I′	R	R	R	R	R	R	R
Spec, A′	R	R	R	R	R	R	R
Spec, Adv′	R	R	R	R	R	R	R
Spec, D′	R	R	R	R	R	Ⓛ	R
C, Compl	R	R	R	R	R	R	R
I, Compl	Ⓛ	Ⓛ	R	R	R	R	R
D, Compl	R	R	R	R	R	R	R
V, θ	Ⓛ	Ⓛ	R	R	R	R	R
A, θ	R	R	R	R	R	R	R
N, θ	R	R	R	R	R	R	R
P, θ	R	R	R	R	R	R	R
Mod, DP	L	L	L	L	L	L	L
Mod, AP	R	R	R	R	R	R	R
AP-Mod, NP	R	R	R	R	R	R	R

We can predict all the entries in the survey given in 122 with five generalizations. First, as is obvious, all Germanic languages are strongly right-leaning languages, i.e. selectors and θ-markers typically take their sister on the right. This is expressed by the following simple parameter:

(123) *Selectors select to the Right.*   (Germanic)

The survey in 122 also shows that there are four exceptions to the generalization in 123. 124a–124d represent the parameters responsible for them.

(124) a. Specifiers take D′ on the Left in Icelandic;
       b. Infls take complements on the Left in G/Du;

As Roger Higgins (personal communication) has pointed out to me, there are even short APs that must occur on the right in certain circumstances:

(iiE)   He bought [[**something**] *old*]

(iiiE)   *He bought [*old* [**something**]]

Structures similar to example (ii) are discussed in Chomsky (1981, 166ff). I have not studied them in detail and do not know whether they exist in any of the other Germanic languages. They will be ignored throughout.

    c. Verbs θ-mark to the Left in G/Du;

    d. CPs modify to the Left in Germanic.

We reverse the sequence of the parameters so as to show their partial ordering by the Elsewhere Condition:

(125) a. Infls take complements on the Left.   (G/Du)

      b. Verbs θ-mark to the Left.   (G/Du)

      c. Specifiers take D′ on the Left.   (Icelandic)

      d. CPs modify to the Left.   (Germanic)

      e. Selectors select to the Right.   (Germanic)

Since the parameters 125a–125d each mention one different grammatical relation, they are not ordered w.r.t. each other. They can therefore apply in any order to the lexicons of those grammars containing them. Their effect will be to set the direction of combination for the mentioned elements and grammatical relations to "Left." Since parameter 125e does not mention any specific grammatical relation or category, it is ordered after all the other parameters by the Elsewhere Condition. It will therefore fill in the value "Right" for every element and grammatical relation that was not affected by one of the previous parameters.

Besides a number of smaller generalizations about modifiers and isolated items like *enough,* the word order in English can be characterized by the following two generalizations:

(126) *The Major Word Order Parameters of English*

      a. CPs modify to the Left.

      b. Selectors select to the Right.

A child learning English would not have to learn very specific information. A few selectors, including relative clauses, take their sister on the left, but the large majority of grammatical relations in English lean rightwards.

Icelandic would be slightly more marked, since, in addition to relative clauses, specifiers of D′ fall out of the big generalization that the language is basically rightwards-selecting:

(127) *The Major Word Order Parameters of Icelandic*

      a. Specifiers take D′ on the Left.

      b. CPs modify to the Left.

      c. Selectors select to the Right.

German and Dutch, finally, come out as most marked among the Germanic languages, since they have more exceptions to the rightward-leaning generalization than any other member of the family.

(128) *The Major Word Order Parameters of German and Dutch*
 a. Infls take complements on the Left.
 b. Verbs θ-mark to the Left.
 c. CPs modify to the Left.
 d. Selectors select to the Right.

The English parameters mention three specific categories/relations, the Icelandic ones five, and the German/Dutch ones seven. Since the sets of parameters in 126, 127, and 128 are the most concise statements allowed in our theory to derive the language-particular word order generalizations in 122, our assumptions entail that a language learner confronted with German or Dutch has to make a greater number of specific observations than one exposed to Icelandic or English. This property can be used as a measure for relative markedness, i.e. we would say that as far as directionality is concerned German and Dutch are more marked than Icelandic or English. This seems to be in accord with our pretheoretic intuition.

2.3 Summary

We have analyzed the basic word order of Germanic as follows: all languages are mostly rightward-selecting, i.e. in a constituent $\gamma = [\alpha\ \beta]$ α selects β to occur to its right. A statement to this effect is entered into lexical entries by the most general directionality parameter that can be formulated in our theory:

(129) *Selectors select to the Right.*

Since there can be additional directionality parameters in an individual grammar (ordered by the Elsewhere Condition), it is possible that there are exceptions to 129. Such exceptions indeed exist in the Germanic languages, although—crucially—they all stay within the limits of variability allowed by our theory of directionality; thus, whereas *modifiers* and *specifiers* are not required to be directionally uniform, all *θ-markers* of the same category have to θ-mark in the same direction. Our theory therefore predicts that of the six logically possible language types listed in 130 the starred one does not exist.

(130)

Direction fixed at the level of	θ-markers	Mod/Spec
Individual morpheme	*	ok
One category	ok	ok
All categories	ok	ok

Universal Grammar thus imposes minimal requirements of uniformity on individual grammars. At least all the members of one category *must* θ-mark in the same direction, and the more categories take the same direction, the more compact the grammar will be. At the level of modifiers and specifiers there is no such minimal requirement, although one would expect there to be some pressure of directional uniformity in this domain as well. The specifiers of A′ in English instantiate this picture directly: all of them precede A′ with the exception of the one isolated item *enough*.

In sum: we predict that all the non-starred language types in 130 are possible natural languages and that the language types closer to the bottom of the table are more unmarked than the ones closer to the top. For the Germanic languages these predictions are borne out, and if our theory is correct, then we should find the same picture in any other natural language we test the theory against.

This concludes our short discussion of the nature of directionality parameters and their predicted effects in the Germanic languages and beyond.

3

The Distribution of Finite Argument Clauses

3.1 Introduction

Having fixed the major directionality parameters of Germanic, we now turn our attention to the distribution and internal make-up of finite argument clauses. We will again follow the strategy of deriving the cross-linguistically uniform properties of these clauses from hypothesized universal aspects of sentence structure and the idiosyncratic ones from the effects of parameters. We will see that the universal projection function and the constraints on parameters inherent in the Saturation Condition leave their characteristic marks on the syntax of argument clauses as well.

3.2 Clauses with and without Overt Complementizers

One property that all finite declarative argument clauses in the Germanic languages have in common is that the complementizer is obligatory in subject sentences, as the examples that follow show.[1]

(1G) *(**Daß**) Hans nicht kommt, ist schade
        that Hans not   comes   is a pity

1. This observation is made and theoretically interpreted in Stowell (1981). Stowell's theory is described in more detail later. See also Holmberg (1988), which is somewhat closer in spirit to the proposals we make.

(2Du)   *(**Dat**) hij komt, verheugt me
        that he comes pleases   me

(3S)   *(**Att**) han var död var en överraskning
        that he   was dead was a   surprise

(4Da)   *(**At**) jeg rejser, er sikkert
        that I   travel   is certain

(5N)   *(**At**) jeg reiser, er sikkert
        that I   travel   is certain

(6I)   *(**Að**) Olafur lofaði   Maríu þessum hring
        that Olaf   promised Mary this   ring
        væri   gagnslaust
        would-be useless

(7E)   *(**That**) John left is a pity

This is however not the case with respect to complement clauses; here we find that some languages require a complementizer while others permit structures without a complementizer:[2]

(8G)   *Peter sagte [**e** Hans Maria geküßt hat]
        Peter said   Hans Maria kissed had

(9Du)   *Piet zei [**e** Jan komen zou]
        Piet said   Jan come   would

(10S)   Vi kunde inte tro   [(**att**) han inte var död]
        we could not believe that he   not was dead

(11Da) Hans siger [(**at**) Peter har mødt Eva]
        Hans says   that Peter has met   Eva

(12N)   Hans sier [(**at**) Peter har moett Eva]
        Hans says   that Peter has met   Eva

(13I)   */ Jón   segir [**e** Olafur hafi séð Egil]
        ok John says   Olaf   has seen Egil

---

2. I should note that the formulation in the text is not literally correct for German. It is not the case that every complement sentence in German must have a complementizer, since the complementizer can sometimes be replaced by the finite verb. What I am stressing here, is that the C-position must not be empty.

Anders Holmberg (personal communication) informs me that there seems to be some dialectal variation with respect to complementizer drop in Icelandic. My own work with informants leads me to the same conclusion.

(14E)   Judy believes [(**that**) she will leave tomorrow]

However, even those languages that allow the overt complementizer to drop when it follows the verb require it to be expressed when the complement clause is topicalized.

(15S)   *(**Att**) han var trött, trodde   jag inte
          that he   was tired thought I   not

(16Da)   *(**At**) han har gjort det, tror   jeg ikke
          that he   has done that believe I   not

(17N)   *(**At**) Eva har skrevet denne boken har   jeg ikke
          that Eva has written this   book have I   not
          sagt
          said

(18I)   *(**Að**) Olafur hafi séð Egil held ég ekki
          that Olaf   has seen Egil think I   not

(19E)   *(**That**) he has done that, I can't believe

In sum, all Germanic languages require an overt complementizer when the clause is (a) a subject sentence or (b) a topicalized sentence. Some require the overt complementizer also when the clause is not topicalized, whereas others allow the complementizer to drop under these circumstances:

(20) *The Obligatoriness of Overt Complementizers in Finite Clauses*

	G	Du	S	Da	N	I	E
Obligatory in SU-sentences	+	+	+	+	+	+	+
Obligatory in Obj-sentences	+	+	−	−		−	±	−
Obligatory under topicalization	+	+	+	+	+	+	+

We will argue that this state of affairs is not the product of accidental stipulations in individual grammars but can be derived from Universal Grammar.

The contrast between the three clause types in 20 is interesting for two reasons. First, there are two rows with uniform entries in 20, suggesting that these properties are not within the domain of parametric stipulation but rather follow from some principle of grammar. Second, it is interesting that the cross-linguistic uniformity or nonuniformity of the behavior of the clause types in 20 correlates directly with their selectional status, i.e. whether they are selected by a lexical head or not. Thus, the nonuniform complement clauses are selected as complements by their governing head, whereas both subject and topic sentences occupy phrase-structure positions outside of the domain of relational and categorial selection of a head.

A pattern such as 20 is prototypically expected in a framework that ties together in the Saturation Condition the grammatical relation of a constituent and its selectional status. According to this hypothesis, the properties of a constituent α can only depend on the properties of another constituent β, if α is selected by β; the latter is only possible if the two constituents stand in a phrase-structural sister configuration. Complements fulfill this condition, but external arguments and sentences in topic position do not. Thus, while the properties of complement sentences are predicted to depend on the properties of the selecting head (including presence or absence of an overt complementizer), this is not the case with subject and topic sentences. Their properties cannot be fixed by selection, because they are not categorially selected (although the trace of the topicalized complement is), which means that their behavior is due either to the properties of their own heads or to universal conditions on sentence structure.

In the following pages I will argue that there are indeed two independently supported principles of the Universal Projection Function that require an overt complementizer for the nonselected clauses while leaving the choice of complementizer in complement sentences open to selection by the governing head. The pattern in 20 is thus seen as one that is not accidental but rather a symptom of our hypothesized principles of form building in natural language. In that, it lends further support to our general approach.

Which invariant properties of the Identical Projection Function might be responsible for the fact that languages must have overt complementizers in finite subject and topic sentences, while there is no such restriction in the case of complements?

The literature contains a number of attempts to derive the distribution of argument clauses with and without overt heads. Both functional[3] and grammatical[4] theories have been proposed.

---

3. These functional hypotheses deny that there is any structural aspect at play here at all. Vater (1973, 21) formulates this account as follows with respect to the Danish complementizer *at:*

> In sum, we can observe that *at* can be omitted when the relation of the subordinate clause to the superordinate one is clearly recognizable even without a conjunction.

This functional account of *that*-drop is implausible for a number of reasons. First, if the overt complementizer is simply a disambiguation device, then it is surprising that all Germanic languages should use exactly the same device, namely requiring an overt complementizer in subject sentences while the complementizer can be empty in complements. One could imagine that some languages have the mirror-image structure of the others, since then subject and object sentences could still be distinguished from each other and from main clauses. Roger Higgins (personal communication) has pointed out, however, that this argument may be invalidated if all Germanic languages behave alike for historical reasons, i.e. no language has innovated. It seems to me that

Higgins's counterargument is only plausible if there are indeed non-Germanic languages that make use of other disambiguation devices. I do not know whether this is the case.

The theory also does not have a good explanation for the fact that several languages under consideration have two types of verbs with respect to complement clauses: one type that requires an overt complementizer in its complement clause (e.g. English *murmur* and one that allows the complementizer to be empty (e.g. English *say*).

It is hard to believe that the nature of the verb governing the sentence should make a difference to the detectability of the grammatical relation of the embedded clause.

The most serious problem that the functional theory of *that*-drop faces, however, is that it cannot account at all for the fact that the complementizer cannot be dropped in subject and topicalized sentences in the SOV-languages Dutch and German. In these languages we find a striking word order difference between main and subordinate clauses, as the following examples from German show:

(iG) Peter *liest* ein Buch   (main clause)
      Peter reads a   book

(iiG) daß Peter ein Buch *liest*   (subordinate clause)
      that Peter a   book reads

There is an obvious difference between these two clause types: the finite verb is in second position in declarative main clauses, while it is in final position in canonical subordinate clauses. Main and subordinate clauses are therefore easily distinguished by word order, so that no disambiguating complementizer would be needed. But as was mentioned above, neither German nor Dutch ever allows *that*-drop, not even in complement clauses. Here we thus *do* have a situation where the relational status of a clause can easily be discovered on the basis of its internal structure, but *that*-drop is still impossible. If this is the case for German and Dutch, then the functional theory of *that*-drop does not really constitute a plausible explanation in the other Germanic languages either.

Bever/Langendoen (1971) propose a functional account of *that*-drop that is subject to the same objections.

4. Following Kayne (1984, Chapter 3), Stowell (1981) proposes to account for the generalizations of *that*-drop in terms of the Empty Category Principle (ECP). There are a number of conceptual and empirical problems with this approach as well, which have led me to search for a more successful alternative.

I will just allude here to some reasons for rejecting the ECP approach. First, Stowell's original theory cannot be stated in more recent formulations of the ECP (cf. Chomsky, 1986b) which apply only to empty categories in chains rather than to all governed empty categories (as the older version of the ECP in Chomsky [1981] did).

On the empirical front there are many severe problems that lead one to revise the first impression that the subject–object asymmetry in complementizer drop is another instance of the subject–object asymmetries induced on the data by the ECP (for a similar argument against the ECP approach to complementizer drop, see Chomsky [1986b, 93 fn. 28]).

First, to get the theory off the ground, it is necessary to postulate an empty complementizer position for all clauses without overt complementizers. This leads to extremely artificial and disadvantageous consequences in the Germanic languages. As an illustration, examine the following two types of subordinate clause from German, both of which feature prominently later in the chapter:

(iG) Ich glaube, [daß Hans krank gewesen ist]
      I   believe that Hans sick   been   is
      'I believe that Hans has been sick'

(iiG) Ich glaube [Hans ist krank gewesen]
       I   believe Hans is   been sick
       'I believe that Hans has been sick'

There are two important differences between the two clause types: (a) one has an overt complementizer, the other one does not; (b) one has the finite verb in final position, the other one has it in second position. Crucially, these two features are not independent as argued in den Besten (1977). Rather, as den Besten showed in meticulous detail, either the complementizer or the finite verb has to appear at the beginning of the sentence, but only one can appear per clause. Thus, the following two sentences are ungrammatical:

(iiiG) *Ich glaube, [e Hans krank gewesen ist]
        I   believe C Hans sick   been   is
        'I believe that Hans has been sick'

(ivG)   *Ich glaube [daß Hans ist krank gewesen]
        I   believe that Hans is   been sick
        'I believe that Hans has been sick'

According to what is now often called "den Besten's description" of the verb-second phenomenon in the Germanic languages, the contrast between (i) and (iii) is due to the requirement that the complementizer position in German cannot be left empty. If there is no overt complementizer, then the verb has to move out of its sentence-final D-structure position and fill the position as in (ii). Example (iv), on the other hand, is ungrammatical, because the finite verb must have moved away from its sentence-final D-structure position. The only landing site it has is Comp (a proposition for which den Besten provides massive evidence, but the position is already filled by the overt complementizer.

With this we return to the issue of complementizer drop. In order for an ECP approach to complementizer drop to work, it must be stipulated that even sentences like (ii) obligatorily contain an empty complementizer position and that the position has to remain obligatorily empty when a verb has moved leftward in the same clause. There is not a single piece of overt justification for either aspect of this propsoal. Even if we are willing to tolerate such abstract postulates in order to bring complentizer drop under the ECP, the damage that these assumptions make to a restrictive explication of verb movement in German should be enough to reevaluate the general strategy.

Other special assumptions will have to be made to save the ECP story. If it is true that complementizers can be dropped in all properly governed clauses, then what is the explanation for the ungrammaticality of the following sentences from Romance whose English translations all allow complementizer drop? (I owe the data to Kurt Kemp.)

(vIt)   Pietro pensa [*(che) lei partira   domani]
         Peter believes that she will-leave tomorrow
(viSp)   Pedro cree [*(que) ella saldra   mañana]
         Peter believes that she will-leave tomorrow
(viiP)   O Pedro acredita [*(que) ela vai sair amanha]
         Peter   believes   that she will leave tomorrow
(viiiFr) Pierre croit [*(qu') elle sortira   demain]
         Peter believes that she will-leave tomorrow

The same question will have to be answered for Dutch and the dialects of Icelandic that never permit complementizer drop. In fact, the Dutch data allow us to make an even stronger case. Compare the following two sentences:

(ixDu)   Piet zei [dat Jan komen zou]
         Piet said that Jan come would

I want to explore a new approach to these phenomena. Let us put some of the above-mentioned facts in a larger perspective by adding a number of observations about the distribution of argument clauses.

As mentioned in footnote 4, German allows the following two types of subordinate clauses, which we also find in the Nordic languages:

(21G) Ich glaube, [daß Hans krank gewesen ist]
       I   believe   that Hans sick   been   is
      'I believe that Hans has been sick'

(22G) Ich glaube [Hans ist krank gewesen]
       I   believe Hans is sick   been
      'I believe that Hans has been sick'

As we saw, the complementizer-introduced clause can appear in subject position and can be topicalized if it is a complement clause. Interestingly, the verb second clause behaves differently in that it patterns with the complementizerless clauses discussed earlier. It cannot occur in subject or topic position either:[5]

(23G) *[Hans ist krank gewesen] ist offensichtlich
       Hans is sick   been   is obvious
      'That Hans has been sick is obvious'

(24G) *[Hans ist krank gewesen] hat Peter t gewußt
       Hans is sick   been   has Peter known
      'Peter knew that Hans has been sick'

(xDu) *Piet zei [e Jan komen zou]
      Piet said   Jan come   would

The second sentence again shows that the complementizer cannot be dropped in Dutch at all. The ECP theory has only one handle on this; it is forced to claim that the complement clause is not properly governed, and hence its head is not properly governed either. This of course predicts that the whole complement clause cannot be moved (with or without overt complementizer), since the trace it leaves behind should violate the ECP as much as the empty element in its head position does in example (x). The grammaticality of the following sentence disconfirms this prediction as well:

(xi Du) [Dat Jan komen zou] zei Piet [CP e]
       that Jan come   would said Piet

5. Note that with parenthetical expressions a verb-second clause can appear in initial position:

(iG) [Hans ist krank gewesen] hat Peter gemeint
      Hans is sick   been   has Peter meant
      'Peter thought Hans had been sick'

Without an intonation break between *gewesen* and *hat*—identifying the last three words as a parenthetical—the sentence is ungrammatical.

I want to claim that these facts can be accounted for insightfully if these asymmetries are tied to the different categorial structure of the clause types; i.e. I assume that the subordinate clause type is 25 is a *nominal* CP while the one in 26 is a *verbal* CP, due to the different categorial nature of their heads.

(25G) Ich glaube, [$_{CP}$ [$_{C'}$ **daß** [$_{IP}$ Hans krank ist]]]
     I   believe   that   Hans sick is

(26G) Ich glaube [$_{CP}$ Hans [$_{C'}$ **ist** [$_{IP}$ t krank t]]]
     I   believe   Hans   is   sick

I take the head of the clause in 25 to be nominal, because it is etymologically related to the demonstrative pronoun *das (that)* and the head of 26 to be verbal for self-evident reasons. The fact that the verbal clause cannot occur in subject position appears less mysterious when seen in the context of the following strong empirical asymmetry between those categories that can serve as complements and those that can perform the external argument function:[6]

(27)	Complement	External Argument
DP	+	+
PP	+	±
AP	+	−
VP	+	−
IP	+	−

We see that although there are no restrictions on the categorial identity of complements, only *nonverbal* expressions can act as external arguments. We can capture this generalization by strengthening the Identical Projection Function with the following universal restriction on the projection clause of external arguments:

(28) *The External Argument Universal*
     External arguments are nonverbal, i.e. [−V].

6. That DP and PP can perform the complement function is standardly assumed. For the other categories, I have the following constructions in mind: AP can occur as a small clause complement after verbs like *find* and *consider*. VP can also be a small clause, e.g. after *see*. And, IP occurs after ECM-verbs like *believe* and *consider*.

If they have the right meaning, then PPs can occupy the subject position:

   (i) *Under the bed* is a nice place to hide

Possibly the following is also a PP subject:

   (ii) *For Bill to leave* would be a disaster

Examples like (i) are discussed in Travis (1984) and Chomsky (1986a, 217 fn 122; cf. Emonds 1985).

This universal law makes the set of expressions allowed in SU-position a proper subset of those allowed in complement positions.[7]

From this account of the paradigm in 27 it also follows that verb-second clauses cannot perform the external argument function; since they are by assumption verbal (i.e. [+V]), they do not satisfy the universal categorial requirement on external arguments; *that*-clauses *can* occur in subject position, however, because they are nominal. Our theory thus derives one aspect of the distribution of argument clauses on the basis of an independently motivated universal principle.

There is one clause-type, however, which is not covered yet. We have banned verb-second subordinate clauses from subject position on the basis that their head C is filled with a verbal category. But what about complementizer-less clauses in Scandinavian in which verb-second has not applied, clauses like 29:

      1   2   3
(29S) Jag vet   [man inte kan lita på Eva]
     I   know one not can rely on Eva

Here the verb is in third position (which is incompatible with analyzing it to be in C^0), so that we have no basis for the claim that the head of CP is verbal. Our account of the absence of verb-second sentences in subject position thus does not carry over to these clauses, so that we have not really solved the problem completely.

I believe that the solution to this problem is the following: although with respect to verb-second sentences like 24 we are forced to assume that they belong to category CP (since I-to-C has overtly applied; cf. the classical arguments in den Besten 1977), there is no comparative evidence that complementizer-less clauses without internal topicalization and subject-aux inversion like 29 have a CP-level at all. Since none of the two potentially available CP-level positions is ever filled with phonetically realizable material and since there is no principle of grammar requiring a CP-node there, we are free to assume that the embedded clause in 29 belongs to category IP. We know independently that heads have the power to c-select IP as a complement from such

---

7. I assume, however, with Koster (1978) that sentences cannot occupy the subject position. This position is exclusively occupied by nonsentential phrases. Later I will propose that sentences in topicalized positions can be linked to a determiner phrase in subject position, giving them the appearance as if they actually occupied this position themselves.

I will continue using the expressions that a sentence "is in subject position" or "is an external argument," trusting that the reader is aware that I mean "binds a DP-trace in subject position" and "binds a DP-trace acting as an external argument."

English constructions as the following:[8]

(30E)   We arrived [$_{PP}$ **before** [$_{IP}$ he left]]

(31E)   *We arrived [$_{PP}$ **before** [$_{CP}$ that [$_{IP}$ he left]]]

(32E)   John **believes** [$_{IP}$ Bill to be sick]
        John **seems**   [$_{IP}$ t to be sick]

There is thus no reason why a finite IP should not be able to perform the complementation function; indeed the grammar would presumably have to be complicated in an ad hoc fashion to block this one category from the complement function while allowing all the others in 27.[9]

Once we make the assumption that complementizer-less subordinate clauses without internal verb movement are IPs, we can give a unified account of the fact that complementizer-less clauses cannot occur in subject position, no matter whether they are V-headed CPs or IPs; finite IPs are always headed by verbal expressions like auxiliaries or moved verbs (a fact which can be captured easily by a rule of canonical structural realization in the sense of Grimshaw 1979). The following two constructions are thus ungrammatical for the same reason. A clause (CP or IP) headed by a verbal constituent cannot serve as an external argument:[10]

$$\begin{array}{ccc} 1 & 2 & 3 \end{array}$$
(33S)   *[$_{CP}$ Han arbetade inte] förvånade alla
         he   worked not   surprised everyone

$$\begin{array}{ccc} 1 & 2 & 3 \end{array}$$
(34S)   *[$_{IP}$ Han inte arbetade] förvånade alla
         he   not worked   surprised everyone

With this we have reduced the first row in 30 to a strengthened version of the Identical Projection Function, namely the constraint on the projection of external arguments in 28. Since external argument sentences do not stand in a relational dependency to a head that could determine their category, this property has to be determined outside of the domain of language-particular

8. In Chomsky (1981) it was still assumed that the complement of ECM and raising verbs is S′ and later undergoes a lexically driven rule of S′-deletion. In later work (cf. Chomsky, 1986b) an analysis in terms of IP-selection is given. We follow this idea here.

9. Bowers (1987) argues on completely independent grounds that finite complement clauses without complementizers should be of category IP rather than CP. He derives the extraction asymmetries between complements with and without *that* by assigning the former clauses to CP and the latter to IP. An algorithm of barriers will then derive the *that*-t effect.

10. The examples are taken from Ejerhed (1982, 147).

relational parameters. 28 imposes a universal requirement on the categories of EA sentences and therefore explains why all the entries in the first row of 20 are identical.

Let us now look for an additional principle of Universal Grammar that will account for the uniformity of the topicalization cases. Since here we find the same split between verbal and nominal clauses, we will try to solve this problem on the basis of their categorial differences as well.

That-clauses can be topicalized much like determiner phrases and there is nothing else to be said about them in this respect. But why should verbal clauses like 26 and 29 be unable to topicalize?

There is a fact about the behavior of IP which might be related to the problem we are presently discussing, namely IP does not undergo *any* of the movement operations available in the Germanic language:

(35E) Topicalization
  *[$_{IP}$ *John is a fool*] I believe that t
  *[$_{IP}$ *He left*] we arrived before t   (cf. 30)

(36E) Extraposition
  *I heard [the claim that t] yesterday [$_{IP}$ *John is sick*]

This suggests that IP cannot be moved at all! Let us in fact make this assumption and try to derive it from Universal Grammar. We will approach the problem in terms of the theory of chains. Take the following well-formedness condition on chain formation:[11]

(37) *The Uniformity Requirement on Chains*
  All members of a movement chain agree in verbal and nominal features, i.e. [V] and [N].

This condition requires that there must not be a clash in the nominal and verbal feature values of the members of a chain. It follows that a PP can only bind a PP-trace etc. Now we impose a second requirement on chains specifically for sentential categories:[12]

---

11. Pesetsky (1982, 127) proposes a similar constraint:

  (i) *Possible Antecedent (def)*
    α is a possible antecedent for β if and only if α and β bear non-distinct values for number, gender and categorial features.

12. To express 38 formally, X-bar theory must be modeled in such a way that there is a feature that exclusively singles out sentential categories. In Webelhuth (1989) I proposed a feature [T] (mnemonic for "truth value") with that function. The concepts "verbal sentence" and "nominal sentence" can be reconstructed in this feature system easily. In the present exposition I will not put the abbreviatory notation to use, however.

(38) *The Sentence Trace Universal*
      Sentences can only bind DP-traces, i.e. traces with the categorial
      specification $[+N, -V]$.

From the interaction of "Uniformity" and the Sentence Trace Universal it
follows that finite IP is not movable at all, since it can never form a well-
formed chain; the latter requires that it leave behind a nominal trace, but the
former only sanctions chains whose members have identical values for the
features [N] and [V]; finite IP cannot satisfy both requirements at the same
time, since it is always verbal.

Besides accounting for the ungrammaticality of 35 and 36, the preceding
theory also explains why verb-second subordinate clauses behave like IPs in
that they cannot be moved: they too cannot satisfy both of the conditions on
chain formation, since they are verbal and hence unable to form a chain with
the nominal trace they are forced to leave behind by the universal principle
38.

3.3 Empirical Consequences of the Sentence Trace Universal

We have reduced the fact that verbal sentences cannot occur in external argument position to a more general property of external arguments, namely the
universal 28 which requires that all external arguments be nonverbal.

Then we have turned to topicalization and have argued that the nontopi-
calizability of verbal clauses can also be reduced to a more general property
of natural language, namely the requirement that sentences leave behind
nominal DP-traces.

As it stands, the Sentence Trace Universal has a rather implausible status.
It was introduced in an ad hoc fashion and conceptually is dubious in that it
requires a set of constituents to leave behind traces that must be categorially
distinct from them—and all that for no reason other than that of capturing
the facts relating to the topicalization of sentences. The latter proposal is especially unusual, given that the whole treatment of long-distance dependencies
in some syntactic theories is based on the premiss that an antecedent and its
trace must be featurally identical.

In categorial grammar, for instance, long-distance dependencies are typically treated with type raising and function composition (cf. Steedman
[1985], Bach [1983]). Take the following example:[13]

(39) a. Category of *depended:* (S|NP)|PP
      b. Category of *He:* S|(S|NP)
      c. Category of *on Mary:* PP

---

13. I ignore the directon of combination in the following illustration.

Depend is a verb that forms VPs (= S|NP) by combining with a PP. Subjects take VP (= S|NP) arguments to form sentences. Instead of combining *depend* with the PP argument directly, the system allows it to function-compose with the subject pronoun:

(40) Category of *He depended:* S|PP

The result is a constituent that combines with a PP to form a sentence; i.e. the crucial result is that the categorial selection of the verb remains constant, even if it composes with other categories. This entails that the element that is interpreted as the first argument of the verb must be of the same category when it appears adjacent to the verb as in 41a and when it combines with it later as a topicalized constituent, as in 41b:

(41) a. He [depended [on Mary]]
      b. [On Mary] [he depended]

The Sentence Trace Universal postulated in 38 is incompatible with this theory of long-distance dependencies as it stands. It requires that a sentence behave like a sentence when unmoved, but like a nominal phrase when moved.

At this point the Sentence Trace Universal has only one argument in its favor; namely it accounts for why verbal sentences cannot be topicalized. At the same time there are reasonable arguments against it, in particular its incompatibility with the widely accepted mechanism of allowing long-distance dependencies, i.e. the claim that a head can have a dependant that satisfies its categorial requirements nonlocally rather than forming a chain with a trace satisfying them locally.

Quite a bit is at stake then in deciding whether the Sentence Trace Universal is correct or not. For this reason I will now lead the reader on a long excursus with independent empirical arguments in support of this unusual proposal. Not all of the arguments originate with us. The following section has benefited substantially from the earlier observations about the distribution of argument sentences in Koster (1978), Williams (1980), Stowell (1981), and Safir (1982, 1985).

3.3.1 Raising, Unaccusative, and Passive Verbs

Note the following English sentences, which contain a raising, unaccusative, and passive verb, respectively:

(42E) It seemed [$_{CP}$ that John was unqualified]

(43E) It turned out [$_{CP}$ that John was unqualified]

(44E) It was objected [$_{CP}$ that John was unqualified]

Each of these verbs governs an internal argument clause. Note that although the subject positions of these sentences are nonthematic, the complements cannot move into them:

(45E) *[$_{CP}$ That John was unqualified] seemed [$_{CP}$ e]

(46E) *[$_{CP}$ That John was unqualified] turned out [$_{CP}$ e]

(47E) *[$_{CP}$ That John was unqualified] was objected [$_{CP}$ e]

The modular theory of Chomsky (1981) and its successors do not have an explanation for this fact, since there is no principle of grammar prohibiting movement in structures like 45–47, and especially since under other circumstances clauses *can* move into subject position. Take the following passive sentence:

(48E) It had been expected [$_{CP}$ that John would be unqualified]

This can be transformed into 49, where the internal argument clause has moved into subject position.

(49E) [$_{CP}$ That John would be unqualified] had been expected [$_{CP}$ e]

We can now demonstrate that there is a second difference between the passive verbs *object* and *expect,* the first of which does not allow its complement clause to move, while the second one does. *Object* also differs from *expect* in that it does not allow a DP-subject:

(50E) *That had been objected [$_{DP}$ e]

(51E) That had been expected [$_{DP}$ e]

We can explain the grammaticality difference between 50 and 51 if we assume that both verbs are subcategorized for a sentence and that *expect* in addition c-selects a DP:

(52) *expect,* [Category is V]

             [Category of Complement is $\begin{Bmatrix} D \\ C \end{Bmatrix}$]

(53) *object,* [Category is V]

             [Category of Complement is C]

The difference between 50 and 51 now follows straightforwardly. 51 is a normal passive sentence with DP-chain formation. In 50, however, the DP in subject position cannot form a chain with the postverbal element, since the verb does not c-select a DP. The sentence thus leads to a violation of the θ-criterion, the argument in subject position being without a θ-role.

With the c-selection frames in 52 and 53 and the assumption that sentences have to leave behind DP-traces, we can also explain the contrast between the two paradigms 44 and 47 vs. 48 and 49. Both verbs allow a postverbal complement clause, since each of them is subcategorized for an internal argument of category CP. The following structures show why only *expect* allows its complement clause to move before the verb.

(54E)　[$_{CP}$ That John would be unqualified] had been expected [$_{DP}$ e]

(55E)　*[$_{CP}$ That John would be unqualified] had been objected [$_{DP}$ e]

54 is possible for the same reason that 51 is allowed. The sentence forms a DP-chain with the postverbal trace. Similarly, 55 is ungrammatical for the same reason that 50 is ungrammatical: the verb *object* does not c-select a DP and will therefore block DP-chain formation; 55 is ruled out by the θ-criterion, since the preverbal argument sentence does not get a θ-role.

Returning to sentences 45–47, we see that the raising and unaccusative verbs neither allow their complement clause to move to preverbal position nor allow a bare DP preverbally.

(56E)　*That fact seemed [$_{DP}$ e]

(57E)　*That fact turned out [$_{DP}$ e]

Compare these sentences to 47 and 50, respectively. In each case we get the paradigm in 58. The verb allows a postverbal complement clause:

(58E)　It seemed [$_{CP}$ that John was unqualified]

The verb does not allow the complement to appear preverbally, although the subject position is nonthematic.

(59E)　*[$_{CP}$ That John was unqualified] seemed [e]

The verb also does not allow a bare DP in subject position.

(60E)　*That fact seemed [$_{DP}$ e]

We will thus assume that all of these verbs c-select only an internal argument of category CP, with the consequence that the complement clause must not move; it cannot form a DP-chain, given that the verb does not license a DP in its complement position.

3.3.2 Other Constructions Where DP Is Not C-Selected

I will now present a number of other constructions in which only a sentence
is licensed but not a DP. In each case we will see that the sentence is non-
movable.

Take the following five examples:

(61E) Mary informed Bill [_CP_ *that John was sick*]

(62E) Mary was unhappy [_CP_ *that John was sick*]

(63E) Bill made the claim [_CP_ *that John was sick*]

(64E) He read a book [_CP_ *that his brother had bought*]

(65E) He is so old [_CP_ *that he cannot walk any more*]

In none of these five different constructions (involving the verb *inform,* an
adjective, a noun, a relative clause, and a result clause) does the sentence alternate with a DP:

(66E) *Mary informed Bill *that fact*

(67E) *Mary is unhappy *that fact*

(68E) *Bill made the claim *that fact*

(69E) *He read a book *that story*

(70E) *He is so old *the walk through the woods*

Because sentences have to leave behind a DP-trace under movement, none
of these five constructions allows the sentence to move away:

(71E) *[_CP_ *That John was sick*] Mary informed Bill [_DP_ e]

(72E) *[_CP_ *That John was sick*] Mary was unhappy [_DP_ e]

(73E) *[_CP_ *That John was sick*] Bill made the claim [_DP_ e]

(74E) *[_CP_ *That his brother had bought*] he read a book [_DP_ e]

(75E) *[_CP_ *That he can't walk any more*] he is so old [_DP_ e]

3.3.3 Platzack on Swedish

Another piece of evidence in favor of our claim that sentences must leave
behind DP-traces comes from Swedish. Platzack (1984) discusses sentences

like the following where a sentence is the complement of an adjective:[14]

(76S) Jag är så glad [$_{CP}$ att du kunde komma]
     I   am so glad   that you could come

Platzack notices that if the complement clause is topicalized, a preposition must be inserted behind the adjective:

(77S) [$_{CP}$ Att du kunde komma] är jag glad *(över) t
       that you could come   am I glad about

This fact becomes immediately understandable once our claim is taken seriously that sentences have to leave behind DP-traces. Imagine that there were no preposition after the adjective in 77. Then the S-structure of the sentence-final AP would be the following:

(78S) [$_{AP}$ glad [$_{DP}$ e]]

This structure is not projectible by the universal clause realizing the complementation relation, since *glad* is not subcategorized for a DP, as the following sentence shows:

(79S)   *Jag är [$_{AP}$ glad det]
      I   am   glad that

Rather, *glad* c-selects a PP headed by the case-marking preposition *över:*

(80S) Jag är [$_{AP}$ glad över det]
     I   am   glad about that

Assuming that sentences have to leave behind a DP-trace, we can explain why *glad* requires the preposition *över* to be overt once its complement sentence has topicalized: if there is a DP in the adjective phrase, then it must be governed by a preposition, whether the DP is overt as in 80 or the trace left by a sentence as in 77.

3.3.4 Preposition Stranding

The Sentence Trace Universal allows us to derive more facts. Take the following English and German sentences, which show that in both languages prepositions can take DP-complements but do not allow complements of category CP:

---

14. Platzack's unpublished manuscript has not been available to me. I have taken the data from Holmberg (1986, 81f), where Platzack's results are reported and the reference is given.

(81E)   We talked [$_{PP}$ about *that fact*] for days

(82E)   *We talked [$_{PP}$ about *that John was sick*] for days

(83G)   Wir sprachen seit Tagen [$_{PP}$ über   *diese Tatsache*]
       we   talked   for days   about that   fact

(84G)   *Wir sprachen seit Tagen [über   *daß Hans krank war*]
       we   talked   for days   about that Hans sick   was

The two languages differ in that English allows the DP to strand the preposition while German generally forbids that.

(85E)   *That fact* we talked [$_{PP}$ about [$_{DP}$ e]] for days

(86G)   *Diese Tatsache* sprachen wir seit Tagen [$_{PP}$ über [$_{DP}$ e]]
      that   fact   talked   we for days   about

The two languages thus differ in that the configuration [$_{PP}$ P [$_{DP}$ e]] is licensed in English but not in German. Note that the English sentence in 82 can be made grammatical by topicalizing the complement sentence.

(87E)   [$_{CP}$ *That John was sick*] we talked [$_{PP}$ about [$_{\alpha}$ e]] for days

Our claim that sentences must bind DP-traces after movement immediately explains the contrast between 82 and 87. α in 87 has to be "DP," and we know from the grammaticality of 85 that the configuration [$_{PP}$ P [$_{DP}$ e]] is licensed in English. Thus, although a preposition that does not c-select a sentence must not govern it, it can govern its trace, if it c-selects a $_{DP}$. We now make the further prediction that the analogue of 87 should be ungrammatical in German; i.e. it should not be possible to save 84 by topicalizing the complement sentence. The reason is that the configuration [$_{PP}$ P [$_{DP}$ e]] is ungrammatical in German (cf. 86). If a sentence has to leave behind a DP-trace, this is the only configuration that is available after topicalization. The prediction is borne out: like DPs, sentences must not strand a preposition in German.

(88G)   *[$_{CP}$ *Daß Hans krank war*] sprachen wir seit Tagen
       that Hans sick   was talked   we for days
    [$_{PP}$ über [$_{DP}$ e]]
    about

These paradigms thus also support our contention that sentences must form chains with DPs.[15]

15. Strictly speaking, the argument just given does not show that sentences *must* leave behind DP-traces, it only shows that they *can* do so. However, this result is compatible with our claim, since if our stronger demand is correct (they *must* leave DP-traces), then the weaker result just achieved follows on logical grounds. If sentences were prohibited from leaving DPs behind and would be required to form chains with empty sentences, then the paradigms given would be mysterious.

3.3.5 ECM Constructions

Another construction in which only DPs can occur while overt sentences are barred is represented by Exceptional Case Marking (ECM) sentences. Note the following contrast:

(89E) John believes [$_{IP}$ *that* to be obvious]

(90E) *John believes [$_{IP}$ *that Bill is sick* to be obvious]

The following sentence shows that the DP-subject of the embedded IP can be topicalized:

(91E) *That* John believes [$_{IP}$ [$_{DP}$ e] to be obvious]

92 shows that 90 can be made grammatical by topicalizing the sentential subject of the lower IP.

(92E) *That Bill is sick* John believes [$_{IP}$ [$_{\alpha}$ e] to be obvious]

The contrast between 90 and 92 is automatically explained if α = DP in 92 as has to be the case if the Sentence Trace Universal is correct.

3.3.6 Resumptive Pronouns

Our Universal allows us to derive a few other seemingly unconnected phenomena. Take the following German sentence:

(93G) Ich bereue (**es**) [$_{CP}$ daß Maria wegfährt]
     I   regret it   that Maria leaves

As the example shows, this sentence contains an optional pronoun.[16] Note what happens when we topicalize the complement clause:

(94G) [$_{CP}$ Daß Maria wegfährt] bereue ich [$_{DP}$ e]
        that Maria leaves   regret I

(95G) *[$_{CP}$ Daß Maria wegfährt] bereue ich [$_{DP}$ **es**]
        that Maria leaves   regret I   it

If the sentence is topicalized, the pronoun has to be dropped. In conjunction with the fact that German does not have resumptive pronouns, our claim about the movement behavior of sentences accounts for the contrast between 94 and 95. The first sentence is grammatical, since the fronted CP can form a chain with the empty DP, which satisfies the definition of "variable," given that it is Case-marked by the verb. 95 has to be ungrammatical, however. The

---

16. For a discussion of whether the pronoun is expletive or referential, cf. Bennis (1986).

overt pronoun cannot form a chain with the topicalized sentence, since German is not a resumptive pronoun language. But by the Sentence Trace Universal the topicalized sentence *must* form a chain with some DP that holds a θ-role. This is not possible, however, since the overt pronoun satisfies the c-selection frame of the verb *bereuen* and this verb c-selects only one DP. There can thus not be a second, empty DP with which the fronted sentence can form a chain, and consequently the sentence is ungrammatical.

3.3.7 Case Agreement

In German, predicate nominals typically agree with their external argument in morphological case if the argument is a determiner phrase. Thus, in the sentence given in 96, the predicate is nominative because it is predicated of the subject of a finite sentence that also carries the nominative case.

(96G)   weil [das] als [ein guter Vorschlag] gilt
        bec. that as a   good proposal   counts
        nom   **nom**

If we embed the construction from 96 under an accusative and infinitive verb (ACI) where the subject comes to be marked with exceptional accusative case, then the predicate has to appear in accusative case as well:

(97G)   weil wir [[das] als [einen guten Vorschlag] gelten] lassen
        bec. we   that as a   good proposal   count let
        acc   **acc**

Note that if we substitute a topicalized sentence for the demonstrative pronoun in 96 and 97 we get exactly the same distribution of morphological case on the respective predicate nominals.

(98G)   [Daß Hans singt] gilt   als [ein guter Vorschlag]
        that Hans sings counts as a   good proposal
                          nom

(99G)   [Daß Hans singt] lassen wir als [[einen guten Vorschlag] gelten]
        that Hans sings let   we as a   good proposal   count
                                   acc

The parallelism between 96 and 97, and 98 and 99 follows straightforwardly from the Sentence Trace Universal, given that this principle requires every moved sentence to form a chain with a determiner phrase. If this principle is operative, then the sentences in 98 and 99 must both contain a sentence-internal DP-trace in the position occupied by the demonstrative pronouns in 96 and 97. Since these traces are A-bar bound, they qualify as variables according to the theory of binding in Chomsky (1981). It also follows from this theory that variables have to be Case-marked. Since we have no independent reason to assume that different Case-marking principles are at play in the two paradigms given above (96 and 97 compared with 98 and 99), it follows immediately that the case distribution should be identical in the paradigms. We can maintain the simple theory of agreement mentioned above: a predicate nominal agrees in case with its external argument, in 96 and 97 this is the overt demonstrative pronoun, in the latter two sentences the DP-trace of the topicalized sentences.[17]

3.3.8 Scrambling

As a final set of arguments, we consider some minimal pairs of German structures involving Scrambling.[18]

We begin by demonstrating that in German, only those verbs that c-select DP in addition to CP allow their complement clause to topicalize. As the following triplets of sentences show, each of the verbs *glauben (believe), wissen (know), behaupten (claim), verstehen (understand), bezweifeln (doubt)* and *vermuten (suspect)* c-select both a DP and a CP and allow their CP to topicalize.

(100G) Ich glaube [*das*]
       I   believe that

(101G) Ich glaube [*daß Hans krank ist*]
       I   believe that Hans sick   is

(102G) [*Daß Hans Krank ist*] glaube ich [$_{DP}$ e]
       that Hans sick   is   believe I

(103G) Ich weiß [*das*]
       I   know that

(104G) Ich weiß [*daß Hans krank ist*]
       I   know that Hans sick   is

(105G) [*Daß Hans krank ist*] weiß ich [$_{DP}$ e]
       that Hans sick   is   know I

17. Alternative explanations for the case agreement facts would seem to have to resort to the dubious claim that sentences *must* be Case-marked, since, as I already pointed out, only the case marking given in the various sentences is grammatical. The claim is dubious because sentences can easily occur in non-Case–marked positions (cf. the examples at the beginning of Section 3.3.1 and also the Swedish example 76).

18. Scrambling is discussed in much greater detail in Chapter 5.

(106G) Ich behaupte [*das*]
        I   claim   that

(107G) Ich behaupte [*daß Hans krank ist*]
        I   claim   that Hans sick is

(108G) [*Daß Hans krank ist*] behaupte ich [$_{DP}$ e]
        that Hans sick   is   claim   I

(109G) Ich verstehe   [*das*]
        I   understand that

(110G) Ich verstehe   [*daß Hans krank ist*]
        I   understand that Hans sick   is

(111G) [*Daß Hans krank ist*] verstehe   ich [$_{DP}$ e]
        that Hans sick   is   understand I

(112G) Ich bezweifle [*das*]
        I   doubt   that

(113G) Ich bezweifle [*daß Hans krank ist*]
        I   doubt   that Hans sick is

(114G) [*Daß Hans krank ist*] bezweifle ich [$_{DP}$ e]
        that Hans sick   is   doubt   I

(115G) Ich vermute [*das*]
        I   suspect that

(116G) Ich vermute [*daß Hans krank ist*]
        I   suspect that Hans sick is

(117G) [*Daß Hans krank ist*] vermute ich [$_{DP}$ e}
        that Hans sick   is   suspect I

Now we turn to some verbs that allow their complement to be realized by
a sentence but not by a DP. In this class are *sich freuen (be happy)*, *informieren*
(inform), *drohen (threaten)*, *sich ärgern (be annoyed)*, *sich wundern (be sur-*
prised). We see that none of the complement sentences can be topicalized,
and the reason is that they cannot be linked to a DP-trace, since the verb does
not c-select a thematic DP:[19]

(118G) *Ich freue   mich [*das*]
         I   am-happy Refl that

---

19. Some of the verbs c-select an expletive reflexive in addition to the complement clause. This
element is glossed "Refl."

(119G) Ich freue   mich [*daß Hans krank ist*]
        I   am-happy Refl   that Hans sick   is

(120G) *[*Daß Hans krank ist*] freue   ich mich [$_{DP}$ e]
        that Hans sick   is am-happy I   Refl

(121G) *Ich informierte ihn [*das*]
        I   informed   him that

(122G) Ich informierte ihn [*daß Hans krank ist*]
        I   informed   him that Hans sick   is

(123G) *[*Daß Hans krank ist*] informierte ich ihn [$_{DP}$ e]
        that Hans sick   is informed   I   him

(124G) *Sie drohten   [*das*]
        they threatened that

(125G) Sie   drohten [*PRO das Lager zu zerstören*][20]
        they threatened   the camp to destroy

(126G) *[*PRO das Lager zu zerstören*] drohten   sie [$_{DP}$ e]
        the camp to destroy   threatened they

(127G) *Ich ärgere   mich [*das*]
        I   am-annoyed Refl   that

---

20. I have smuggled one non-finite sentence into the set of finite argument clauses to show that it behaves like a nominal sentence either because control sentences are universally nominal CPs or because they are nominal IPs due to their lack of tense. In any event, the current paradigm shows that they must be analyzed as sentences falling under the Sentence Trace Universal. Verb phrases, on the other hand, behave differently. Take the following German expression:

(iG) Er geht [$_{VP}$ einkaufen]
      he goes   shopping

The verb *gehen (go)* plausibly takes a VP-complement in German. The VP does not alternate with a DP:

(iiG) *Er geht [*das*]
       he goes that

Nevertheless, the VP in (i) can be topicalized:

(iiiG) [$_{VP}$ Einkaufen] geht er [$_{VP}$ e]
        shopping   goes he

The VP after *einkaufen* thus behaves differently than the control infinitive after *drohen* in the main text, which patterns with finite nominal *sentences*. More arguments to that effect are provided in Koster/May (1982).

(128G)   Ich ärgere   mich [*daß Hans krank ist*]
          I   am-annoyed Refl   that Hans sick   is

(129G)   *[*Daß Hans krank ist*] ärgere   ich mich [$_{DP}$ e]
          that Hans sick   is   am-annoyed I   Refl

(130G)   *Ich wundere   mich [*das*]
          I   am-surprised Refl   that

(131G)   Ich wundere   mich [*daß Hans krank ist*]
          I   am-surprised Refl   that Hans sick   is

(132G)   *[*Daß Hans krank ist*] wundere   ich mich [$_{DP}$ e]
          that Hans sick   is   am-surprised I   Refl

The facts fall out as expected. Those verbs that c-select both DP and CP allow their complement clause to topicalize; those that only take CP disallow topicalization. For the following discussion, let us call the first type of verb "class I" and the second one "class II."

There are many other interesting differences between the two verb classes that can be derived from the claim that moved sentences have to leave behind DP-traces. The following examples show again that both verb classes behave alike in that they can appear with an extraposed complement sentence:[21]

(133G)   Ich kann nicht glauben [*daß Hans krank ist*]
          I   can   not   believe   that Hans sick   is

(134G)   Ich kann mich nicht freuen   [*daß Hans krank ist*]
          I   can   Refl   not   be-happy   that Hans sick   is

We know already that only the first verb allows its complement sentence to move all the way to the beginning of the matrix sentence, while the second verb blocks this. Note that we find exactly the same asymmetry when we try to move the complement sentence into the middle field of the German sentence:[22]

21. I have added a modal auxiliary and a negation to both sentences, because it is easier to prepose the complement sentence in the subsequent examples if the matrix sentence ends in a heavy constituent.

22. The term "middle field" stems from traditional grammar (cf. Drach, 1937) which segments the German clause into three fields as follows:

(i)   Initial | Middle | Final
       Field | Field | Field
          Finite   Non-finite
          Verb   Verb(s)

The finite verb demarcates the boundary between the initial field and the middle field, and the non-finite verb seperates the middle field and the final field.

(135G) weil ich [$_{CP}$ *daß Hans krank ist*] nicht glauben
        bec. I   that Hans sick   is   not   believe
        kann
        can
        'I cannot believe that Hans is sick'

(136G) *weil ich [$_{CP}$ *daß Hans krank ist*] mich nicht freuen   kann
        bec. I   that Hans sick   is   Refl   not   be-happy can
        'I cannot be happy that Hans is sick'

This difference systematically distinguishes all verbs of classes I and II. Let us put this discovery in the form of a generalization:

(137) *A verb allows its complement clause to appear in the middle field if and only if it c-selects DP.*

We can now put this observation together with those that we made earlier and arrive at the following generalization about complement clauses in German ("MF" is short for "Middle Field"):

(138) *Verb Classes and Complement Clauses*

	Class I	Class II
CP can follow V	+	+
V c-selects DP	+	−
CP topicalizable	+	−
CP can occur in MF	+	−

What is interesting about the data in 138 is that the distribution of complements of class II verbs is a proper subset of that of class I verbs; that is, all clauses can occur in the final field (i.e. at the end of the sentence), but class I verbs in addition allow their clauses to appear in TOP and in the middle field.

These fields are reconstructed in our theory as follows:

(ii) $\dfrac{[_{CP} \ \text{SPEC}}{1} \ \dfrac{C}{2} \ [_{IP} \ \text{SU} \ [_{VP} \dfrac{\text{OBJ}}{3} \ \dfrac{V]}{4} \ \dfrac{X]}{5}$

(iii) Initial field   = 1
       Finite verb   = 2
       Middle field   = 3
       Non-finite verbs   = 4
       Final field   = 5

Thus, whereas earlier in the text we tried to move a complement clause from position 5 to position 1, we are now witnessing the same asymmetry between class I and class II verbs by trying to move from the postverbal position 5 to position 3—that is, to a position between the complementizer/finite verb and the right bracket of VP.

This suggests that the final field position is in some sense unmarked, whereas the other two are special. This intuition is supported by another interesting difference between complement clauses in these two positions. Take the following two sentences with a class I verb that allows its complement to be on either side:

(139G) weil ich geglaubt habe [*daß Maria den Jungen liebt*]
        bec. I   believed have that Maria the boy   loves

(140G) weil ich [*daß Maria den Jungen liebt*] geglaubt habe
        bec. I   that Maria the boy   loves believed have

Note that we get a sharp contrast between the two sentences when we try to extract from the complement clause:

(141G)   Wen hast du   geglaubt [*daß Maria t liebt*]
          who have you believed   that Maria   loves

(142G)   *Wen hast du   [*daß Maria t liebt*] geglaubt
          who have you   that Maria   loves believed

Extraction from the "extraposed" clause is easy for those speakers of German who can extract over a complementizer, and it is doubtful in my dialect, where long extraction is limited by subjacency. However, for me, the second sentence is markedly worse, and this judgment is supported by speakers who can freely extract from 141.

This means that the postverbal position, which we called "unmarked" above, is a position where the complement clause can be extracted from, while the "marked" middle field position is an extraction island.

If we put this fact together with the observations in 138, then the analysis in 143 strongly suggests itself.

(143) *Complement clauses are base-generated in the final field, i.e. after the verb.*

143 explains all the facts we have collected. It predicts that both verb classes allow their complement in the final field, since that is their base-generated position. Furthermore, it predicts the extraction facts right away: extraction from postverbal position 141 is possible, since the clause is θ-governed in the sense of Chomsky (1986b), and no barriers are crossed (modulo the subjacency difference between the northern and southern dialects mentioned earlier). The position in the middle field in 142, however, is derived and therefore is not a θ-position. The clause in this position is treated like an adjunct, and extraction will be blocked by some version of Huang's (1982) Adjunct Condition, e.g. Chomsky's (1986b) calculus of barriers.

The correlation between the last two rows in 138 and selection of DP is also predicted when we bring the Sentence Trace Universal into play. The reader can easily see this from inspection of the following schema:

(144) [$_{VP}$ V   CP]

Since, by hypothesis, German verbs θ-mark their complement clauses to the right while they take all other complements on the left, a complement clause that appears to the left of the verb must have been moved.

(145) [$_{VP}$ CP$_k$ V   [$_\alpha$ e]$_K$]

Note now, that the structure in 145 is ungrammatical, since by the Sentence Trace Universal α = DP. But verbs in German do not license any DPs to their right, as the following difference between 146 and 147 shows:

(146G)   weil Peter [$_{VP}$ *das Buch* las]
           bec. Peter   the book read

(147G)   *weil Peter [$_{VP}$ las   *das Buch*]
           bec. Peter   read the book

There is thus only one way for a complement clause to "move" to the left; it has to appear in a position where it gets to c-command an empty DP:[23]

(148) [$_{VP}$ CP$_k$ [$_{DP}$ e]$_k$ V]

The structure of a grammatical sentence with a complement clause of a class I verb in the middle field (cf. 140) is thus the following:

(149G) weil ich   [[*daß Maria den Jungen liebt*]$_k$ [$_{DP}$ e]$_k$ geglaubt
       bec. I   that Maria the boy   loves   believed
       habe
       have

From this set of assumptions it follows straightforwardly that only class I verbs allow their complement clause to appear to the left of the verb, either in the middle field or in the topic position. Only those verbs c-select a DP besides their argument clause and therefore license the configuration needed for the complement clause to form a chain under "movement."

(150) [$_{VP}$ DP V]

23. I have put the word "move" in quotation marks, because I am of course assuming that there is no sentence trace after the verb; that is, the complement clause forms a chain exclusively with the empty DP to the left of the verb.

In our discussion of basic word order in Chapter 2 we assumed that *all* complements of verbs in German are base-generated to the left of the verb, and this was expressed by the following directionality parameter value:

(151) *Verbs θ-mark to the Left.*

Now we see that we have to add a more specific directionality parameter that bleeds 151 in case the θ-marked element is of category C.

(152) *Verbs θ-mark CPs to the Right.*

151 and 152 together now predict that verbs θ-govern CPs to the right and expressions of all other categories to the left. Both are possible directionality parameters as defined in Chapter 1.

The assumptions we have made give a consistent analysis of the distribution and the extraction possibilities of the complement clauses of verb classes I and II. The theory makes the following predictions about these clauses:

(153) They can occur postverbally with all verbs, because of 152;
- they are not extraction islands when they occur postverbally because they are θ-governed in this position according to 152;
- they cannot be moved away from postverbal position because they would have to leave behind a postverbal DP-category, which is not licensed in German/Dutch, since verbs govern DPs to the left in these languages;
- they can occur to the left of the verb adjoined in the middle field of DP-selecting verbs because they can form a chain with an empty DP to the left of the verb;
- they cannot occur to the left of non-DP-selecting verbs, since verbs do not have sentential categories to their left, nor can they be related to an empty DP-position;
- if the clause can occur to the left of the verb, then it is an extraction island, since not it but the empty DP with which it forms a chain is θ-governed;
- a clause that can occur in the middle field can occur in the topic position, and if it cannot occur in the middle field, then it cannot be topicalized, since in both cases it has to be linked to an empty DP.

To make these predictions, three language-particular statements were necessary in addition to the contribution of Universal Grammar (the Sentence Trace Universal and the Adjunct Condition).

(154) Verbs θ-mark DP to the Left;
verbs θ-mark CP to the Right;
that-clauses can adjoin in the middle field.

The first stipulation is needed independently to account for the distribution of DP-complements (cf. 146 vs. 147). The discussion of Scrambling in Chapter 5 will show that the third statement is also needed on independent grounds. This means that only the second parameter is needed specifically to derive the seven generalizations in 153.

The crucial aspect of this analysis is that it depends on the Sentence Trace Universal. Without it the systematic differences between the two verb classes would remain mysterious.

3.4 Conclusion

We began the previous subsection by noting that the Sentence Trace Universal was rather unusual for conceptual reasons, and that it was in conflict with well-established theories of long-distance dependencies.

Now we have seen that, despite this, the principle is of extraordinary explanatory value in the analysis of a large number seemingly unconnected phenomena of the syntax of Germanic. Here is the list of predictions that the Sentence Trace Universal was seen to make in conjunction with certain language-particular parameters ("AC" is short for "argument clause"):

(155) Raising, passive and unaccusative verbs allow their AC to move into subject position iff they c-select DP;
- verbs allow their AC to topicalize iff they c-select DP (*say* vs. *inform*);
- adjectives do not allow their AC to topicalize, since they do not c-select DP;
- ACs of nouns cannot be topicalized, since nouns do not c-select DP;
- relative clauses cannot be topicalized, since they do not alternate with DPs;
- result clauses cannot be topicalized, since they do not alternate with DPs;
- in Swedish, a preposition that c-selects DP has to be inserted after an adjective if the AC of the adjective is topicalized;
- in English, ACs cannot be governed by prepositions; they can strand the preposition, however, since DPs can do so too;

- in German, ACs cannot be governed by prepositions and can also not strand them, since DPs cannot do so either;
- in English, ACs cannot appear as the subject in an ECM-construction; they can be topicalized, however, since DPs can serve as the subject in ECM-constructions;
- in German, predicate nominals show the same case distribution when they are predicated of a DP or of an AC;
- in German, an AC in the final field can co-occur with a co-referential pronoun in the middle field; when the AC is topicalized, however, the pronoun has to drop, since the sentence has to form a chain with an empty DP, German lacking resumptive pronouns;
- in German, all ACs can appear in the final field;
- in German, an AC in the final field is not an extraction island (modulo non-bridge verbs);
- in German, an AC can occur in the middle field iff its governor c-selects DP;
- in German, an AC in the middle field is an extraction island, since it has "moved" to an adjunct position;
- in German, an AC can occur in the topic position iff it can occur in the middle field.

With these results we conclude our analysis of the distribution of nominal (i.e. complementizer-introduced) and verbal argument clauses (the latter coming in two types, the verb second clauses and the IP-type). I remind the reader which positions each of these finite clause types can occupy in the phrase structure of all seven Germanic languages:

(156)	Nominal Clauses	Verbal Clauses
Complement	+	+
External argument	+	−
Topic	+	−

We had set out to explain the data in 156 by recourse to properties of the Identical Projection Function. To this end we postulated two principles, the External Argument Universal and the Sentence Trace Universal, here repeated:

(157) *The External Argument Universal*
External arguments are nonverbal, i.e. $[-V]$.

(158) *The Sentence Trace Universal*
Sentences can only bind DP-traces, i.e. traces with the categorial specification $[+N, -V]$.

The first universal predicts the grammaticality judgments of the following paradigm, which is representative of all Germanic languages:

(159S)   [$_{CP}$ *Att* [$_{IP}$ *han inte arbetade*] förvånade alla
              that   he   not   worked   surprised   everyone

(160S)   *[$_{CP}$ *Han arbetade* [$_{IP}$ *inte*]] förvånade alla
              he   worked   not   surprised   everyone

(161S)   *[$_{IP}$ *Han inte arbetade*] förvånade alla
              he   not worked   surprised   everyone

The first sentence contains a subject clause headed by a nominal complementizer. Since the whole sentence is nonverbal, this structure complies with 159. In the second example the underlined clause has a V in C-position making the subject-CP verbal. This is prohibited by 157, and hence the sentence is ungrammatical. Finally, in the third case we have tried to make an IP serve as the external argument of the main verb. Since finite IP is also verbal, it behaves like the verbal CP in the example before and leads to the ungrammaticality of the sentence. In sum, the External Argument Universal 157 accounts for 159–161 and is independently motivated, since it derives the data in 27.

The Sentence Trace Universal 158 predicts the following paradigm, which is also representative of all Germanic languages:

(162S)   [$_{CP}$ *Att* [$_{IP}$ *han inte arbetade*] trodde vi t
              that   he   not worked   thought we

(163S)   *[$_{CP}$ *Han arbetade* [$_{IP}$ *inte*]] trodde vi t
              he   worked   not   thought we

(164S)   *[$_{IP}$ *Han inte arbetade*] trodde vi t
              he   not worked   thought we

All three sentences contain a topicalized clause. Only the first one is grammatical, since it is nominal, due to the nominal complementizer. The others are verbal, either because verb movement to C has applied [163], or because the clause is a finite IP.

That all topicalized clauses must be headed by a complementizer is thus also predicted on universal grounds within our theory; in fact, it is only one more reflex of the operation of the Sentence Trace Universal, which in the last subsection was shown to give a unified analysis of a large number of independent phenomena.

The second and third rows of 156 are thus completely derived by two properties of the Identical Projection Function: it can only project nonverbal external arguments, and it can only make sentences head chains that are terminated by a nominal expression.

The first row is explained as well, since neither of the two universals applies to unmoved complement clauses, and there is no other universal principle restricting the categorial realization of such a clause. Also, the complementation relation is of course the only one in 156 where a clause would be in a selected position. Therefore, we predict correctly that languages (and dialects) can differ in this respect; in fact, even that different heads in one language can impose different categorial requirements on their sisters.

The data in 156 are thus entirely derivable from the properties of the system of principles and parameters that we have developed. That external arguments and topicalized sentences cannot be categorially selected by a verb is a consequence of the Saturation Condition, which prevents a constituent from categorially selecting a nonsister. This gap is filled by the two universal principles introduced above.

The Saturation Condition thus imprints its locality effects on the distribution of argument clauses much like it predicts that the availability of pro-drop correlates at most with the sister constituent of *pro,* or that a directional statement may only mention the categories of sister constituents.

In the next chapter we demonstrate that besides contributing to the properties of pro-drop, WH-movement, directionality, and the distribution of argument clauses, the Saturation Condition also leaves its unmistakable mark on the phenomenon of pied piping.

4

Pied Piping

4.1 The Theoretical Relevance of the Pied Piping Phenomenon

In Chapter 3 we dealt with some problems in the syntax of clausal arguments. Before we turn to nonclausal arguments in the next chapter, we will concern ourselves here with the phenomenon of S-structure pied piping.

I will show that the data from the Germanic languages suggests a strong correlation between the grammatical relation that an element bears in a phrase marker and its capacity to pied-pipe its mother constituent, i.e. to cause its mother to move along with it into an operator position. To the extent that this claim is correct, the phenomenon of pied piping leads to valuable insights into the characterization of such universal building blocks of phrase structure as the complementation relation, modification, and specification. This may be an important result for two reasons: first, because it allows us a kind of reduction in the language-acquisition process, which is pronounced desirable in the following discussion from Chomsky (1981, 9 ff) under the rubric of "epistemological priority":

> Any theory—in particular, a theory of UG—may be regarded ideally as a set of concepts and a set of theorems stated in terms of these concepts. We may select a primitive basis of concepts in terms of which the theorems are derivable. . . . The primitive basis must meet a condition of epistemological priority. That is, still assuming the idealization to instantaneous language acquisition, we want the primitives to be concepts that can plausibly be assumed to provide a preliminary, prelinguistic analysis of a reasonable selection of data. . . . But it would be unreasonable to incorporate, for example, such notions as "subject of a sentence" or other grammatical relations within the class of primitive notions, since it is unreasonable to suppose that these notions can be directly applied to

linguistically unanalyzed data. Rather, we would expect that such notions would be defined in UG in terms of a primitive basis that meets the condition of epistemological priority.

Given Chomsky's argument, a correlation between grammatical relations which do not meet the condition of epistemological priority but are successful components of linguistic analysis and the linear order effects of pied piping (which do meet the condition in the case where an element is a pied piper) is a desirable result. This correlation may help the language learner to deduce certain aspects of the "hidden" relational structure over a string from its observable linear order.

The second reason for viewing a strong correlation between grammatical relations and pied piping as an important result is that it allows us to formulate further nontrivial restrictions on language variation.

This book pursues the goal of formulating the general theory of language— Universal Grammar—as a network of strong correlations among individual properties of grammatical systems; if two properties A and B of an individual grammar are correlated by a universal principle, then they cannot fluctuate independently of each other, so that all those logically possible individual grammars that do not follow the universal requirements are excluded in principle. This elimination of possible options at the universal level thus leads to more specific expectations as to the structural properties of existing and possible natural languages than could be achieved in a framework which excludes the nonexisting structures at the level of individual grammars.

In the following sections I will investigate the pied piping capacity of most of the phrase-structure positions of the Germanic languages one by one.

It will be argued (once a few interfering factors have been identified and eliminated) that an examination of the Germanic data leads to a pattern that suggests descriptive generalizations about pied piping that can be derived from independently motivated modules, e.g. the θ-criterion, the definition of the modification relation, etc. Pied piping thus emerges as a phenomenon that has the same status as passive or raising in that neither Universal Grammar nor individual grammars make reference to these constructions as a whole; rather they are derived from a modular theory of grammar that imposes strong cross-linguistic constraints on their properties and also predicts their range of cross-linguistic variation.

4.2 Pied Piping Possibilities in Germanic

We will begin by examining the scope of the pied piping phenomenon in Germanic sentences.

First we look at the behavior of determiner phrases. The first set of sentences below shows that the specifier of a determiner phrase can pied-pipe the DP in all languages of the Germanic family:

(1G)   [*Wessen* Buch] hast du gelesen
        whose   book have you read

(2Du) [*Welk* boek] heb je   gezien
        which book have you seen

(3S)   [*Vilken* bok] köpte han
        which book bought he

(4Da) [*Hvilken* bog] købte han
        which   book bought he

(5N)   [*Hvilken* bok] leser du
        which   book read you

(6I)   [*Hvers* móður] hittir þú
        whose mother met   you

(7E)   [*Whose* book] did you read

In German, Dutch, and Norwegian we find possessor sentences like 8–10 in which a name precedes a possessive pronoun followed by a noun phrase:

(8G)   Peter sein Vater
        (Dative)
        Peter his father
        'Peter's father'

(9Du) Jan z'n vader
        Jan his father
        'Jan's father'

(10N) Per sin bil[1]
        Per his car
        'Per's car'

The following sentences show that the position preceding the determiner is a pied piper:

(11G) [*Wem* sein Vater] ist gestorben
        who his father is died

---

1. This sentence is quoted from Fiva (1984) where the construction is discussed in more detail.

(12Du) [*Wie* z'n boek] is dit
        who his book is this

(13N)   [*Hvem* sin far]   er doed
        who   his father is dead

There is one other—so far also unmentioned—construction in which an
element belonging to a determiner phrase can appear before a definite determiner. Take the following German sentence:[2]

(14G) weil er [die Gerüchte über Chomsky] geglaubt hat
       bec. he the rumors   about Chomsky believed has

The string *über Chomsky* can also precede the string *die Gerüchte:*

(15G) weil er [über Chomsky die Gerüchte] geglaubt hat
       bec. he about Chomsky the rumors   believed has

That the PP at least *can* stay within the determiner phrase, even when it
appears to the left of the determiner, is shown by the following example,
where the whole DP has been topicalized:[3]

(16G) [über Chomsky die Gerüchte] hat er geglaubt
       about Chomsky the rumors   has he believed

Let us now investigate whether the position occupied by the PP *über
Chomsky* in 16 is a pied piper. The following sentences show that it is not:

(17G) *[*über wen*   das Buch] hat Hans verloren
        about whom the book has Hans lost

(18Du) *[*Van wie* het boek] ligt op de tafel
        of   who the book lies on the table

So far we have established that all and only DP-positions to the left of the
head of a determiner phrase are pied pipers. Let us now turn to the positions
on the right of the head of DP. We are assuming that the determiner and its
NP-complement form a constituent D'. We cannot test whether the NP can

---

2. I am grateful to Thilo Tappe for pointing this construction out to me and for extremely fruitful discussions about the structure of noun/determiner phrases in German. Many of the results
on the latter reported here are immediately derived from Tappe's so far unpublished work on these
issues.

3. I should note here that both the preceding and the following sentence are only possible in
very colloquial style and might not even be accepted by all speakers of German. For Tappe and
me these sentences are possible, however, especially if the object of the preposition is stressed, i.e.
über CHOMSKY die Gerüchte.

pied-pipe the D′ and the DP, because there do not seem to exist any question words of category NP, i.e. the following configuration is not instantiated:[4]

(19) [$_{D'}$ D   NP]
         [+WH]

There exists one other position after the head of the determiner phrase, however. I will assume, without argument here, that the following temporal and local adverbial modifiers are adjoined to DP:

(20E) [$_{DP}$ [$_{DP}$ the party] last night]

(21E) [$_{DP}$ [$_{DP}$ the airport] in New York]

This position is not a pied piper in any Germanic language:

(22G)   *[Die Party *wo*]   war ein Erfolg
            the party where was a   success

4. Reis (1985) notes that such phrases *are* possible in echo questions in German:

(i)Du hast [ein was] gekauft?
   you have a   what bought

The bracketed constituent can even move to the main clause operator position (with the echo interpretation maintained).

(ii) [Ein was] hast du t gekauft?
      a   what have you bought

It remains unclear however, whether the WH-word in this sentence type is really marked with the feature [+ WH] instead of just having the phonological form typical of WH-words. Note that (ii) probably involves topicalization of a constituent in an echo question, because it can be shown with the following sentence that the fronted constituent in (ii) does not play the role of a WH-operator:

(iii) * Ich frage mich [[ein was] du t gekauft hast]
        I   ask   myself a   what you bought have
        'I ask myself what you bought'

In (iii) we have moved the bracketed constituent into the operator position of a subordinate clause, which through semantic selection of the governing verb needs to be interpreted as a real question and is incompatible with a topicalized constituent, as shown by (iv).

(iv) * Ich frage mich [[ein Auto] du t gekauft hast]
        I   ask   myself a   car   you bought have

When checking the pied piping possibilities of a phrase it is thus important to ensure that the element is moved to a position that can only be occupied by an interrogative/relative operator and not also by a topicalized phrase with a question/relative word in it leading to an echo question. (I am grateful to Angelika Kratzer for bringing this to my attention.)

Bowers (1987) contains a discussion of echo questions in English. I will disregard echo questions throughout, since I have not studied them in detail.

(23Du)   *[De party *waar*] was een succes
            the party where was a   success

(24S)   *[Partyt   *var*] var lyckat
            the party where was a success

(25Da)   *[Festen   *hvor*] var vellykket
            the party where was a success

(26N)   *[Festen   *hvor*] var vellykket
            the party where was a success

(27I)   *[Veislan   *hvar*] var vel heppnuð
            the party where was successful

(28E)   *[The party *where*] was a success

We can formulate our findings now as follows: a DP can be pied-piped by a DP that it dominates but not by a PP.

Now we turn to noun phrases. All Germanic languages allow PPs to function as arguments of nouns. In no case is pied piping possible:

(29G)   *Ich   frage mich   [die Gerüchte über *wen*] ihn schockiert
            I   ask   myself   the rumors about who him shocked
            haben
            have

(30Du)   *Ik   informeerde [de geruchten over *wie*] hem geschokt
            I   inquired   the rumors   about who him shocked
            hebben
            have

(31S)   *Jag   vet   inte   [ryktena   om   *vem*] har chockerat
            I   know not   the rumors about who has shocked
            honom
            him

(32Da)   *Jeg ved   ikke   [rygterne   om   *hvem*] har chokeret ham
            I   know not   the rumors about whom has shocked him

(33N)   *Jeg spoer meg selv [ryktene   om   *hvem*] ham sjokkert
            I   ask   myself   the rumors about whom have shocked
            har
            him

(34I)   *Ég   veit   ekki   [sögusagnirnar um   *hvern*] hafa skelft
            I   know not   the rumors   about whom have horrified
            hann
            him

(35E)   *I asked [the rumors about *whom*] shocked him

As indicated at the beginning of this chapter, we will hypothesize that the pied piping capacity of a constituent correlates with the grammatical relation that it bears. Before we formulate this hypothesis in more detailed form, we look at a final paradigm involving noun phrases. We assume that attributive adjective phrases are adjoined to the noun phrase they modify. The following sentences show that such adjective phrases cannot turn the noun phrase into a pied piper of the DP:

(36G)   *[Die *wie* alten Bücher] hat Hans verloren
         the how old   books   has Hans lost

(37Du)   *[De *hoe* oude boeken] heeft Hans verloren
         the how old   books   has   Hans lost

(38S)   *[*Hur* gamla böcker] har Hans förlorat
         how old   books   has Hans lost

(39Da)   *[De *hvor* gamle bøger] har Hans tabt
         the how old   books has Hans lost

(40N)   *[De *hvor* gamle boekene] har Hans mistet
         the how old   books   has Hans lost

(41I)   *[*Hve* gömlu bókunum] tyndi hann
         how old   the books lost   he

(42E)   *[The *how* old books] has John lost

With this behavior of determiner and noun phrases we formulate the following tentative descriptive generalizations:

(43)   Specifiers are pied pipers.
       Modifiers are not pied pipers.
       Complements are not pied pipers.

All the data presented so far are covered by these generalizations. That only DPs can pied-pipe DP follows from an arguably universal restriction that specifiers of DP have to be DPs themselves, but not, for instance, PPs. If the PPs in 17–18 cannot be specifiers, then they have to be modifiers of the DP and will hence not be able to pied-pipe the whole DP, because modifiers in general are not pied pipers. The ungrammaticality of 22–28 is also accounted for, since the relevant adverbials are modifying the DP and therefore do not qualify as pied pipers. The impossibility of 29–35 follows from the claim that complements, like modifiers, are never pied pipers.

Let us now go through the other phrase-structure positions in Germanic to see whether the generalizations in 43 can be upheld.

Specifiers of AP are pied pipers, as expected:

(44G)   [*Wie* alt] ist Hans
         how old is Hans

(45Du)   [*Hoe* laat] is het
         how late is it

(46S)   [*Hur* stort] är ert   hus
         how big   is your house

(47Da)   [*Hvor* stort] er dit   hus
         how big   is your house

(48N)   [*Hvor* langt] er det til Bergen
         how far   is it   to Bergen

(49I)   [*Hve* gamall] er hann
         how old   is he

(50E)   [*How* old] is John

Likewise, complements of adjectives are well-behaved in all languages under consideration:

(51G)   *[Stolz *auf wen*] ist Hans
          proud of whom is Hans

(52Du)   *[Trots *op wie*]   is Hans
          proud of whom is Hans

(53S)   *[Trogen *vem*]   är Hans
          faithful whom is Hans

(54Da)   *[Stolt   *af hvem*] er Hans
          proud of whom is Hans

(55N)   *[Stolt   *av hvem*] er Hans
          proud of whom is Hans

(56I)   *[Stoltur *af hverjum*] er Jón
          proud of whom   is Jón

(57E)   *[Proud *of whom*] is John

All Germanic languages allow PP-complements of adjectives to follow the head. In addition, in German and Dutch, they can also precede the head.[5]

5. That these structures are possible in German and Dutch but in no other Germanic language will follow from the theory of scrambling developed in Chapter 5.

Even in this position they are not pied pipers:

    (58G)   *[*Auf wen*   [sehr stolz]] ist Hans
                of whom very proud is Hans

    (59Du) *[*Op wie*   [heel trots]] is Hans
                of whom very proud is Hans

Specifiers of adverbial phrases do pied-pipe and support our theory:

    (60G)   [*Wie* schnell] ist Hans gelaufen
                how fast   is Hans run

    (61Du) [*Hoe* snel] heeft Hans gelopen
                how fast has   Hans run

    (62S)   [*Hur* fort] har Hans sprungit
                how fast has Hans run

    (63Da) [*Hvor* stærkt] løb Hans
                how fast   ran Hans

    (64N)   [*Hvor* fort] loep Hans
                how fast ran Hans

    (65I)   [*Hve* hratt] hefur Jón hlaupið
                how fast   has Jón run

    (66E)   [*How* fast] did John run

Complements of verbs behave like those of nouns in not having the capacity to pied-pipe the VP:

    (67G)   *[*Was* gelesen] hat Hans
                what read   has Hans

    (68Du) *[*Wat* gelezen] heeft Hans
                what read   has Hans

    (69S)   *[Läst *vad*] har Hans
                read what has Hans

    (70Da) *[Læst *hvad*] har Hans
                read what has Hans

    (71N)   *[Lest *hva*] har Hans
                read what has Hans

    (72I)   *[Lesið *hvad*] hefur Jón
                read what has Jón

(73E)   *[Read *what*] has John

Manner adverbials, here taken as modifiers of some verbal projection (maybe the VP), do not pied-pipe, as predicted:

(74G)   *[*Wie* die Tür geschlossen] hat Hans
          how the door closed   has Hans

(75Du) *[*Hoe* de deur gesloten] heeft Hans
          how the door closed   has   Hans

(76S)   *[Stängt dörren   *hur*] har Hans
          closed the door how has Hans

(77Da) *[Lukket døren   *hvordan*] har Hans
          closed the door how   has Hans

(78N)   *[Lukket doeren   *hvordan*] har Hans
          closed the door how   has Hans

(79I)   *[Lokað dyrunum *hvernig*] hefur Jón
          closed the door how   has Jón

(80E)   *[*How* closed the door] has John

Now we come to a paradigm that will force us to modify our descriptive generalization in 43. As the following sentences show, complements of prepositions *can* typically pied-pipe the whole prepositional phrase, in violation of 43:

(81G)   [Mit *wem*] hat Hans gesprochen
          with whom has Hans spoken

(82Du) [Van *wie*] heb je die   schaar gekregen
          from whom have you those scissors gotten
          'Who did you get those scissors from'

(83S)   [Till *vem*] gav du boken
          to   whom gave you the book

(84Da) [Til *hvem*] gav du bogen
          to whom gave you the book

(85N)   [Til *hvem*] skriver du
          to whom write   you

(86I)   [Við *hvern*] talaði hún
          with whom talked she

(87E)   [To *whom*] did John talk

88 is the new descriptive generalization.

(88) Specifiers are pied pipers.
Modifiers are not pied pipers.
Complements of nonprepositional heads are not pied pipers.

We proceed with an examination of the behavior of modifiers of prepositional phrases. Take structures like the following:

(89E) He went [downstairs [into the kitchen]]

The adverbial modifier cannot pied-pipe the PP and therefore behaves like all other modifiers:[6]

(90G)   *[*Wohin* in   die Küche] ist er gegangen
            where into the kitchen is he gone

(91S)   *[*Vart* in   i   köket] gick Hans
            where into the kitchen went Hans

(92Da) *[*Hvor* ind i   køkkenet] gik Hans
            where into the kitchen   went Hans

(93N)   *[*Hvor* inn i   kjoekkenet] gikk Hans
            where into the kitchen   went Hans

(94I)   *[*Hvert* i   eldhúsið]   fór Jón
            where into the kitchen went Jón

(95E)   *[*Where* into the kitchen] did John go

In German the adverbial modifier can also appear to the right of the prepositional phrase.

(96G) [In   die Küche *hinunter*]   ist er gegangen
         Into the kitchen downstairs is he gone

Also in this position, it is not a pied piper.

(97G) *[In die Küche *wohin*] ist er gegangen
         In the kitchen where is he gone

Since modifiers of PPs behave as expected, we leave the nonclausal categories at this point and test our descriptive generalization 88 against the sentential categories.

We have to cover six possibilities: complements of I^0 and C^0, specifiers of I' and C', and modifiers of projections of I and C.

---

6. I am grateful to Fred Landman (personal communication) for pointing out to me that this construction does not exist in Dutch.

One correct result of these tests can already be predicted on the basis of our assumptions in the previous chapter: no constituent will ever cause IP to move, since IP is an unmovable category in principle. However, we must take into consideration that IP, although not a mover itself, could cause a dominating constituent to move, i.e. CP. Abstractly, these sentences would have structures like the following:

(98) $[_{CP}$ that $[_{IP} \ldots WH \ldots]]_i$ did John V t_i

The following English examples instantiate the above structure:

(99) *[That who met John] did Mary know t

(100) *[That John met who] did Mary know t

(101) *[That John left when] did Mary know t

These structures are all sharply ungrammatical compared to

(102) [What] did Mary know t ?

(103) [Which story] did Mary know t ?

and therefore establish that IP cannot pied-pipe CP, no matter where the WH-word is embedded within IP. The structure 98 will so clearly be ungrammatical in the other Germanic languages that we do not give their counterparts of 99–101 here.

The cases that we just discussed take care of all IP structures and the constellation in which a CP would be pied-piped by the IP-complement of its head-C^0. Two structures remain: a modifier that pied-pipes CP, and a specifier. I have not been able to find an example of the first kind, i.e. a configuration in which an adverb has to be taken as adjoined to CP rather than IP or VP. Until an instance of this configuration can be found, our generalization in 88 is not testable in this case.

This leaves specifiers of C'. Can a WH-phrase in the specifier of C' pied-pipe the whole CP out of its DS position into an operator position? The answer seems to be no:[7]

7. Contrary to the assumptions made here, it has been argued in van Riemsdijk (1985) and Webelhuth (1984) that a relative pronoun in German *can* pied-pipe the whole relative clause. Arguments against this view have been presented in Haider (1984), Grewendorf (1986), and Huybregts (1987). The latter authors propose that what looks like a pied-piped clause has really been topicalized with subsequent extraction of the relative pronoun.

Although it still seems to me that the van Riemsdijk/Webelhuth position is the right one, I have chosen to ignore these examples here, since an argument based on them would inherit the uncertain status of their analysis.

In any event, since I am arguing that specifiers can, in principle, pied-pipe, it would not come as a big surprise to me if examples of CP pied piping by a specifier could be found.

The reader may consult van de Velde (1977) for a thorough description of the phenomenon.

(104G)   *[*Wer* ein Buch gelesen hat] wußte Hans t
          who a   book read   has knew Hans

(105Du)   *[*Wie* er   een boek gelezen heeft] weet   Hans t
          who there a   book read   has   knows Hans

(106S)   *[*Vem* har läst boken]   visste Hans t
          who has read the book knew Hans

(107Da)   *[*Hvem* der   har læst bogen]   vidste Hans t
          who   there has read the book knew Hans

(108N)   *[*Hvem* har lest en bok] visste Hans t
          who   has read a   book knew Hans

(109I)   *[*Hver* hefur lesið bókina]   vissi Kjartan t
          who has   read the book knew Kjartan

(110E)   *[*Who* had left for Scotland] did Hans know t

With these examples we conclude our overview of the pied piping possibilities
of Germanic and sum up all the grammaticality judgments:

(111) *Pied Piping in Germanic Questions*

	G	Du	S	Da	N	I	E
Spec							
DP	+	+	+	+	+	+	+
AP	+	+	+	+	+	+	+
ADVP	+	+	+	+	+	+	+
CP	−	−	−	−	−	−	−
Mod							
DP	−	−	−	−	−	−	−
NP	−	−	−	−	−	−	−
VP	−	−	−	−	−	−	−
PP	−	−	−	−	−	−	−
Compl							
DP	−	−	−	−	−	−	−
NP	−	−	−	−	−	−	−
AP	−	−	−	−	−	−	−
VP	−	−	−	−	−	−	−
PP	+	+	+	+	+	+	+
CP	−	−	−	−	−	−	−

The descriptive generalization that emerges at this point (and will be further
improved below) is the one given in 112.

(112) Specifiers of nonclausal categories are pied pipers.
Modifiers are not pied pipers.
Complements of nonprepositional heads are not pied pipers.

With this result in mind, we turn to some apparent counterexamples in English relative clauses in Section 4.3, and a closer look at what might be special about specifiers of clauses and complements of preopositions in Section 4.4.

4.3 Relative Clauses in English

Until now all the presented examples of pied piping occurred in constituent questions. Of course, we also find this phenomenon in relative clauses.

(113E) the man [whose brother] we met

In general, the pied piping possibilities in relative clauses mirror those in questions, but as is well known, this is not always the case in English. Thus, Ross (1967, 109) presents the following examples:

(114E) Reports [the covers of which] the government prescribes the height of the lettering on almost always put me to sleep

(115E) Reports [the lettering on the covers of which] the government prescribes the height of are a shocking waste of funds

(116E) Reports [the height of the lettering on the covers of which] the government prescribes should be abolished

In all these cases it appears as if a complement to a noun can pied-pipe the whole noun phrase and then the determiner phrase to the beginning of the sentence. Complements of adjective phrases seem to have this capacity as well in English:[8]

(117E) This is the kind of woman [proud of whom] I could never be

These cases are not covered by the generalization that we arrived at in the previous section. There we found that a complement to a nonprepositional head does not have the capacity of pied piping.

How should these examples be treated? We could pursue the option of modifying the universal feature percolation mechanisms slightly so that the relevant examples are let in. But this is not easy, since all the counterexamples

---

8. This fact and examples similar to the one given in the text were brought to my attention by Craig Thiersch (personal communication).

presented are actually ungrammatical in all the other Germanic languages, where testable:

(118G) *der Präsident, [ein Bild von *dem*] an der Wand hing
        the president a   pict. of whom at the wall hung

(119Du) *de president, [een foto van *wie*] aan de muur hing
         the president a   pict. of whom at   the wall hung

(120S) *presidenten [en bild av *vem*] hängde på väggen
        the president a   pict. of whom hung on the wall

(121Da) *præsidenten [et billede af *hvem*] hænger paa væggen
         the president a picture of whom hangs on the wall

(122N) *presidenten [et bilde av *hvem*] hang paa veggen
        the president a picture of whom hung on the wall

Moreover, as already stated, the counterexamples are all of the same type in that they only occur in relative clauses, never in questions:

(123E) *I asked Bill [proud of whom] he has always been

If we were to capture English examples like 117 through a manipulation of feature percolation, then not only would we have to parametrize the percolation mechanism so as to allow English an option that the other languages do not have, but also we would have to assume different percolation conventions depending on whether a REL-feature moves or a WH-feature does. Such a proposal is not very attractive, especially if one shares our view that the syntactic properties of a complex constituent should be universally predictable from the syntactic properties of its parts. Allowing different percolation mechanisms would entail that one and the same pair of constituents could be projected to different complex constituents in two languages. This is exactly the state of affairs we would like to avoid.

All these considerations suggest that the universal theory should be left as it is and that the English relative clauses should be taken care of in some language-particular fashion that is independent of the percolation mechanism.

The phenomenon under discussion has a third marked property in addition to the ones just mentioned, i.e. that the construction occurs in only one Germanic language, and here only in one specific environment, relative clauses. This third property is that the construction has a rather "bookish" sound to it. Jespersen (1927, Part III, p. 182), for example, comments as follows (emphasis added):

> The natural place of a relative pronoun, like that of an interrogative pronoun and of a conjunction, is at the beginning of the clause. But while this rule is uni-

versal with conjunctions . . . there are a good many exceptions with the *wh*-pro-nouns, because other tendencies of word order may come into conflict with the front-position of these pronouns. This is especially true of *literary* English, which in accordance with the classical languages favors complicated relative constructions *foreign to natural colloquial speech.*

I believe that an approach to the English examples should account for why they are possible at all but should also express the fact that they are exceed-ingly rare (at least in the context of the Germanic languages), and that they only occur in relative clauses but not in questions. A manipulation of feature percolation mechanisms would only do the first, i.e. restate the English facts. It would not shed any light on why the structures should be so exceptional, and would also not explain why they are displayed in relative clauses but not in questions rather than the opposite.

I will therefore propose that Universal Grammar does not license these structures as pure relative clauses at all and that precisely this is the reason for their stylistic markedness. That the phenomenon is restricted to relative clauses gives an important clue to its analysis, especially in the light of the following observation brought to my attention by Roger Higgins (personal communication): the exceptional "pied piping" is only possible if the con-stituent that moves along with the "pied piper" is independently topicaliza-ble. Thus, note the contrast between the following two topicalization con-structions (the second example was contributed by Higgins):

(124E)   [Proud of John] he has never been t
(125E)   *[To leave] I want t

Thus, although the AP in 124 can be topicalized independently of pied pip-ing, the infinitive of 125 is barred from topicalization for some reason. Note, now, that we get the same grammaticality distribution in the exceptional pied piping construction:

(126E)   his wife [proud of whom] he has never been t
(127E)   *his wife [to leave whom] he wanted

The parallelism in grammaticality between 124, 125 and 126, 127 is probably not accidental and suggests that the exceptional cases of pied piping are indeed instances of topicalization in which what looks formally like a relative pronoun is interpreted as an indexical pronoun, much like *her* in the follow-ing discourse sequence:

(128)   His wife is intelligent. But, [proud of her] he has never been.

The second sentence in this discourse begins with the structure that forms the relative clause in 126, but in this case the pronoun is anaphoric to the discourse antecedent *his wife*. In discourse representation systems like those presented in Kamp (1981) and Heim (1982) the clause containing the anaphoric pronoun would be treated as an open sentence which is predicated of the discourse referent introduced in the previous sentence. It is noteworthy that relative pronouns have a similar semantic function. Montague (1973), for example, also treats relative clauses as open sentences that are predicated of a referent, namely the entity or class of entities that also satisfies the predicate denoted by the head noun of the relative clause. Indexical pronouns and relative pronouns are thus somewhat similar in their semantic effect, and it therefore is not implausible that the English "relative clauses" which Universal Grammar (according to our conception) does not allow, are formed as structures involving topicalization, in analogy with the sentences involving indexical personal pronouns. What looks like a relative pronoun formally seems to be able to take on the semantics of an indexical pronoun.[9]

The nonexistence of analogous WH-pied piping examples would become understandable, when one considers that question words function very differently from anaphoric and relative pronouns. They do not turn the sentence containing them into an open sentence which is then predicated of a discourse referent. Rather, they are logical operators that restrict the range of a variable. Both anaphoric and relative pronouns, however, are themselves variables that get bound either in a discourse or by the operator, which also binds an argument of the predicate denoted by the head of the relative clause. It is thus not surprising that WH-operators cannot take on the meaning of an anaphoric pronoun, while this is easier for relative pronouns. The latter two are both logical variables, while the former is an operator, a very different semantic entity.

To sum up my proposal concerning the English "relative clauses": the counterexamples to our generalization 112 are all of the same type; namely they only occur in relative clauses but not in WH-questions, and those sentences are stylistically highly marked. Furthermore, none of the counterexamples is grammatical in any other Germanic language discussed here. I have argued, therefore, that Universal Grammar should not cover these sentence types as relative clauses at all. Rather, they should be projected as structures involving topicalization. That they are only found in relative clauses is accounted for by assuming that the relevant examples are built in analogy to sentences involving anaphoric pronouns, which have a very similar semantic function to relative pronouns but no semantic relation to question opera-

9. For a more detailed proposal of this sort, cf. Sells (1983). Apparently Cinque (1982) contains the earliest suggestion along these lines.

tors.[10] And, finally, that the constructions are highly marked stylistically can be attributed to the fact that there is a mismatch between the form of these structures as relative clauses and their interpretation, which applies a semantic rule of discourse anaphora to relative pronouns that usually exclusively fall into the domain of sentence grammar.

In the following discussion I will assume that the sentence types discussed in this subsection are irrelevant for a theory of pied piping, and consequently they will be ignored.

4.4 The Pied Piping Generalizations

4.4.1 Introduction

With the English "relative clauses" out of the way, we now return to our generalization in 112, repeated below for convenience:

(129) Specifiers of nonclausal categories are pied pipers.
       Modifiers are not pied pipers.
       Complements of nonprepositional heads are not pied pipers.

In this section I will further refine the generalization, but I will maintain that the description we ultimately end up with holds for instances of pied piping in both questions and true relative clauses.

An inspection of 129 shows that there are two elements that are, in principle, pied pipers: (1) specifiers of nonclausal expressions, and (2) complements of prepositions. The problem that we face at this point is that these two types of expressions do not form a natural class with respect to any syntactic phenomenon that I know of. It is thus not obvious how to characterize the possible pied pipers in an insightful way, i.e. in a way other than just stipulating the observed facts, e.g. by inventing a constructional feature [+ Pied Piping] and assigning it to the relevant expressions.

The strategy that I am going to follow at this point is to reexamine the subgeneralizations in 129, especially the specifier and complement clauses. The next two subsections are dedicated to this task. The resulting observations will lead us to the conclusion that the possible pied pipers still do not

10. The phenomenon under discussion thus probably falls under the cases that Chomsky (1981, 8) discusses briefly in the following paragraph (my emphasis):

Furthermore, each actual 'language' will incorporate a periphery of borrowings, historical residues, inventions, and so on, which we can hardly expect to—*and indeed would not want to*—incorporate within a principled theory of UG.

form a natural syntactic class, and neither do the elements that are *not* possible pied pipers. However, it will turn out that the elements that are *not* pied pipers will automatically be singled out by two independently motivated modules of our version of the Principles and Parameters system, namely the definition of modification and the θ-criterion. All those elements that are not prevented from being pied pipers by either of these modules will then be shown to have the capacity for playing this role in phrase structure.

4.4.2 Specifiers

Above we claimed that all specifiers of nonclausal constituents are pied pipers. Here we will reexamine this claim by testing it against more data, concluding that the generalization is false as stated. Rather, we will find that some specifiers of nonclausal constituents are pied pipers and some are not, and that the two different classes of elements are distinguishable by the θ-criterion.

Our claim that specifiers of nonclausal constituents are pied pipers was based on examples like the following:

(130E) [*How* sick] is John t

(131E) [*How* quickly] did John open the door t

(132E) [*Whose* book] did John read t

However, so far we have ignored cases where a specifier of a nonclausal category is *not* a pied piper. In the following I will contrast a paradigm in which the potential pied piper specifies a D′ containing a deverbal noun with one in which the D′ contains a gerund:

(133E) The Democratic voters resented [Atwater's harsh *attack* on Dukakis] most

(134E) The Democratic voters resented [Atwater's harshly *attacking* Dukakis] most

Note that these two types of DPs behave differently with respect to pied piping as observed in Williams (1975). According to his judgment and that of my informants, only the deverbal noun can be pied-piped, whereas the gerund blocks pied piping:

(135E) I wonder [whose harsh *attack* on Dukakis] the Democratic voters resented t most

(136E) *I wonder [whose harshly *attacking* Dukakis] the Democratic voters resented t most

The following sentences illustrate the same phenomenon. From the underlying structures

(137E) The administration objected to [Bill's frequent *travels* to Chicago] on financial grounds

(138E) The administration objected to [Bill's frequently *traveling* to Chicago] on financial grounds

we can only get a well-formed question through pied piping if the deverbal noun is pied-piped but not in the case of the gerund:

(139E) [Whose frequent *travels* to Chicago] did the administration object to on financial grounds

(140E) *[Whose frequently *traveling* to Chicago] did the administration object to on financial grounds

Since the potential pied pipers in 135–136 and 139–140 are all specifiers, it is not enough to say that all specifiers of nonclausal categories are pied pipers. There has to be a crucial difference between the specifiers in 135, 139 as compared to the ones in 136, 140. I would like to suggest that this difference relates to θ-theory, in particular, that the specifiers of the derived nouns are not θ-marked while those of the gerunds are.

Independent evidence for this view is available from a number of sources.[11] First of all, if the specifier of a nongerundive noun is not θ-marked while that of a gerund is, then these structures should get different interpretations when the specifier is not expressed overtly. The following examples show that this is correct:

(141E) The Democrats resented [the attack on Dukakis]

(142E) The Democrats resented [PRO attacking Dukakis]

In the first case, since the noun *attack* does not θ-mark the specifier, its reading is free when it is left unexpressed. The sentence can mean that the Democrats resented somebody else's attack on Dukakis. The second sentence cannot have this meaning, since *attacking* has to assign its agent θ-role to a specifier, which has to be realized as PRO if it is not overt. In that case PRO is in a control environment, however, and the sentence can only mean that the Democrats resented their own attacking of Dukakis.

Second, if *attack* does not θ-mark its specifier while *attacking* does, then it should be possible to fill the specifier position with a nonargument in the first case, while doing so in the second should lead to a violation of the θ-criterion.

11. I am drawing on insights here in Lebeaux (1986), Grimshaw (1986), and Chomsky (1986a).

This is also correct, as the following examples demonstrate:

(143E)   The Democrats resented [*yesterday's* attack on Dukakis]

(144E)   *The Democrats resented [*yesterday's* attacking Dukakis]

Third, if the specifier position of the gerund is an argument position whereas that of the noun is not, then one would expect the former to be a possible landing site for DP-movement while the latter is not. Williams (1982) has provided evidence that this is the case:

(145E)   *Everybody resented [*John's* semblance [t to be lazy]]

(146E)   Everybody resented [*John's* seeming [t to be lazy]]

Finally, for the same reason, the first construction should not allow expletive elements in specifier position while the second one should. Examples confirming this prediction are given below (cf. Chomsky, 1986a):

(147E)   *Everybody resented [*its* obviousness that John is so lazy]

(148E)   Everybody resented [*its* being so obvious that John is so lazy]

The case for specifiers of gerunds being θ-marked while not those of non-gerundive nominals is therefore quite strong. Since it is exactly the specifiers of gerundive nominals that fail to be pied pipers, we will assume that it is their status as heads of θ-chains that prevents them from taking along their mother constituent under movement to an operator position.

With this result, we turn to the complements of prepositions: *θ-marked specifiers of nonclausal constituents are not pied pipers.*

4.4.3 Complements

In this subsection we reevaluate the claim that complements of prepositions are in principle pied pipers while complements to other heads are not. I will argue that this generalization is correct as it stands but fails to capture the essential property distinguishing prepositions from the other heads.

The situation we face with respect to prepositions is partly similar and partly different from the exceptional case of "relative clause" pied piping in English discussed in Section 4.3. On the one hand the PP cases, much like the "relative clauses," clearly fall outside our first larger generalization in 43 that complements are not pied pipers. On the other hand, however, the PP case differs in that it is not associated with any of the three marked features of the "relative clauses"; i.e. PP pied piping is not restricted to one Germanic lan-

guage but occurs in all of them, PP pied piping is not restricted to one particular environment unlike the "relative clauses", and the PP case also does not
have the "bookish" flavor to it that the "relative clause" examples have, at
least not in languages without preposition stranding, e.g. German and Dutch.

It would thus not be fruitful to claim that the PP cases are so exceptional
that they do not bear on a theory of pied piping. Such a proposal would simply
lack the kind of justification we have given for excluding the English "relative
clauses" from consideration.

Given our generalization that complements of prepositions are the only
complements that can pied-pipe, while specifiers in principle are pied pipers,
one obvious approach would try to unify these two cases by making what
looks like a complement of a preposition into a specifier, either by base-generating the relevant DPs as specifiers, or by base-generating them as complements and then moving them up into the specifier position of the PP.[12]

However, even if the significant technical difficulties that such a proposal
entails could be overcome, such a theory would in my opinion still be unsat-
isfactory as long as it does not give a principled answer to the question of why
prepositions behave differently from the other heads.

Therefore I will pursue a different approach here, an approach that challenges one central assumption of θ-theory but seems to be motivated strongly
enough to warrant consideration. I intend to argue that a number of interesting differences between prepositions and other X-bar theoretic heads can be
derived from the claim that prepositions are exempt from the θ-theoretic
requirement in Chomsky (1981, 36) that a head must θ-mark all its complements.[13] According to my proposal, prepositions—even the semantically
active ones—would differ from the heads of category V, A, or N in that they
can take complements without θ-marking them themselves. The contribution of a preposition that appears to assign a particular θ-role would then be
one where the preposition "solicits" the θ-role from some other head; i.e. the
presence of an appropriate preposition is a condition on the θ-role assignment
by the verb (or any other head) rather than a consequence of the preposition
being a θ-role assigner itself.[14]

12. Harbert (1989) takes this route as a reaction to a previous version of the present chapter.

13. Postal/Pullum (1988) argue that the restriction should be given up even for other heads.
The proposal here does not go that far, and in my view it is worth testing which of their examples
are relevant for θ-theory at all, since many of them appear to be idioms (which are exempt from
the θ-criterion by definition) or might involve embedded small clauses.

14. This would have to work as follows. Idiosyncratic prepositions are treated in analogy to
oblique cases; that is, *depend* must be followed by a PP headed by *on* in order to assign its internal
θ-role; grammatically, there is no difference to a verb like *helfen* (help) in German which is also
restricted in that it can only assign its internal θ-role to a DP headed by a datively marked D. A

In the following paragraphs I will show that the assumptions above account for a variety of typical differences between prepositions and other heads. At the same time I will demonstrate that in each case where the set of heads is partitioned into prepositions and all other elements by some property, prepositions behave functionally as if they were affixes, in particular, inflectional case affixes. According to my proposal this is not surprising, since the function of soliciting a θ-role without θ-marking is, of course, exactly that performed by affixes marking some oblique Case, e.g. the ablative in classical Latin or the different cases in Finnish. Stripping adpositions of the θ-marking capacity would turn them into what their name suggests, namely morphemes whose major function it is to form-ally identify the elements they are associated with as constituents that can enter certain relations, i.e. receive a certain thematic role.

The first advantage of assuming that prepositions are θ-role solicitors rather than θ-role assigners is that the functional equivalence of affixes and prepositions typical in natural language becomes understandable. Thus, there are many examples in the Germanic languages alone where a verb will only assign a specific θ-role to an argument that has a certain form, e.g. appears in dative rather than accusative case. The German verbs *begegnen* (meet) and *finden* (find), for instance, differ in that the former assigns one of its semantic roles only to a DP that is marked DATIVE, whereas the latter only θ-marks DPs with ACCUSATIVE shape. This is a mere formal difference between the

---

technical mechanism for the selection of idiosyncratic prepositions has been proposed in note 21, Chapter 1.

Selections of PPs that are not headed by idiosyncratic prepositions would be done by just c-selecting a PP without specifying a particular head for it. The semantic sort of the preposition then has to be compatible with the θ-role assigned by the governing head; that is, if the θ-role *location* is assigned, the preposition has to have a locational meaning. If this is not the case, the sentence will be semantically anomalous, as the contrast between the following two examples illustrates:

(i)   John lives [PP in Paris]

  θ:Loc

(ii) * John lives [PP to Paris]

  θ:Loc

If the governing head has more than one θ-role to assign, the identity of the preposition will determine which θ-role it is compatible with. Thus, if *talk* is combined with *to*, then it will assign *goal*, and if it is followed by *about*, it will assign *patient*.

In my understanding, the informal proposal concerning prepositions above is an extension of the theory of adverbs presented in McConnell-Ginet (1982) on both syntactic and semantic grounds. If true, this would be of some interest, since then the proposal would have some independent support.

two verbs that is not derivable from any other of their properties (e.g. their meanings), or from the "meanings" of the two morphological cases.

The postulated functional symmetry between case affixes and prepositions can now be illustrated by pairs of verbs that differ in requiring two separate prepositions in their θ-governed complement. Thus, *hoffen* (hope) requires the preposition *auf* (on) in German, while *abhängen* (depend) requires *von* (of). Again, this difference is of a completely formal kind that is not predictable from any other property of these two verbs. In sum, claiming that prepositions assign a thematic role to their complement would make it less understandable why prepositions behave very much like affixes, elements that are not taken to assign θ-roles.[15]

Second, a theory in which prepositions are θ-role solicitors through their form and meaning but do not assign θ-roles themselves has a natural explanation for the relative tendency of prepositions to lose their meaning; in this respect prepositions differ sharply from transitive heads of categories V, N, or A, which seem to be semantically empty only in idiomatic expressions. But again, prepositions are very similar to inflectional affixes in this respect, since, at least in the modern Germanic languages, one cannot assign a meaning to the different morphological cases any more. If—as we claim—prepositions share with case affixes the ability to solicit a θ-role from a governing head just through their presence but do not θ-mark themselves, then they are not required to carry any semantic information. They are thus predicted to behave differently from the θ-marking heads, since the assignment of θ-roles by a head presupposes that the head can combine the denotation of the θ-receiver with its own denotation to describe a situation.

The third property that classifies prepositions with case affixes against the θ-marking heads is nonstrandability. The θ-marking heads can be stranded by their complements in all Germanic languages, e.g. by WH-movement. There is never an issue whether a language allows "verb stranding" or "adjective stranding." In contrast "preposition stranding" cannot be taken for granted, since there are many languages that do not allow the configuration

15. Note that a claim opposite mine would not be very plausible. Thus, somebody might agree with me that affixes and prepositions are functionally equivalent but might hold the view that they both do assign thematic roles rather than not doing so.

Such a claim would entail that there exists some version of "internal" θ-marking, since the affixes in most languages are contained within the θ-marked phrase. A related problem is that case is frequently distributed within a determiner phrase; that is, it may be realized on the head determiner, adjectives, and the noun. Thus, it seems best to me to maintain the view in the main text that both affixes and prepositions are what they appear to be at first sight, namely form-al markers that may have to be present for a constituent to receive a certain θ-role.

[$_{pp}$ P e]. For instance, we saw in Chapter 3 that German does not allow a preposition to be stranded by a nonpronominal DP. In that respect prepositions of course behave like affixes, which can never be stranded either. Thus, it is impossible to extract the stems of a datively marked DP and leave all the dative affixes behind. That prepositions differ from the other heads in frequently not allowing their complement to move away may be accounted for in an ECP framework like that of Chomsky (1986b), by assuming that an empty category in complement position has to be θ-governed by a lexical head. This assumption would make the nonstrandability of prepositions the normal case and would require some (thematic) reanalysis for those cases where prepositions can be stranded, along lines similar to what is proposed in Hornstein/Weinberg (1981).

Until now we have presented three properties in which prepositions typically differ from other syntactic heads but behave like affixes. I showed that a unified explanation of these differences is possible if we assume that prepositions are syntactic heads that take complements but fail to θ-mark them. There is a fourth and a fifth difference that I would like to incorporate into this account.

The fourth difference relates to the concerns of this chapter, namely categorial transparency. Thus, as we saw above, prepositions typically differ from the other heads in allowing the operator feature of their complement to percolate to their common mother node. Thus, although the PP-node in [$_{pp}$ to whom] can inherit the [+ WH] feature from *whom,* this is not the case for the VP-node in [$_{VP}$ see whom]. Case affixes, however, typically pattern with prepositions again, rather than with the θ-marking heads. For instance, the English genitive marker *-s* is transparent for the [+ WH] feature in the DP to which it is attached.

(149E) [[$_{DP}$ [$_{DP}$ which person] s] book] did you read t

The embedded DP *which person* in 149 is marked for the feature [+ WH] and can percolate it to the DP *which person's,* since the genitive affix is categorially transparent for the WH-feature. Prepositions and affixes thus pattern together again against the syntactic heads N, V, and A.

In Section 4.5 I will suggest that the categorial transparency of prepositions is also a function of their inability to assign θ-roles. This status as "syntactic affixes," i.e. syntactic X^0-heads with the nonthematic marking function of affixes, makes them behave differently from the θ-marking heads and allow their complement to pied-pipe them to an operator position while the other heads do not.

This leaves us with one last property of prepositions that typically makes them different from all other syntactic X^0-heads: uniformity of the directionality of government.

In Chapter 1, when we developed a restrictive theory of parameters, we mentioned that the head–complement relation differs from specification and modification in that all X^0-heads of a language have to take their complements in the same direction, whereas this is not the case for the other two grammatical relations. It is often necessary to stipulate the direction of combination for individual specifier or modifier morphemes, e.g. English adverbs, or Romance adjectives.

To account for this difference we proposed that the head–complement relation is different from the other two in that it involves θ-marking. Consequently, we suggested that the correct range of parametrization can be predicted if the directions of specification, modification, and complementation can be stipulated on a morpheme-particular basis, whereas the direction of θ-marking is a property of a whole major syntactic category, not of individual morphemes.

As noted in Chapter 1, this theory introduces a slight redundancy into the system in that it allows (in fact, requires) individual X^0-heads to stipulate a direction of complementation that cannot be used, since in order to θ-mark its complement the head will be subject to the direction of θ-marking, which is stated not for the individual head but for the whole category it belongs to.

With the assumptions of this chapter we can demonstrate that the directions of complementation are not fully redundant in that they can always be predicted from the morpheme-independent directions of θ-marking. The reason is that adpositions do take complements but fail to θ-mark them. Accordingly, our theory predicts that adpositions do *not* have to satisfy the direction-of-θ-marking-parameter but just the direction-of-complementation parameter, whose requirements are weaker in that it allows an individual head to fix its own direction of combination. Put more simply, our theory predicts that adpositions should differ from all other syntactic heads in that not all members of their class in a language have to take their complements in the same direction.

Interestingly, this prediction is fulfilled, since—as mentioned in footnote 18 of Chapter 1—languages can indeed have both prepositions and postpositions, although they do not seem to have verb systems in which some transitive verbs take their complement on the left while others take it on the right. German and Dutch are examples of this state of affairs. Thus, although German is mostly a prepositional language,

(150G) weil Peter das Buch [$_{PP}$ *an* Maria] schickte
bec. Peter the book   to Maria sent

it also has a stock of postpositions:[16]

> (151G) weil Peter [$_{PP}$ dem Haus *gegenüber*] steht
>   bec. Peter   the house opposite   stands
>   'Peter is standing opposite to the house'

I conclude that the existence of languages with both pre- and postpositions in the (hypothesized) absence of languages with nonuniform nominal, verbal, and adjectival heads supports our assumptions that the direction of θ-marking is a uniform property of major categories, and that prepositions as non-θ-markers do not fall under this uniformity requirement. They can fix their direction of combination on an individual basis by attaining a "direction of complementation" statement.

We set out to explain why complements of prepositions have the capacity to pied-pipe their mother node, while complements of other heads do not have this ability. We rejected the proposal to make complements of prepositions into specifiers, since it would not do justice to the typically idiosyncratic role that prepositions play in phrase structure. We identified five properties in which prepositions typically differ from the other X^0-heads and pattern with inflectional affixes where relevant:

(152)	N,V,A	P	Affixes
1. Semantically empty	−	+	+
2. Idiosyncratic selection	−	+	+
3. Non-strandable	−	+	+
4. Categorially transparent	−	+	+
5. Directionally not uniform	−	+	n/a

In our view the pattern in 152 is not accidental and can be considered symptomatic of one principled difference between prepositions and the other X^0-heads: prepositions are θ-role solicitors, but the other heads are θ-role assigners. Then, all five generalizations in 152 can be derived from this proposal. We have already sketched how this would be done for all but the fourth, the pied piping property. This gap will be closed in Section 4.5.

16. Note that the sentence in the text probably also has a bracketing:

> (i)   weil Peter dem Haus [gegenüber steht]

That the elements in brackets in the text example can form a constituent is shown by their ability to move together to the topic position:

> (ii) [$_{PP}$ Dem Haus gegenüber] steht Peter t

Also, the morphological case of *dem Haus* is dependent on *gegenüber,* arguing that the postposition is the head of the constituent.

With this theory of prepositions we now return to our principled concern, namely the investigation of the pied piping capacity of complements.

We had started out this section by examining why it is that prepositions can be pied-piped while other X^0-heads cannot. The result of the above considerations suggests that there is nothing particular about prepositions with respect to pied piping; rather, the difference between Ps and the other heads falls out from the more major contrast that prepositions lack the ability of the other heads to θ-mark their complements.

We can thus restate our generalization concerning complements and pied piping in such a way that reference to prepositions is avoided in favor of reference to θ-marking:

(153) A θ-marked complement is not a pied piper.

4.4.4 Summary of the Generalizations

Let us now draw together the various strands of our long fact-finding mission. We now have four generalizations:

(154) a. A modifier is not a pied piper.
b. A θ-marked specifier is not a pied piper.
c. A θ-marked complement is not a pied piper.
d. A specifier of C′ is not a pied piper.

Section 4.5 will derive all four generalizations on the basis of our assumptions about X-bar theory and other independently motivated principles such as the θ-criterion and the Bijection Principle from Koopman/Sportiche (1982).

4.5 Deriving the Generalizations

We will derive the pied piping generalization from Section 4.4.4 in three steps. Section 4.5.1 will derive 154a, 4.5.2 will deal with 154b and 154c, and 4.5.3 will take care of the final sub-generalization.

4.5.1 Modifiers

I would like to suggest that the failure of modifiers to pied-pipe their mother nodes is due to the part of the Saturation Condition that deals with the phrase-structural realization of modifiers, and the following well-formedness condition on operator chains:

(155) *The head of an operator chain has to be an operator.*

One of the requirements for qualifying as an operator will naturally be that the candidate carry an operator feature. Descriptively speaking, we will say that an element α pied-pipes its mother node β (or a node dominating its mother) if, by percolating an operator feature to β, it turns β into an operator; the derived operator will then be able to satisfy the condition in 155 and will therefore be able to move into an operator position:

(156) $\beta[+ \text{WH}]$
                              |
                              $\alpha[+ \text{WH}]$

We define the following subset of the categorial properties as "operator features":

(157) *Definition of "Operator Feature"*
      α is an operator feature iff $\alpha \,\epsilon\, \{[+ \text{WH}], [+ \text{Rel}]\}$.

We allow each expression to have at most one operator feature.

There are two more ingredients that we have to state as parts of our theory of pied piping before we can give the definition of modification that will derive that modifiers are never pied pipers.

First, we present the Bijection Principle that was originally proposed in Koopman/Sportiche (1982). For purely expository purposes, I have slightly changed its wording:[17]

(158) *The Bijection Principle (BP)*
      (i) Every syntactic operator binds exactly one syntactic variable;
      (ii) Every syntactic variable is bound by exactly one syntactic
           operator.

Second, we have to give a definition of "syntactic operator" that is referred to in BP. Above we had already mentioned one condition for being an operator, that of carrying an operator feature. But this condition can only be necessary and not sufficient, as the grammaticality of the following sentence shows:

(159E) [How sick] is John t

Note that in this sentence there are two constituents that are marked $[+ \text{WH}]$ (*how* and *how sick*), but there is only one variable. Thus it cannot be the case that every phrase marked $[+ \text{WH}]$ is a syntactic operator, since then 159

---

17. The original statement of the BP was formulated as follows:

   (i) *The Bijection Principle* (Koopman/Sportiche, 1982, 146)
       There is a bijective correspondence between variables and A-bar positions.

should violate clause (i) of BP. In fact, since only the higher constituent binds a variable in 159, we have to conclude that if a constituent α turns a constituent β into a syntactic operator, then α ceases to be a syntactic operator itself. Put differently, only the highest element in a percolation chain of operator features will be an operator. We can reach that result by giving a relational definition of "syntactic operator in γ." Syntactic operators will then only be those phrases that (a) carry an operator feature, and (b) are dominated by a nonoperator:

(160) α is a syntactic operator in γ if
a. γ dominates α,
b. α is a maximal projection,
c. α carries an operator feature,
d. α is immediately dominated by β in γ s.t.
1. β does not carry an operator feature, or
2. β is not a syntactic operator in γ.

I restate the intuition behind 160 in words: only the highest element in a percolation chain involving an operator feature is a syntactic operator, with one exception: if the highest element is a root clause, then the element from which it received the operator feature will be the operator, since the root clause cannot satisfy clause (a) of the definition, given that there is no γ in which it could be an operator.

According to 160, there is only one syntactic operator in 159, namely the AP. The AdvP loses its syntactic operator status by percolating its operator feature to the AP, which satisfies the definition of "syntactic operator in CP." We predict that 159 satisfies BP, since every syntactic operator binds one syntactic variable, and every syntactic variable is bound by one syntactic operator.

With these preliminaries we can now give the definition of modification from which it will follow that modifiers are never pied pipers. In fact, our preliminary definition in Chapter 1 already has this effect (for ease of exposition we ignore direction of combination, since it plays no role in feature percolation):

(161) *The Projection of the Modification Relation*
If a. α is a member of category YP,
b. β is a member of category X and bar level n,
c. α modifies expressions of category X and bar level n,

then δ, the constituent formed by concatenating α and β, is an expression that inherits all the grammatical features and specifications of β and none of α.

The definition is formulated as an acceptance condition, i.e. it first defines two constituents α and β with certain properties and then accepts these elements as the immediate subconstituents of a new expression δ. The remaining properties of δ are determined in the last clause. We define the modification relation as one that is completely recursive on the properties of the modified element; i.e. all the properties of the mother node (category, bar level, relational information, θ-role information, and operator features, etc.) are inherited from the modified element. The modifier, on the other hand, does not contribute any information to the mother node it shares with the modified element.

It is this recursive property that makes our theory predict that modifiers are never pied pipers. To pied-pipe a dominating expression α, a constituent β has to turn α into a syntactic operator through the percolation of an operator feature. Since the universal instance of the Saturation Condition that defines the phrase-structure realization of modifiers prevents these elements from contributing *any* information to a dominating expression, it prevents them from percolating an operator feature in particular. The following percolation configuration, which would be necessary for a modifier to pied-pipe its mother node, is thus not projectible from our version of the realization of modification relations:

(162)

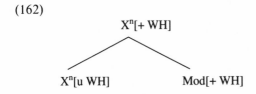

$X^n[+ \text{WH}]$

$X^n[\text{u WH}]$ $\text{Mod}[+ \text{WH}]$

Let us walk through a prototypical instance of a modification relation to realize the full consequences of the interaction of the various principles that we have invoked. We begin with the following basic example:

(163E) John will [[$_{VP}$ give a talk] *there*]

Since the adverb in 163 can move along with the VP, we assume that it modifies the whole VP in that sentence.

(164E) He promised to give a talk in Maryland, and [$_{VP}$ give a talk *there*] he did t

However, although the whole VP can move in principle (cf. 164), the adverb cannot pied-pipe the VP:

(165E) *[[$_{VP}$ Give a talk] *where*] will John t

The reason is that *where* in 165 is in a percolation island and cannot turn its mother node VP into an operator. Since the VP also does not have any other operator features, it does not satisfy the definition of "syntactic operator in γ," which means that the variable at the end of the sentence is not bound by an operator and violates BP. There is a second BP violation in 165: the adverb *where* satisfies the definition of "syntactic operator in γ" but does not bind a variable.

The following two sentences differ from the previous ones in that the modifier here is embedded within an NP. However, the grammaticality judgments remain the same, and our explanation is exactly parallel:

(166E)   John will enjoy [$_{DP}$ [the party] *there*]

(167E)   *[$_{DP}$ [The party] *where*] will John enjoy t

We sum up our major expectations for the behavior of modifiers cross-linguistically with respect to pied piping: since a modifier with an operator feature cannot percolate its operator feature, it always satisfies the definition of "syntactic operator in γ" and has to satisfy BP. Consequently, if the modifier is not in an extraction island, it has to move to an appropriate operator position; if the modifier is in an extraction island, the sentence is ungrammatical:

(168E)   *No extraction island:*
    a. I [[$_{VP}$ gave a talk] *there*]
    b. *Where* did you give a talk t?

(169E)   *Extraction island:*
    a. [$_{SU}$ [The party] *there*] annoyed me
    b. *Where did [the party t] annoy you?

Three components interact to achieve this result: the definition of modification, BP, and the definition of "syntactic operator in γ."

4.5.2 θ-Marked Phrases

Having accounted for 170a, we will now concern ourselves with the derivation of 170b and 170c:

(170)   a. A modifier is not a pied piper.
    b. A θ-marked specifier is not a pied piper.
    c. A θ-marked complement is not a pied piper.
    d. A specifier of a clausal constituent is not a pied piper.

These two generalizations can be combined into the following larger one:

(171)   A θ-marked phrase is not a pied piper.

As in our discussion of modifiers, we begin by stating the parts of the Saturation Condition that deal with the projection of complementation and specification relations. Since at least some non-θ-marked complements and specifiers *can* pied-pipe their mother node by turning it into a syntactic operator, we have to change our percolation conventions from Chapter 1 slightly to allow these elements to percolate an operator feature to an immediately dominating node. The required new definitions are given below (direction of combination is ignored again, since it does not influence feature percolation):

(172) *The Projection of the Complementation Relation*

    If a. α is a member of category X and bar level 0,

       b. β is a member of category YP,

       c. α takes members of YP as complements,

  then d. δ, the constituent formed by concatenating α and β, is an expression with the following grammatical properties:

   (i) the category of δ is inherited from α,

   (ii) the bar level of δ is 1,

   (iii) δ inherits all selectional properties of α except the one satisfied by α's sister β,

   (iv) if present, δ inherits the operator feature of β.

(173) *The Projection of the Specification Relation*

    If a. α is a member of category YP,

       b. β is a member of category X and bar level 1,

       c. α specifies members of category X,

  then d. δ, the constituent formed by concatenating α and β, is an expression with the following grammatical properties:

   (i) the category of δ is inherited from β,

   (ii) the bar level of δ is 2,

   (iii) δ inherits all selectional properties of β,

   (iv) if β has an operator feature, then δ inherits this feature and none from α,

   (v) if β has no operator feature but α does, then δ inherits the operator feature of α.

For our present concerns it is important that the final clause of 172 says that an X'-constituent inherits the operator feature of the complement if there is one. And that the final two clauses of 173 say that a phrase inherits the operator feature of its X'-head if the latter has one; otherwise, i.e. if the specified element does not make use of this option, the specifier can percolate its operator feature to the mother node, if it has one.

To derive 171, we now only have to add the θ-criterion, which is based on the definition of syntactic argument in 175:

(174) *The θ-Criterion*

(i) Every syntactic argument occurs in exactly one chain that terminates in a θ-position.

(ii) Every θ-position terminates a chain that is headed by exactly one syntactic argument.

(175) α is a *syntactic argument* only if

a. α is a maximal projection,

b. α is not expletive, and

c. α does not carry any operator features.

The X-bar theoretic clauses in 172–173 interact with the θ-criterion and the definition of syntactic argument to derive the generalization we are interested in: θ-marked phrases cannot pied-pipe. The explanation runs as follows.

To be a pied piper, a specifier or complement has to percolate an operator feature to its mother node:

(176)

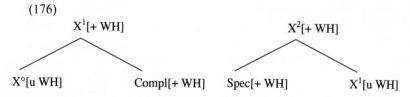

However, every such specifier or complement cannot be a member of a θ-chain, since the θ-criterion requires heads of θ-chains to be syntactic arguments, which according to the definition in 175 must not carry any operator features. Consequently, a θ-role receiver cannot be a pied piper:

(177E) *θ-marked complement*

a. John will [$_{VP}$ meet *Mary*]
+θ

b. *[$_{VP}$ meet *whom*] will Mary t
+θ

(178E) *θ-marked specifier*

a. The administration objected to
[*John's* [frequently traveling to Chicago]]
+θ

b. *[*Whose* [frequently traveling to Chicago]] did the
+θ
administration object to t

Both 177b and 178b are ruled out, since the θ-criterion is violated within
the fronted constituent.

However, non-θ-marked specifiers and complements can in principle pied-
pipe, since they are not subject to the θ-criterion. In Section 4.4.2 we provided
evidence that the specifier of the following nongerundive DP is not θ-marked,
and—as we can see—it is indeed capable of pied-piping its mother node, in
contrast to the one of the gerundive DP in 178b above:

(179E) *Non-θ-marked specifier*
    a. The administration objected to
       [*John's* [frequent travels to Chicago]]

$$-\theta$$

    b. [*Whose* [frequent travels to Chicago]] did the

$$-\theta$$

      administration object to t

Example 179b is grammatical, since all principles of the modules of Universal Grammar are obeyed. The θ-criterion within the fronted constituent is
satisfied, since *whose* does not receive a θ-role from *travels* and therefore does
not have to satisfy the definition of "syntactic argument"; i.e. it does not have
to be free of operator features. Second, BP is satisfied as well. *Whose,* although
carrying the feature [+ WH], is not an operator, since it percolates the WH-
feature to its mother node by X-bar theory, which is possible, since its X′ sister
does not carry any operator feature. There is thus only one syntactic operator
in 179, namely the fronted DP. Since this DP binds a variable and there is no
other variable in the sentence, both parts of BP are satisfied.

Finally, we show that the θ-criterion also predicts the difference between
the pied piping behavior of complements to prepositions and that of complements to other X°-heads. We remember from Section 4.4.3 that there is good
evidence for the claim that complements of prepositions are not θ-marked by
the preposition while the complements of the nonfunctional heads are θ-
marked. It is easy to see that this prior difference is exploited by the θ-criterion
in allowing complements of prepositions to pied-pipe while blocking this for
the others. Thus compare 180 with 181.

(180E) *[$_{VP}$ see *whom*] did John t

$$+\theta$$

(181) [$_{PP}$ to *whom*] did John talk t

$$-\theta$$

180 violates the θ-criterion, since *see* cannot assign its internal θ-role to
whom, given that the latter does not satisfy the requirement that syntactic

arguments be free of operator features. 181, however, is grammatical, since *whom* is not θ-governed in this sentence and therefore does not have to fulfill the defintion of syntactic argument. The sentence also passes BP: there is only one syntactic operator in 181—namely, *to whom*—and this phrase binds one variable as required.

With respect to pied piping, the behavior of complements and specifiers can be summed up as follows: if the element is θ-marked, then it has to move by itself if it is not in an extraction island,

(182E) *Who* will John meet t
     [Op]   [Var]

since otherwise the sentence would violate the θ-criterion:

(183E) *No extraction island*
    John will [$_{VP}$ meet   who]
                        [+ WH]
                     $+\theta$

If the element is in an extraction island, then the sentence is ungrammatical, since movement would violate a movement constraint (cf. 184b), and the unmoved structure violates the θ-criterion (cf. 184a):

(184E) *Extraction island*
    a. * The administration objected to
        [whose [frequently traveling to Chicago]]
        [+ WH]

                   $+\theta$
    b. * *Whose* did the administration object to
        [t [frequently traveling to Chicago]]

Non-θ-marked complements and specifiers can pied-pipe their mother node (with the exception of specifiers of clausal categories to which we will turn promptly), since they can carry operator features and pass them up. Elements of this sort that are contained within a movement island must pied-pipe; otherwise their mother would violate BP.

(185E) *Extraction island*
    [How sick] is John t

Since *how* cannot be extracted from the AP, it is not in a position to bind a variable to satisfy BP. Therefore it must percolate its operator feature to its mother node in order to lose its own operatorship. This in turn forces the AP to move, since it now has to bind a variable to satisfy BP.

Finally, languages with preposition stranding have two choices. The ungrammaticality of 186 due to BP (the PP does not bind a variable),

(186E) *John talked [_PP_ to whom]
                            [Op]

can be overcome in two ways. The complement of the preposition can move into an operator position:

(187E) *Who* did you talk [_PP_ to t]

Since the trace of *who* does not carry any operator features, the PP in 187 is not an operator and therefore can be assigned the goal θ-role of *talk*. BP is also satisfied, since *who* is an operator and binds a variable.

The second option to save 186 is to move the whole PP:

(188E) [_PP_ To whom] did you talk t

The fronted constituent in 188 has the following structure:

(189)

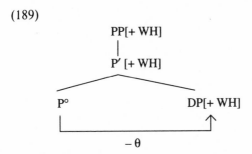

The DP does not satisfy the definition of "syntactic argument" and hence may not head a θ-chain; however, since prepositions do not θ-mark their complements, the θ-criterion does not apply to the DP. The DP also does not satisfy the defintion of "operator in γ," since it percolates its operator feature. Therefore, it is also exempt from BP and does not have to bind a variable. In contrast, the whole fronted PP does satisfy the definition of "operator in γ" and therefore has to bind a variable. Since it does so in 188, the sentence is grammatical.

This concludes our discussion of 171.

4.5.3 Specifiers of C'

The earlier sections have derived the first three subgeneralizations of 170. In this section, we will show that the fourth subgeneralization, repeated below, also follows from BP:

(190) A specifier of C′ is not a pied piper.

190 describes the case where we first move a WH-phrase into the specifier of some subordinate clause,

(191E) Mary knew [$_{CP}$ *who* [$_{C'}$ e [$_{IP}$ John met t]]]

with the subsequent attempt of the WH-specifier to pied-pipe the whole subordinate clause into the specifier position of a higher clause:

(192E) *[$_{CP}$ *Who* [$_{C'}$ e [$_{IP}$ John met t]]] did Mary know t ?

This sentence type is invariably ungrammatical (but see footnote 7) in all the Germanic languages. We have not shown yet why this should be the case, since the examples discussed so far were all different in some respect. 192 is certainly not ungrammatical because of the definition of modification, since it does not contain any modifers; also, all the examples above in which a specifier illicitly pied-piped a constituent were ungrammatical, because the specifier was an argument of its sister constituent and the fronted constituent violated the θ-criterion (cf. 178). 192 cannot be ungrammatical for this reason, since neither *who* receives a θ-role nor does *who e John met t*. Instead, both the internally moved element and the sentence it pied-pipes bind a variable in an argument position and therefore are not arguments themselves. The θ-criterion is thus satisfied in 192.

But this last property mentioned, namely that there are two variables in 192 that have to be bound, "breaks the sentence's neck." By clause 158ii of BP, every variable must be bound by a syntactic operator. Close inspection of 192 will reveal that this condition is not fulfilled, due to our definition of "syntactic operator in γ." The phrase *who* within the fronted constituent is marked [+ WH]; it is therefore a potential syntactic operator, but only if it does not percolate its operator feature up to its mother node (i.e. the fronted clause). If it does so, then it loses its operator status and the variable that it binds violates clause 158ii of BP. For the whole clause in 192 to move, however, it must be a syntactic operator according to the well-formedness condition on operator chains in 155. The only possible source for an operator feature for the whole clause is its specifier, which would—as we just saw—violate BP itself if it were to percolate. Therefore, the whole clause has to stay in its argument position as in 191.

To prevent the specifier in 192 from percolating its operator feature to the whole sentence, we have to invoke the last two clauses of the definition of specification 173 at this point, which say that a specifier can only percolate its operator feature if its sister is unmarked for the relevant feature. Then, if the WH-complementizers in the Germanic languages are marked [− WH], their clauses can never be turned into operators by a specifier. These assumptions thus derive 190, the final part of the pied piping generalization.

I want to conclude this discussion of sentences and pied piping by pointing out two side effects of our theory.

First, the above derivation of 190 allows us to explain an interesting conflict between c-selection and s-selection that has gone unnoticed so far in the literature, as far as I am aware. Note the following paradigm of a verb like *determine* that semantically selects an interrogative complement, which can be syntactically represented either by a CP or a DP:

(193E) We determined [$_{CP}$ who e the name belonged to t]

(194E) We determined [$_{DP}$ the name]

(195E) *We determined [$_{DP}$ whose name]

The interesting fact is that 195 is ungrammatical. Thus, although *determine* takes an interrogative complement (as shown by 193), and it also takes DP-complements (as shown by 194), it does not allow the DP-complement to take on the form of an interrogative phrase.

Our theory can explain all the grammaticality judgments in 193–195 without any further additions. From our discussion of 192 we know that the phonologically inert WH-complementizer in 193 is marked [− WH], and hence blocks the attempt of its specifier to percolate the feature [+ WH] to the whole clause. This clause is thus an argument and can receive the patient θ-role assigned by *determine.*

194 is also grammatical, although *name* is unmarked for the feature WH. Since there is no specifier that could turn the DP into an operator, it is also an argument and therefore compatible with the θ-role assigned by the verb.

195 is ruled out by the θ-criterion, however. Maintaining the assumption with respect to 194 that *name* is not marked for the feature WH, the specifier turns *whose name* into a constituent marked [+ WH]. However, although such a constituent can occur in the operator position of a sentence such as

(196E) [$_{DP}$ Whose name] was mentioned t

where it does not have to satisfy the θ-criterion, it cannot occur in the complement position of a verb that assigns a θ-role. In contrast to 193–194, 195 is thus ungrammatical by the θ-criterion.

Of course, our theory also predicts that 195 can be saved by moving the operator into an operator position, thus freeing the θ-position for its argument trace:

(197E) [$_{DP}$ Whose name] did you determine t

The second interesting fact that our theory explains is rather similar to the one just treated. Grewendorf (1988) mentions that a German assertion verb like *wissen* has the following three properties: (i) It semantically selects a question,

(198G) Ich weiß, [wen Hans t getroffen hat]
       I   know who Hans   met   has

(ii) It syntactically allows both a verb-final and a verb-second declarative argument clause (cf. Chapter 3),

(199G) Ich weiß, [daß Hans Maria getroffen hat]
       I   know that Hans Maria met   has

(200G) Ich weiß, [Hans hat t Maria getroffen v]
       I   know Hans has   Maria met

but (iii) it only allows a verb-final clause when it combines with an interrogative argument clause:

(201G) Ich weiß, [wen e Hans t getroffen hat]
       I   know who   Hans   met   has

(202G) *Ich weiß, [wen hat Hans t getroffen v]
       I   know who has Hans   met

The puzzling fact is the ungrammaticality of 202. If—as claimed in Grimshaw (1979)—categorial and semantic selection are autonomous, then *wissen*, if it allows an interrogative complement and verb-second complements, should also allow interrogative verb-second complements. The ungrammaticality of 202 becomes even more surprising when we note that the embedded clause in 202 makes a fine main clause question:

(203G) [CP Wen hat Hans t getroffen v]
        who has Hans   met

All these German facts are automatically explained by the assumptions we have made above, if we make one further stipulation: unlike the embedded WH-complementizer, the verb-second clause complementizer is unmarked for the feature WH. Such a proposal is not that unusual if we take into account that verb-second sentences are usually main clauses, i.e. not argument clauses; unlike the complementizer of embedded clauses, the main clause complementizer does not have to prevent a specifier marked with an operator feature from destroying the argument capacity of the whole clause.

If that is correct, then both 199 and 200 should be grammatical, since neither subordinate clause carries an operator feature and can thus receive the

θ-role patient from *wissen*. 201 and 203 should also be grammatical, the first one because its complementizer percolates the feature [− WH] to the whole clause, which therefore qualifies as an argument compatible with the θ-role assigned by the verb, the second one because it is a root clause that is not assigned a θ-role; the root clause thus does not have to satisfy the definition of "syntactic argument," which it indeed does not do since it inherits the feature [+ WH] from its specifier.

Crucially, however, the specifier cannot turn the root clause 203 into an operator in γ, since there is no dominating γ available in which the root clause could be an operator. According to clause 160d2 of the definition of "syntactic operator in γ," only the specifier of the root clause is an operator and it binds a variable as required by BP. The whole root clause also satisfies BP, since it is not an operator in any γ (despite its being marked [+ WH]) and therefore does not have to bind a variable.

202, however, falls victim to the θ-criterion. If we embed the root clause in 203 under a verb, then the embedded clause will be marked [+ WH], exactly like the main clause in 203. Again, like the former, it does not satisfy the definition of "syntactic argument." With respect to the main clause, this did not have any consequences, since it is not θ-marked. But the embedded clause in 202 violates the θ-criterion, which requires that thematic roles only be assigned to elements free from operator features.

With this demonstration that the side effects of our theory of pied piping eliminate two unsolved nontrivial problems in the theory of syntactic and semantic selection we conclude our analysis.

4.6 Summary and Discussion

In this chapter we have studied the pied piping behavior of most of the phrase-structure positions in the Germanic languages. In our initial survey we found a rather complex array of data that pointed toward a generalization that grouped together a set of elements not characterizable as a natural syntactic class. The generalization was that specifiers of nonclausal constituents and complements of prepositions are pied pipers. In addition, complements of nouns and adjectives appeared to be pied pipers in English, but only in relative clauses.

In a first effort to systematize the data, we excluded the English "relative clauses" as irrelevant for a theory of pied piping, by showing that the relevant phenomena were highly marked, both internal to English and even more so in the context of the other Germanic languages.

What we were left with at this point was the description that some complements are pied pipers while some are not (those of prepositions), and that the specifiers of nonclausal constituents can pied-pipe as well. In a second "attack" on the previous generalizations, we extended our data coverage by adding examples showing that not even all specifiers of nonclausal constituents behave the same way. We found that argument specifiers are not pied pipers while nonargument specifiers are.

With this finding, an alternative view of the data emerged that allowed us to characterize the two sets of expressions that are or are not pied pipers, but only if we made the assumption that prepositions are not θ-markers. We set out to establish this fact by showing that it would explain an interesting set of syntactic properties of prepositions that are otherwise unaccounted for. With these assumptions the set of pied pipers could now be captured negatively, namely as those expressions that are neither modifiers nor receivers of θ-roles.

In the final section we demonstrated that this negative characterization of pied pipers could be derived from the interaction of a number of modules:

(204)   The theory of operator chains
         X-bar theory
         the θ-criterion
         the Bijection Principle
         the definitions of "syntactic argument" and "syntactic
         operator in γ."

All of these modules or principles have to be stated independently of the specific phenomenon of pied piping, for sentences without any operator chains, or sentences where a noncomplex operator moves without pied-piping any other constituent.

Besides observing that our theory accounts for a rather complex array of empirical data from seven languages, it is worth emphasizing that its empirical success crucially relies on the interaction of different modules.

Thus, as we have seen, the class of pied pipers cannot be characterized as a unified set of elements that have some positive property in common. Rather, we have to refer to two *negative* properties: the pied pipers are the elements that (i) are *not* modifiers and (ii) are *not* θ-role receivers.

Such a state of affairs is exactly what one would expect in a principles and parameters approach based on the premise that the allowable phrase structures of a language result from the interaction of a set of grammatical modules that each impose construction-independent well-formedness conditions. That it is necessary to invoke a double-negative characterization of pied pipers strongly implies that this phenomenon is not a "construction." Rather, pied piping is an epiphenomenon that is the result of the interaction of substantive principles of grammar that are not construction-specific. Although not easy to establish, once the generalizations are found it is obvious that at least three such principles or modules clearly leave their fingerprints on this phenomenon: X-bar theory (the definitions of the saturation configurations), the θ-criterion, and the Bijection Principle.

We conclude that "Pied Piping" can be added to the set of terms including "passive" and "main clause" whose role has been reduced to that of descriptive notions that are convenient in the classification of construction types but that have no status in the theory itself. Chomsky (1981, 7) writes (emphasis added):

> In early work in generative grammar it was assumed, as in traditional grammar, that there are rules such as "passive", "relativization", "question formation", etc. These rules were considered to be decomposable into more fundamental elements: elementary transformations that can compound in various ways, and structural conditions (in the technical sense of transformational grammar) that are themselves formed from more elementary constituents. In subsequent work, in accordance with the sound methodological principle of reducing the range and variety of possible grammars to the minimum, these possibilities of compounding were gradually reduced, approaching the rule Move-α as a limit. But the idea of decomposing rules such as "passive", etc., remained, though now interpreted in a rather different way. *These "rules" are decomposed into the more fundamental elements of the subsystems of rules and principles. . . .* This development, largely in work of the past ten years, represents a substantial break from earlier generative grammar, or from the traditional grammar on which it was in part modelled. It is reminiscent of the move from phonemes to features in the phonology of the Prague school, though in the present case the "features" (e.g., the principles of Case, government and binding theory) are considerably more abstract and their properties and interaction much more intricate. *The notions "passive", "relativization", etc., can be reconstructed as processes of a more general nature, with a functional role in grammar, but they are not "rules of grammar."*

We have decomposed the "rule" or "convention" of pied piping into the principles of feature theory, θ-theory, and operator theory, i.e. modules of grammar motivated independently of the pied piping phenomenon, since they build the foundation stone of all phrase structure.

I wish to conclude by formulating one theorem that can be derived from the assumptions of this chapter:

(205) The antecedent of a constituent in a θ-position is not a pied piper.

This proposition has to be true in our theory, as can be shown as follows. There are two possibilities for the status of the antecedent of the θ-position in 205. It either is in an argument position and hence forms an argument chain with the θ-position (DP-movement), or it is in an operator position and forms an operator chain with the θ-position (WH-movement). In either case the antecedent is not a possible pied piper.

In the first case it would violate the θ-criterion, since as the head of an argument chain it must be an argument, i.e. free of operator features.

In the second case, the antecedent must be an operator in order to form an operator chain with the trace in the θ-position. Then, should the antecedent percolate its operator feature to its mother and turn it into an operator, it would lose the operator status itself and hence would violate BP.

Thus, whatever the status of the antecedent of a trace in a θ-position, it cannot be a pied piper. That means that whenever an argument moves out of its DS position, our theory predicts it not to be a pied piper. I have pointed out this consequence here, because in the next chapter we will have occasion to test it against the data of four free word order constructions in the Germanic languages.

5

The Syntax of Arguments and Sentence-Internal Chain Formation in Germanic

5.1 Introduction

In this chapter we return to our analysis of the head-complement relation. The reader will remember that some of the most important predictions of our theory derive from the overarching principle governing all saturation phenomena, the Saturation Condition:

(1) *The Saturation Condition*
   a. Any well-formedness condition on saturation mentions only properties of the two elements of the saturation process;
   b. any two elements in a saturation process form a constituent.

As was shown earlier, especially in Chapter 1, this condition is both conceptually plausible and of great explanatory value in that it allows us to account for, in a unified manner, a number of empirically attested restrictions on what should count as a possible parameter of natural language. The principle is thus a very desirable one, and any counterevidence that it faces should be examined carefully for its validity.

In this chapter I present four constructions from the Germanic languages that, on appearance, seem to challenge the correctness of the condition. All of these constructions involve free word order phenomena like those in the following German sentences:

(2G) weil Peter *das Buch* **wahrscheinlich** *gelesen* hat
    bec. Peter the book probably   read   has
(3G) weil *das Buch* **niemand** *gelesen* hat
    bec. the book nobody read   has

In both 2 and 3 the italicized direct object is not in the phrase structure position that it should occupy according to the Saturation Condition. Thus, according to 1b and the complementation clause of X-bar theory, the head verb and its direct object should form a constituent of the form given in 4.

(4)

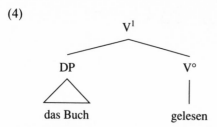

Given our theory of constituency, if the DP in 2 and 3 forms a V' with the verb, then no other constituent would be allowed to intervene between the verb and the object. But, as is easy to see, in 2 an adverb separates the two constituents, and in 3 the external argument of the verb intervenes.

German is a language that appears to have relatively free word order of nominal arguments on the sentence level. Thus, if a verb has three nominal arguments, a subject and two objects, then all six logically possible orders of these elements are indeed grammatical in certain circumstances.

The existence of the free word order structures in German and similar constructions in other Germanic languages that I will turn to below thus make it necessary to reevaluate the benefits of our assumption that all head-complement configurations are universally governed by the Saturation Condition in 1. At this point we face two options. We can give up the Saturation Condition and allow the base generation of structures like 5 where a head and its complement do not form a constituent by themselves. Let us refer to this proposal as the "Base Generation Hypothesis" ("EA" is short for "External Argument"):

(5)

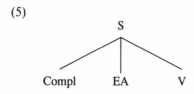

The base generation hypothesis has been put forward in a number of contexts, among them Hale (1983) and Haider (1981, 1985).

Since the base generation hypothesis is inconsistent with the Saturation Condition, and its adoption would lead to a loss of the explanatory consequences of this principle, we may examine an alternative account of the existence of free word order structures like 2–3, a proposal that I will call the "Movement Hypothesis." It denies that a direct object can be base-generated without forming a constituent with the verb and holds instead that if a complement is nonadjacent to its head, then the complement has been dislocated from its D-structure position while leaving a trace. A sentence like 3 would be assigned the following structure compatible with the Saturation Condition:

(6)

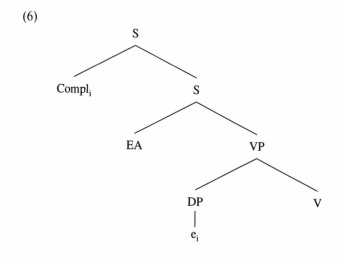

Works that assume structures like 6 include de Haan (1979), Saito/Hoji (1983), and Webelhuth (1984, 1986, 1987, 1990). If it is possible to maintain that sentences like 2–3 are indeed assigned structures involving a sentence-internal chain, then the free word order phenomenon of German would, against all appearances, not put the validity of the Saturation Condition in jeopardy. In fact, if there is evidence for the chain in these sentence types, then these structures would lend *strong support* to the Saturation Condition, since its validity would automatically predict that configurations like 5 are not possible phrase structures of natural language and therefore would not be postulated by a language learner. In that case the free word order structures would actually be an important piece of evidence against theories where the Saturation Condition does not hold.

Before turning to a section that will investigate the question of whether 5 or 6 are the correct structures underlying sentences like 2 and 3, I will introduce three additional constructions from the Germanic languages that pose the same problem as the free word order sentences of German.

The first one is the Heavy-NP Shift construction which can be found in all the Germanic SVO-dialects:

(7E) I *threw away* **yesterday** *the book that his father bought*

Another construction in Germanic where a head and its complement are not adjacent can be found in adjective phrases. Take the following Swedish sentence (cf. Holmberg, 1986, 168):

(8S) Hunden var tillgiven sin husse
      the dog was devoted his master
      'The dog was devoted to his master'

The nominal complement of the adjective can also appear to the left of the head:

(9S) Hunden var *sin husse* tillgiven
      the dog was his master devoted
      'The dog was devoted to his master'

This fact as such does not threaten our definition of complementation yet, since this might just mean that an adjective can take its complement on either side. However, the following sentences show that such a solution is not feasible. When the adjective phrase has a specifier, then the specifier *must* intervene between the complement and the adjective; adjacency between the two is impossible:

(10S)   Hunden var *sin husse*   **mycket** *tillgiven*
        the dog was his master very   devoted

(11S)   *Hunden var **mycket** *sin husse*   *tillgiven*
        the dog was very   his master devoted

Structures like 10 can thus not be reconciled with a definition of complementation that satisfies the Saturation Condition, if the complement is assumed to occur in its D-structure position.

The final construction to be considered here involves the word order of object DPs in Scandinavian. I will illustrate this with examples from Swedish quoted from the insightful work of Anders Holmberg on this phenomenon. Note the contrast between 12 and 13–14 showing that pronouns in Swedish can occur before sentence adverbs within IP, but nonpronominal DPs cannot (the verb in these examples has moved out of the VP to Comp, as it does in all main clauses):[1]

(12S)   Han köpte   *den* **inte** [$_{VP}$ v]
          he   bought it   not

(13S)   *Han köpte   *boken*   **inte** [$_{VP}$ v]
          he   bought the book not

(14S)   Han köpte   **inte** [$_{VP}$ v *boken*]
          he   bought not   the book

That the pronoun in 12 behaves in a special way relative to the full DP is also shown by the fact that PPs always pattern with the latter; that is, they have to appear within the VP, following the negation:

(15S)   *Jag tror [$_{PP}$ *på det*] **inte** [$_{VP}$ v]
          I   believe in it   not

(16S)   Jag tror   **inte** [$_{VP}$ v [$_{PP}$ *på det*]]
          I   believe not   in it

Thus, the positioning of full DPs as in 14 and of PPs as in 16 is compatible with the Saturation Condition under the standard assumption that the verb occupies the position of the trace in D-structure. Subordinate clauses like those in 17 and 18, where the verb is not subject to the verb-second constraint and hence has not moved to Comp, indeed show the verb to the right of the negation and adjacent to its complements:

(17S) att   han **inte** [$_{VP}$ köpte   *boken*]
          that he   not   bought the book

(18S) att   jag **inte** [$_{VP}$ tror [$_{PP}$ *på det*]]
          that I   not   believe in it

1. This assumption, now known as "den Besten's description of the verb-second phenomenon" dates back to the ground-breaking work of den Besten (1977) wherein an earlier proposal in Koster (1975) is developed and supported with the strongest empirical evidence available to date.

This set of assumption lies at the basis of almost all recent work on verb movement, among others Thiersch (1978), Koopman (1983), den Besten/Moed-van Walraven (1985), Platzack (1986), Chomsky (1986b), Pollock (1988), and the contributions to Haider/Prinzhorn (1985).

A second strand of research on verb movement was initiated by Travis (1984), where den Besten's description was maintained but its domain of application restricted to a subset of the verb-second effects. These proposals have influenced Baker (1988), and Diesing (1990).

We will consistently abstract away from verb displacement phenomena in the discussion of argument movement and will examine the word order behavior of arguments relative to the D-structure position of the verb, whether the verb occupies this position in S-structure or not.

The only problematic case that remains is the first example above (12), that is, the sentence type containing a pronoun preceding the sentence adverb. Since the D-structure position of the verb in 12 is after the negation, the pronoun should follow the negation also in order to form a constituent with the empty verb. This type of example is therefore in potential conflict with the Saturation Condition, like the three other Germanic constructions introduced earlier.

5.2 Free Word Order Structures in German and Constraints on Movement

In the previous section I noted that if we want to maintain the version of the complementation relation that is compatible with the Saturation Condition, then we are forced to postulate some sentence-internal movement operations of arguments in German. In order to motivate this approach, it is necessary to examine carefully the different empirical predictions of what I have called the "base generation hypothesis" and the "movement hypothesis." Given the theoretical advantages of the Saturation Condition and its empirical success in other areas of the grammar (for example in predicting the correct range of parametrization of pro-drop, WH-movement, and directionality), the movement hypothesis is clearly preferred over the base generation hypothesis on conceptual grounds, since it is compatible with the Saturation Condition, whereas the base generation hypothesis is not. The only advantage that can be listed for the base generation hypothesis is that, at first sight, it is empirically successful in generating the different word orders of German without invoking sentence-internal movement operations.

In the following subsections I will destroy this one apparent advantage of the base generation hypothesis by demonstrating that German is *not* a free word order language in the sense that the serialization of constituents is independent of syntactic constraints. Rather, I will show that the first impression of German as a free word order language according to the base generation hypothesis is misguided and has to give way to an analysis where German is a free word order language in the same sense that, for instance, English is a WH-movement rather than a WH-in-situ language.

The arguments undermining the plausibility of the base generation hypothesis will all be based on the crucial difference between the base generation and the movement hypothesis, namely that the latter postulates the existence of an antecedent-trace relation within free word order structures while the former does not. These different predictions are testable, since German, like English, is a WH-movement language and therefore exhibits a number of diagnostics for the existence of antecedent-trace relations outside the free word order phenomenon. Among these diagnostics are constraints on movement like those presented in Ross (1967) and later work, e.g. the subject condition, the ECP, and the coordinate structure constraint. Each of the subsequent subsections presents evidence that WH-movement in German is only well-formed in a certain set of syntactic environments while it is blocked by a general movement constraint in others. Simultaneously it will be demonstrated that the free word order phenomenon is systematically displayed only in those syntactic environments that also license WH-movement, but that there are no free word order structures in environments where WH-movement is blocked. This will be interpreted as evidence that German is a free word order language in the same sense that languages can have overt WH-movement, but not in the sense that its sentences are unstructured, base-generated strings of constituents that are somehow exempt from the strict well-formedness conditions on the phrase structure of languages with rigid word order. In sum, since the one piece of support for the base generation analysis—namely its impressionistic empirical success—will be shown to collapse under careful scrutiny, it fails both on conceptual and empirical grounds relative to the movement hypothesis. The Saturation Condition, initially motivated on other grounds, thus also finds support from the converging conceptual and empirical evidence of free word order phenomena and is thereby further strengthened in its already substantial explanatory value.

5.2.1 Extraction from PP and the Left Branch Condition

To demonstrate that the existence of free word order structures is not independent of the well-formedness of WH-movement, we begin by examining the word order behavior of complements. The first two sentences below show that the complements of verbs and adjectives can be WH-moved.

(19G) [Welches Buch] hat niemand t gesehen
      which   book has nobody   seen

(20G) [Auf wen] war Hans noch nie [stolz t]
      of   whom was Hans never   proud

The following pair shows that for each sentence derived by WH-movement of such a complement there is a corresponding free word order structure:[2]

---

2. I have inserted focus particles in some of the sentences to make them more natural. Thus, it is usually only possible to move a nominal object before an agentive subject if the subject is focused (cf. Lenerz, 1977; Höhle, 1982). We will disregard the focus properties of the various sentences here, but will come back to them in later sections of this chapter. Here we are only interested in the fact that certain word orders are possible at all.

(21G) weil   [das Buch] niemand t gelesen hat
       bec.   the book   nobody   read   has

(22G) weil   [auf seine Kinder] auch Hans   [sehr stolz t] war
       bec.   of his   children also Hans   very proud   was

With respect to extraction of complements from DP we have to distinguish
two cases: extraction of prepositional complements and extraction of genitive
DPs. The former can be extracted by WH-movement while the latter cannot:[3]

(23G) [Über wen]   hat sich niemand [einen Film t] angeschaut
       about whom has refl nobody   a   movie   watched
       'whom did nobody watch a movie about'

(24G) *[Wessen] hat sich Hans [einen Film t] angeschaut
       whose   has refl Hans a   movie   watched

We find exactly the same state of affairs in the free word order structures:
prepositional complements can be separated from the rest of the DP within
the middle field, but genitives cannot:

(25G) weil sich [über   England] niemand [einen Film t]
       bec. refl about England nobody   a   movie
       angeschaut hat
       watched   has
       'because nobody watched a movie about England'

(26G) *weil sich [Faßbinders] Hans [einen Film t] angeschaut hat
       bec. refl Faßbinder Hans a   movie   watched   has
       'because Hans watched one of Faßbinder's movies'

Two different cases also have to be distinguished in the case of extraction from
PP. The complement of a preposition can only be WH-moved if it is pronominal, but not if it is a full DP, as the following contrast illustrates:[4]

(27G) *Wessen Freiheit haben die Leute lange [für t] gekämpft
       whose freedom have the people long for   fought

3. The verb *anschauen* (watch) is optionally reflexive. The reflexive is glossed "refl." A grammatical declarative counterpart of 24 would be (i).

   (iG) Hans hat sich einen Film Faßbinders angeschaut
        Hans has refl a   movie Faßbinder watched
                                   gen
        'Hans watched one of Faßbinder's movies'

4. Apparently some speakers of German do not allow preposition stranding at all. Crucially,
however, those speakers *never* allow stranding so that the main observation, namely that speakers
will treat the free word order structures like WH-movement structures, is not challenged.

(28G)   Wo   haben die Leute lange [t für] gekämpft
         where have   the people long   for fought
         'What did the people fight for for a long time'

We find exactly the same grammaticality distribution when we consider sentences in which the object of a preposition induces a free word order structure; only the pronominal object can appear before the subject in the middle field; the nominal object has to stay adjacent to the preposition.

(29G) *weil [ihre Freiheit] die Leute lange [für t] gekämpft haben
        bec. their freedom the people long   for   fought   have
        'because the people have fought for their freedom for a long time'

(30G) weil [da]   die Leute lange [t für] gekämpft haben
        bec. there the people long   for fought   have

Moreover, there are two circumstances under which even the pronoun cannot be extracted from the prepositional phrase: (a) if the whole prepositional phrase occurs to the left of the negation and (b) if the prepositional phrase is itself embedded within a prepositional phrase:

(31G) *Wo   hat Peter [t mit] *nicht* gerechnet
        where has Peter   with not   counted
        'What did Peter not expect to happen'

(32G) *Wo   ist er [$_{PP}$ bis [$_{PP}$ t hin]] gefahren
        where is he   to   up   driven
        'Where did he drive to'

Under these circumstances the free word order structures are blocked as well:

(33G) *weil da   Peter [t mit] *nicht* gerechnet hat
        bec. there Peter   with not   counted   has
        'because Peter did not expect this to happen'

(34G) *weil da   jemand [$_{PP}$ bis [$_{PP}$ t hin]] gefahren ist
        bec. there somebody to   up   driven is
        'because somebody drove all the way up there'

We can conclude that with respect to complements the parallelism between WH-movement and the free word order structures is perfect.

Now we turn to specifiers. We know that in many languages specifiers cannot be extracted by WH-movement (cf. the Left-branch Condition from Ross

(1967) and later work within the Extended Standard Theory). I illustrate this with English examples:

(35E) *Whose did you see [t brother]

(36E) *How is John [t proud of his children]

(37E) *How did John leave [t quickly]

The constraint is also operative in German; specifiers of DP, AP, and AdvP cannot be WH-moved.

(38G) *Wessen wurde [t Auto] gestohlen
       whose was   car   stolen
       'Whose car was stolen'

(39G) *Wie ist Hans [t stolz   auf seine Kinder]
       how is Hans   proud of his   children
       'How proud is Hans of his children'

(40G) *Wie ist Hans [t schnell] gelaufen
       how is Hans   fast   run
       'How fast did Hans run'

The equivalent free word order structures are all ungrammatical as well:

(41G) *weil [meines Bruders] gestern [t Auto] gestohlen wurde
       bec. my   brother's yesterday car   stolen   was
       'because my brother's car was stolen yesterday'

(42G) *weil [sehr] Hans [t stolz   auf seine Kinder] ist
       bec. very Hans   proud of his   children is
       'because Hans is very proud of his children'

(43G) *weil [sehr] Hans [t schnell] gelaufen ist
       bec. very Hans   fast   run   is
       'because Hans ran very fast'

This brings us to the last case: the WH-movement behavior of modifiers. The first example below shows that a modifier of DP cannot be extracted by WH-movement and the second one that the standard of comparison cannot be moved away leftwards from the adjective phrase either (I use topicalization to the operator position here, since the two modifiers cannot be questioned easily):

(44G) *[Mit langen Haaren] kennt Peter [einen Studenten t]
       with long hair   knows Peter a   student
       'Peter knows a student with long hair'

(45G) *[Als Peter] ist Maria [größer t]
      than Peter is Maria taller
      'Maria is taller than Peter'

The free word order equivalents of 44 and 45 share the sharp ungrammaticality of these sentences.

(46G) *weil [mit langen Haaren] Peter [einen Studenten t] kennt
      bec. with long hair Peter a student knows
      'because Peter knows a student with long hair'

(47G) *weil [als Peter] Maria [größer t] ist
      bec. than Peter Maria taller is
      'because Maria is taller than Peter'

All in all, then, complements, specifiers, and modifiers can be WH-moved if and only if they can occur separated from their sister constituents in the free word order structures.

It is important that the restrictions on WH-movement illustrated above are typically *constraints on movement* and not on interpretive rules involving, for example, binding. Thus, the left-branch condition, although it prevents specifiers from being extracted, does not block binding of specifiers, as the following examples show:

(48E) They$_k$ liked [$_{DP}$ each other's$_k$ pictures]

(49G) weil jeder$_k$ [$_{DP}$ seine$_k$ Mutter] liebt
      bec. everybody his mother loves
      'because everybody loves his mother'

In the English example the reciprocal on the left branch of the DP is bound by the subject of the sentence, and in the German case the possessive pronoun can be interpreted as a variable bound by the subject quantifier.[5]

The same is true for the restriction on preposition stranding in German. Although movement of a nonpronominal DP out of a prepositional phrase is impossible, binding of the object of the preposition from outside the PP is allowed:

(50G) weil wir [über einander] gelacht haben
      bec. we about each other laughed have
      'because we laughed about each other'

---

5. I have used a pronoun in the DP, because German does not have possessive reflexives or reciprocals.

5.2.2 The Specificity Constraint on Extraction from DP

As is well known, extraction from DP depends on the specificity of the determiner phrase in many languages. Take the following examples from English (cf. Chomsky, 1986b):

(51E) *Who did you see [John's picture of t]
(52E) Who did you see [three pictures of t]

The subsequent sentences show that WH-movement out of a DP in German—as in English—is only possible if the DP is nonspecific.

(53G) *[Von wem] werden [Peters Bilder t] veröffentlicht
       of   whom are   Peter's pictures published

(54G) [Von wem] werden [weniger Bilder t] veröffentlicht
       of   whom are   fewer   pictures published

When we try to construct the free word order analogues to the above WH-movement sentences, we find that only those structures are available that involve a nonspecific DP:

(55G) *Ich wünschte daß [von Brigitte Bardot] [Peters
       I   wished   that of Brigitte Bardot   Peter's
       Bilder t] veröffentlicht werden
       pictures published   are
       'I wished that Peter's pictures of Brigitte Bardot were
       published'

(56G) Ich wünschte daß [von Brigitte Bardot] [weniger
       I   wished   that of Brigitte Bardot fewer
       Bilder t] veröffentlicht werden
       pictures published   are
       'I wished that fewer pictures of Brigitte Bardot were
       published'

5.2.3 The Coordinate Structure Constraint

Another principle restricting movement but not interpretive rules is Ross's Coordinate Structure Constraint; as the following examples show, WH-movement of only one conjunct of a coordinate structure is impossible, whereas exclusive binding into one conjunct is easily possible:

(57G)   weil jemand   [Hans und Maria] angemeldet hat
        bec. somebody Hans and Maria   registered   has
        'because he registered Hans and Maria'

(58G) *[Wen] hat jemand [t und Maria] angemeldet
      who   has somebody and Maria registered

(59G) weil jemand [sich   und Maria] angemeldet hat
       bec. somebody himself and Maria registered   has

Crucially, there are no free word order structures that break up coordinate structures; that is, these structures pattern with the movement phenomenon, not with the interpretive one:

(60G) *weil [Hans] jemand [t und Maria] angemeldet hat
       bec. Hans somebody and Maria registered   has

There is another version of the coordinate structure in which the second conjunct is extraposed to the end of the clause together with the coordinator:

(61E) John read a book yesterday [and a newspaper]

(62G) weil jemand   Hans angemeldet hat [und Maria]
      bec. somebody Hans registered   has and Maria

Although, probably for semantic reasons, the first conjunct can still not be WH-moved, it can at least be topicalized to the clausal operator position:

(63E) [A book] John read t yesterday [and a newspaper]

(64G) [Hans] hat jemand t angemeldet [und Maria]

In the split coordination construction the conjunct left in the clause is thus in principle "a free agent" for movement. We find that the free word order structure is possible again under these circumstances as well:

(65G) weil [Hans] jemand t   angemeldet hat [und Maria]
      bec. Hans somebody registered   has and Maria

5.2.4 The Subject Condition

The next constraint on movement stemming from Ross' work that I want to discuss is the Subject Condition. It distinguishes English sentences like those in 66 and 67.

(66E) Who did you read [a book about t]
(67E) *Who did [a book about t] annoy you

In German we can illustrate this condition with the following minimal pair involving extraction out of the subject of an unaccusative verb in the first case and the subject of an intransitive verb in the second one:[6]

6. The sentences are modeled on similar ones in Grewendorf (1988), who shows convincingly that *gefallen* is an intransitive verb, that is, that its subject is an external argument. Consult also the seminal works on ergativity in German (den Besten, 1985a,b).

(68G)   [Über wen]   ist dir [eine Geschichte t] eingefallen
         about whom is you a   story   occurred
         'About whom did a story occur to you'

(69G) ?*[Über wen]   hat dir [eine Geschichte t] gefallen
         about whom did you a   story   please
         'About whom did a story please you'

Note that a free word order equivalent of the first sentence exists, while there
is none for the second one.

(70G)   weil [über   Hans] dir [eine Geschichte t] eingefallen ist
         bec. about Hans you a   story   occurred   is
         'because a story about Hans occurred to you'

(71G) ?*weil [über   Hans] dir [eine Geschichte t] gefallen hat
         bec. about Hans you a   story   pleased has
         'because a story about Hans pleased you'

Also in this case it can be shown that the interpretive rules of binding are not
affected by whether the bindee is embedded within an internal or an external
argument.

(72G)   weil jeder$_k$ glaubt, daß uns
        bec. everybody believes that us
        [eine Geschichte über   ihn$_k$] eingefallen ist

        a   story   about him occurred   is
        'because everybody believes that a story about him occurred to
        us'

(73G)   weil jeder$_k$ glaubt, daß uns
        bec. everybody believes that us
        [eine Geschichte über   ihn$_k$] gefallen hat

        a   story   about him pleased has
        'because everybody believes that a story about him pleases us'

5.2.5 Anti-Crossover Effects

A further well-known property of WH-movement is the anti-crossover effect.
Note that in both of the following sentences where the subject pronoun c-
commands the name within the object-DP we get a violation of Principle C
of the Binding Theory of Chomsky (1981):

(74G) *weil er$_k$ [die Behauptungen, die   Hans$_k$ während der
        bec. he   the claims   that Hans during   the

Konferenz gemacht hatte] zurücknehmen mußte
conference made   had   take-back   had-to
'because Hans had to take back the claims that he had made during the conference'

(75G) *weil er$_k$ [die Behauptung, daß Hans$_k$ während der
bec. he   the claim   that Hans during   the
Konferenz geschlafen hatte] zurücknehmen mußte
conference slept   had   take-back   had-to
'because he had to take back the claim that Hans had slept during the conference'

The previous sentences differ in that in the first case the name is embedded within a relative clause, whereas in the second one it occurs within a complement sentence to the head noun of the direct object. This makes a difference, because when the respective determiner phrases are topicalized, co-reference between the pronoun and the name becomes possible in the first case whereas it is still blocked in the second one.[7]

(76G) [Welche der Behauptungen, die Hans$_k$ während der
which-of the claims   that Hans during   the
Konferenz gemacht hatte] mußte er$_k$ zurücknehmen
conference made   had   had-to he back-take
'Which of the claims that Hans had made during the conference did he have to take back'

(77G) *[Wieviele   der Behauptungen, daß Hans$_k$ während
how many-of the claims   that Hans during
der Konferenz geschlafen hatte] mußte er$_k$ zurücknehmen
the conference slept   had   had-to he back-take
'How many of the claims that Hans had slept during the conference did he have to take back'

When we examine the equivalent free word order structures we find the same sharp contrast in co-reference potential between the pronoun and the name.

(78G) ? weil [manche der Behauptungen, die Hans$_k$ während
bec. some-of the claims   that Hans during
der Konferenz gemacht hatte] er$_k$ zurücknehmen mußte
the conference made   had   he back-take   had-to

7. This observation was presented in Lebeaux (1989).

'because some of the claims that Hans had made during the conference he had to take back'

(79G)   *weil [manche der Behauptungen, daß Hans$_k$ während
        bec. some-of the claims   that Hans during
        der Konferenz geschlafen hatte] er$_k$ zurücknehmen mußte
        the conference slept   had   he back-take   had-to
        'because some of the claims that Hans had slept during the con-
        ference he had to take back'

The first sentence is unnatural because we have moved a heavy phrase to the IP-initial position, which is usually reserved for the subject clitic; every other sentence with the same structure would meet the same judgment, independently of the question of co-reference. Abstracting away from this heaviness effect, we find that where co-reference is possible in the WH-movement examples it is also possible in the free word order structure and that if co-reference is blocked, then it is blocked in both cases: thus, the WH-movement structures and the free word order structures behave identically with respect to the anti-crossover effect.

5.2.6 Parasitic Gaps

This leads us to a final property that is found exclusively in movement structures: parasitic gaps. We know from other Germanic languages (cf. Taraldsen [1981], Engdahl [1983, 1984], Chomsky [1982b, 1986b]) that parasitic gaps, as their name suggests, are only licensed in sentences that contain another gap, usually referred to as the "real" gap. This explains the contrast between 80, which does not contain a real gap and the question 81, the relative clause 82, the Heavy-NP-shift construction 83, and the complex adjectival construction 84, which each contain an operator-bound real gap:[8]

(80E)   *He filed the article [without reading e]

(81E)   Which article did he file t [without reading e]

(82E)   The article [O [he filed t [without reading e]]]

(83E)   John offended t [by not recognizing e immediately] his favorite uncle from Cleveland

(84E)   This book is too interesting [O [PRO to put down t [without having finished e]]]

---

8. Sentences 83 and 84 are taken from Chomsky (1982b, 45ff).

Although the parasitic gap phenomenon is much more restricted in German than in English and the Scandinavian languages, the contrast between the initial three sentence types just discussed is also found in German.

(85G) *weil er [ohne PRO vorher e zu untersuchen] den Patienten
bec. he without   first   to examine   the patient
operierte
operated
'because he operated on the patient without first examining him'

(86G) ? Welchen Patienten hat er [ohne PRO vorher e zu
which   patient   has he without   first   to
untersuchen] t operiert
examine   operated
'Which patient did he operate on before first examining'

(87G) ? der Patient, den er [ohne PRO vorher e zu
the patient who he without   first   to
untersuchen] t operierte
examine   operated
'the patient who he operated on before first examining'

Felix (1985) makes the important observation that the sentence in 85 with a gap in the adjunct clause becomes grammatical if the object precedes the adjunct (for similar observations in Dutch, cf. Bennis/Hoekstra [1985], Bennis [1986], Koster [1987a], Huybregts/v. Riemsdijk [1985]). The reason for this is that the object can be taken to be adjoined in the middle field, c-commanding both its trace and the gap in the adjunct clause. Since neither of the two gaps c-commands the other, the resulting structure represents the parasitic gap configuration:

(88G) ? weil er den Patienten [ohne PRO vorher e zu
bec. he the patient   without   first   to
untersuchen] t operierte
examine   operated
'because he operated on the patient without first examining'

It does not matter whether the object immediately precedes the adjunct clause or not, as long as it is to its left. In the first of the following sentences the accusative pronoun immediately precedes the adjunct; in the second one it is separated from it by a temporal adverb and in the last one by the subject of the sentence. All sentences are equally good.

(89G)   ? weil jemand   ihn [ohne PRO vorher e zu untersuchen] t
bec. somebody him without   first   to examine
operierte
operated
'because somebody operated on him without first examining
him'

(90G)   ? weil jemand   ihn gestern [ohne PRO vorher e zu
bec. somebody him yesterday without   first   to
untersuchen] t operierte
examine   operated
'because somebody operated on him yesterday without first
examining him'

(100G) ? weil ihn jemand   [ohne PRO vorher e zu untersuchen] t
bec. him somebody without   first   to examine
operierte
operated
'because somebody operated on him without first examining
him'

5.2.7 Summary of Sections 5.2.1–5.2.6

The previous six subsections have established that the free word order structures of German exhibit the following properties:

(101)   They display the same preposition stranding behavior as WH-movement contexts.
They obey the Left-branch Condition.
They obey the Specificity Constraint on extraction from DP.
They obey the Coordinate Structure Constraint.
They obey the Subject Condition.
Like WH-movement, they show anti-crossover effects.
They contain parasitic gaps.

Before we discuss the relevance of these findings, we present one more piece of evidence that the free word order structures are very similar to expressions derived by WH-movement. The argument is based on language acquisition data.

5.2.8 Evidence from Language Acquisition

Among the syntactic phenomena that have been studied extensively for their role in language acquisition is WH-movement. This book is not the place to review the literature, so I will restrict myself to quoting an observation about the acquisition of WH-movement constructions by German children (emphasis added):

> Probably the children first learn to question single constituents; syntactic markers of interrogative clauses do not yet appear at this stage. Only the rising intonation distinguishes these utterances from declaratives. . . . During the second phase the children acquire the relevant types of interrogative clauses, *however in the beginning still without the corresponding adult overt markers (= the interrogative pronoun and INVERSION).* (Clahsen, 1982, 79)

What is important for our current concerns is that Clahsen found a temporal asymmetry in the acquisition of base-generated structures and those involving movement; that is, it takes German children longer to acquire those constructions involving a long-distance dependency than those that do not. It is consistent with Clahsen's observation to state that movement operations add a factor of grammatical complexity to a construction which makes it harder to acquire.

Whatever factors may be responsible for this increased difficulty, it is interesting that in the same study Clahsen mentions that free word order structures display it as well (emphasis added):[9]

> Before the acquisition of V-restriction II [the restriction that the finite verb has to be in second position in main clauses; G.W.] *the children prefer an order of the complements in which the object appears adjacent to the verb.* After the acquisition of V-restriction II this constraint is given up, i.e. now adverbials can also stand between the object and the verb. (Clahsen 1982, 70)

In sum, this section has drawn on data from real language acquisition by German children that supports the view that free word order structures—as far as the acquisition sequence of base-generated and movement structures are concerned—pattern with the movement structures rather than with the base-generated ones.

9. I am very grateful to Harald Clahsen for pointing out these facts concerning the acquisition of Scrambling after a talk at the Meeting of the Linguistic Society of Germany in 1987. My earlier theory (published as Webelhuth, 1987) tried to give a purely universal account of Scrambling within the parameter model. Clahsen's data led me to weaken the theory by relegating some of the properties of Scrambling to the individual grammars so that it became understandable why children have problems acquiring them. Another motivation for a weakening of the universal theory was that there are differences between scrambled sentences from one language to the next as far as adjunction sites and the categorial scope of the process is concerned (cf. Ross, 1967). For example, although German and Dutch allow Scrambling on the IP-level, they allow very little free word order within DP, although other languages like classical Latin and Warlpiri do. In the new framework of this book, these differences are easy to state, and the parameter is still easy to acquire on the basis of positive evidence, since one can assume that a child can distinguish adjectives from prepositions and so forth.

With this additional, grammar-external, piece of evidence we now turn to an evaluation of the relevance of the properties of free word order structures discussed so far.

5.2.9 Consequences of the Syntactic and Acquisitional Properties of the Free Word Order Structures

All the syntactic aspects of free word order structures that we have summarized in Section 5.2.7 and the acquisitional observation quoted in 5.2.8 are properties of *expressions derived by movement.* The following survey compares the behavior of sentences involving WH-movement with those involving free word order structures:

(102)

Constraint	WH-mvt	Free Word Order
1. PP extracted from DP	+	+
2. Pronoun strands P	+	+
3. Extraposed coordinate structure	+	+
4. Acquired late	+	+
5. Anti-crossover effect	+	+
6. Genitive extracted from DP	−	−
7. Modifier extracted from DP	−	−
8. DP strands P	−	−
9. Stranding before negation	−	−
10. Stranding out of two PPs	−	−
11. Extraction of specifiers	−	−
12. Extraction from specific DP	−	−
13. Coordinate structures	−	−
14. Extraction from SUs	−	−

As is obvious, there is a complete parallelism between the two types of constructions; that is, it is misleading to speak of German as a "free word order language" without further qualification. Rather, there are very severe constraints on free word order in German, and those constraints have to be stated independently to give a descriptively adequate account of the relationship between a WH-antecedent and its trace in the language. I conclude that the observations above—that only those non-local word orders are possible that can be derived without violating constraints on movement—defeat the argument that the existence of free word order refutes the prediction of the Saturation Condition that every complement must form a constituent with its head. In contrast, the scope of the free word order phenomenon strongly vindicates the adoption of the Saturation Condition beyond its role in pro-drop,

WH-movement, and directionality, in that it automatically predicts the conditions under which free word orders will be found (in conjunction with other modules of the grammar). This sets our theory apart further from theories in which the Saturation Condition does not hold, and where the base generation hypothesis is a permissible analysis. These theories cannot be said to be explanatory with respect to the free word order phenomenon, at least in German.[10]

5.3 The Properties of Sentence-Internal Chains

Having argued in detail that the free word order structures of German should be accounted for by a movement process,[11] we will assume without further argument that such an analysis carries over to the other three constructions

---

10. The reader will of course be aware that we have not shown that these more powerful theories will not be necessary on other grounds. One obvious candidate is the analysis of languages (like Latin and Warlpiri) with much more extreme word order freedom than that found in German. Also, it is equally possible that other languages with semi-free word order (e.g. Hungarian, Slavic) will not behave like German. It does appear, for instance, that although WH-movement and free word order structures in general pattern together, in Slavic there are a few constructions (obviously meriting further careful study) where they behave differently. There may also be languages without independent movement rules against which to test Scrambling. But in my view, the recent history of the study of German makes it advisable to refrain from relaxing principally attested well-formedness conditions in some languages but not in others, even at the risk of temporarily underdetermining the apparent descriptive generalizations found. Up until very recently, it was naturally taken for granted that German should be described as a language without major constraints on the word order behavior of arguments. In fact, there are many research papers and reference grammars of German with explicit statements to that effect (cf. Eisenberg, 1986), and a paper like Webelhuth (1984)—challenging that consensus—was still received with as much skepticism even among theoreticians as Saito's and Hoji's work on Japanese (cf. the references in the bibliography). Short of giving an analysis of the type that I am giving here prototypically for German for all other free word order languages, it is of course impossible to prove that there are no languages that need to be described in terms of the base generation analysis. But it is of some significance that the descriptive generalization of German as an unrestricted free word order language turned out to be false, even though it has gone unchallenged by generations of linguists. Languages like Warlpiri may eventually also be captured by a theory incorporating the Saturation Condition, especially, as Jelinek (1984) has shown, if the role that morphology and pro-drop play in these languages is better understood.

11. A number of authors have used other evidence for this conclusion, among them Scherpenisse (1986) and Fanselow (1986). Tappe (1984) contains a noteworthy discussion of the syntax of stressed and unstressed pronouns. The reader should also consult the important paper Thiersch (1982).

Webelhuth/den Besten (in preparation) crucially relies on the movement hypothesis in a theory of topicalization in the Germanic languages.

presented in Section 5.1. We now turn to an investigation of the exact properties of the chains formed in each of the constructions.

Recent versions of the theory of Government and Binding (cf. Aoun [1985], Chomsky [1986a, 1986b], Webelhuth [1987]) acknowledge two kinds of chains: operator chains and argument chains. The prototypical constructions involving such chains are WH-movement and Passive/Raising respectively. The survey in 103 gives an overview of some of the typical properties of the two chain types:

(103) *Properties of Operator and Argument Chains*

	O-Chains	A-Chains
1. Moves DP	+	+
2. Moves PP	+	−
3. Mover lacks Case	+	−
4. Licenses parasitic gaps	+	−
5. Strands prepositions	+	−

The chain types are similar in that they can both be headed by a DP. However, they differ in that only operator chains can contain prepositional phrases, only the head of an operator chain can move to a position where it is not Case-marked, only heads of operator chains can license parasitic gaps and strand prepositions.

In what follows we will systematically compare the four instances of sentence-internal movement in Germanic with both WH-movement and DP-movement to establish whether the created chain has the properties of an operator or an argument chain. The result will be that Scrambling and Heavy-NP Shift pattern with WH-movement and should thus be analyzed in terms of operator chains, while Object Shift and AP-adjunction pattern with DP-movement and require an analysis in terms of argument chains. The overall results will be collected in a survey after the empirical evidence has been presented.

We will present the data following the order of the properties listed in 103.

5.3.1 DP Can Undergo the Movement Process

5.3.1.1 WH-Movement

(104E) [DP *Which book*] did John read t ?

5.3.1.2 Scrambling

(105G) weil Hans [DP *das Buch*] wahrscheinlich t gelesen hat
       bec. Hans   the book probably   read   has

5.3.1.3 Heavy-NP Shift (HNPS)

(106E) John gave t to Mary [DP *all the books he could find*]

5.3.1.4 DP-Movement

(107E) [DP *The books*] were stolen t

5.3.1.5 Object Shift

(108S) Han köpte [DP *den*] inte v t]]
       he   bought it   not

5.3.1.6 AP-Adjunction

(109S) Jag har   varit [DP *min hustru*] trogen t
       I   have been   my wife   faithful

As the reader can see, all constructions can involve a moved DP. This is not surprising since both operator and argument chains can be headed by a determiner phrase. From now on, however, the six examined constructions will fall into two groups, one group displaying the properties of operator chains, the other one displaying the properties of argument chains.

5.3.2 PP Can Undergo the Movement Process

Examples 110, 111, and 112 show that Scrambling and HNPS pattern with WH-movement in that they can involve movement of a prepositional phrase.

5.3.2.1 WH-Movement

(110E) [PP *To whom*] did you talk?

5.3.2.2 Scrambling

(111G) weil er [PP *mit ihr*] nicht t tanzen wollte
         bec. he   with her not   dance wanted
         'bec. he did not want to dance with her'

5.3.2.3 Heavy-NP Shift

(112E) He talked t yesterday [PP *to all the applicants from India*]

DP-movement, Object Shift, and AP-adjunction do not follow the first group; PP-movement is excluded:

5.3.2.4 DP-Movement

(113E) *[PP *At Mary*] was looked *t*

5.3.2.5 Object Shift

(114S) *Jag tror   [$_{PP}$ *på det*] inte t
       I   believe   in it   not

5.3.2.6 AP-Adjunction

(115S) *Han var [$_{PP}$ *mot sin hustru*] trogen t
       he   was   to   his wife   faithful

5.3.3 The Moved Element Is in a Non-Case Marked Position

The definition of DP-chains in Chomsky (1981) requires that the overt head of an argument chain occupy a Case-position. For operator chains such a condition is not called for, since—as example 116 shows—a WH-word does not land in a position where Case can be assigned.

5.3.3.1 WH-Movement

(116E) *Whom* do you think that John met *t*

The operator position of a root clause is not considered a position to which the accusative case borne by the WH-word can be assigned. We thus conclude that the WH-word is not in a Case-marked position. Scrambling and HNPS behave in the same way.

5.3.3.2 Scrambling

(117G) weil [$_{IP}$ *den Jungen* [$_{IP}$ niemand t *gesehen* hat]]
      bec.   the boy   nobody   seen   has

In this German sentence the direct object has been moved to the left of the external argument of the verb. Like the clausal operator position, this adjoined position is one that usually is not considered to be eligible for accusative Case assignment.

5.3.3.3 Heavy-NP Shift

(118E) He had given *t* to John [*all the books he could find*]

The same holds for HNPS. There is no evidence that an English verb can assign accusative Case to a DP following a prepositional object of the verb.[12]
The three remaining constructions show a different pattern.

---

12. In fact Stowell's (1981) adjacency condition on Case assignment was explicitly formulated to rule out such nonadjacent Case marking.

5.3.3.4 DP-Movement

We look at DP-movement first. In 119 a DP has been moved to the subject position of a tensed IP which is assigned nominative Case. The sentence is grammatical.

(119E) *John* seemed [$_{IP}$ *t* to have been killed *t*]
       [+C]   [−C]

If the movement stops at the intermediate subject position, i.e. the subject of a non-tensed sentence which is not assigned Case, then the sentence is ungrammatical.

(120E) *It seemed [$_{IP}$ *John* to have been killed *t*]
       [+C]   [−C]

Phenomena like these motivated Chomsky (1981) to include the Case-marking condition on DP-chain formation.

5.3.3.5 Object Shift

Object Shift can be shown to pattern with DP-movement. Although there are slight dialectal differences among the Nordic languages with respect to Object Shift, one element of the process remains constant across all languages: the shifted object must land within the c-command domain of its Case-assigning verb. This has a number of consequences, including the following:

(a) In Mainland Scandinavian (MLS), Object Shift can only apply in main clauses, as 121 shows. The subsequent sentence illustrates that subordinate clauses do not allow the construction:

(121S)   Han [$_{C'}$ *köpte* [$_{I'}$ *den* [$_{I'}$ inte v t]]]
       he   bought it   not

(122S) *att han [$_{I'}$ *den* [$_{I'}$ inte [$_{I'}$ *köpte* t]]]
       that he   it   not   bought

This fact can be explained as follows: detailed analyses of MLS have shown (cf. den Besten [1977], Platzack [1986], Holmberg [1986]) that the finite verb occupies different positions in main and subordinate clauses. In main clauses it occupies the Comp-position and is thus able to c-command and Case-mark the landing site of Object Shift which is I′ in MLS. In subordinate clauses, however, the verb remains in Infl and thus does not c-command the landing site of the shifted object, under the strict definition of c-command (involving the concept "first branching node") from Reinhart (1976).

(b) In Icelandic, where the landing site of Object Shift is VP rather than I', the construction is possible both in main and in subordinate clauses, since even a verb in the Infl of a subordinate clause c-commands the shifted object:

(123I) Jón [$_C$ keypti [$_{VP}$ *hann* ekki]]
John   bought   it   not

(124I) að   hann [$_I$ keypti [$_{VP}$ *hann* ekki]]
that he   bought   it   not

(c) Object Shift may not apply when other reasons prevent the verb from moving to a position c-commanding the landing site of the shifted object; one reason can be the existence of an auxiliary in Infl. Since the verb must at least move to Infl in Icelandic and through Infl to Comp in MLS to Case-mark the shifted object, an auxiliary in Infl blocks the verb from achieving this position and hence prevents the application of Object Shift as well.

(125S) *Varför *har* studenterna den inte *läst*
why   have the students it   not read

(126I) *að Jón *hefur* bókina   ekki *keypt*
that John has   the book not   bought

We thus have good evidence that the head of the chain involved in Object Shift must be in a position that can be Case-marked at S-structure and hence behaves like a DP-chain.

5.3.3.6 AP-Adjunction

In the case of AP-adjunction the question whether the moved DP lands in a Case-marked position is not testable, since the moved DP is assigned oblique Case by the adjective at D-structure and "takes" this Case with it to its S-structure position. We thus cannot say more than that the moved DP does have Case in its S-structure position and at least in this respect patterns with DP-movement and Object Shift.

(127G) Er ist [$_{AP}$ *seiner*   *Frau* [$_{AP}$ sehr treu *t*]]
                    [+ OBL]
he is   his   wife   very faithful

5.3.4 The Movement Licenses Parasitic Gaps

So far we have found that all six constructions can involve movement of a DP and that WH-movement, Scrambling, and HNPS pattern against DP-movement, Object Shift, and AP-adjunction in (1) also allowing PPs to move and in (2) not requiring that the moved element land in a Case-marked position. Now we turn to the question of whether the moved element licenses parasitic gaps. The example sentences in subsequent sections show that the first three constructions can indeed contain parasitic gaps.

5.3.4.1 WH-Movement

(128E) *What* did John file *t* [without having read *e*]

5.3.4.2 Scrambling

(129G) ? weil er *den Artikel* [ohne PRO vorher *e* zu lesen] *t* ablegte
        bec. he the article   without first   to read   filed
        'because he filed the article without first having read it'

5.3.4.3 Heavy-NP Shift

(130E) John offended t [by not recognizing e immediately]
        his favorite uncle from Cleveland
        (from Chomsky [1982b])

Things are different when we look at the final three construction types.

5.3.4.4 DP-Movement

DP-movement does not license parasitic gaps, as is well-known.

(131E) * The article was filed *t* [without having read *e*]

5.3.4.5 Object Shift

Object Shift behaves like DP-movement.

(132S) *Jag kastade *den* inte *t* [innan jag hade läst *e*]
        I   threw   it   not   before I   had read
        'I didn't throw it away before I had read it' (from Holmberg
        [1986, 173])

5.3.4.6 AP-Adjunction

As far as I can see it is not possible to test whether the AP-adjunction construction can contain parasitic gaps, since the movement of the complement is too local to construct a potential parasitic gap configuration.

We conclude that the first three constructions pattern together again.

5.3.5 The Mover Can Strand a Preposition

5.3.5.1 WH-Movement

(133E) *Who* did John talk [$_{PP}$ *to* t]

5.3.5.2 Scrambling

(134G) weil *da*   niemand [_PP_ *t gegen*] war
bec. that nobody   against was

5.3.5.3 Heavy-NP Shift

HNPS falls out of the paradigm this time. Although both WH-movement and Scrambling can strand prepositions, this is not possible with HNPS.

(135E) *John spoke [_PP_ *to* t] of his troubles *just about everyone who asked* (from Kayne [1984, 200])

It is noteworthy that there does not seem to exist any rightward movement (e.g. extraposition, etc.) that can strand a preposition. I will assume in the analysis that follows that it is this property of HNPS that is responsible for the effect, not its operator chain forming property. I will not be able to offer a further explanation for this constraint, however.

None of the other constructions allows the stranding of a preposition.

5.3.5.4 DP-Movement

In DP-movement, preposition stranding is only possible under very special, often lexically governed, circumstances (cf. Hornstein/Weinberg [1981]). Native speakers of English find sentences like the following dubious:

(136E) ?*The bridge* was slept under *t*

The remaining constructions do not allow preposition stranding at all.

5.3.5.5 Object Shift

(137S) *Jag tror   *det* inte [_PP_ *på* t]
I   believe it   not   in
(from Holmberg [1986, 165])

5.3.5.6 AP-Adjunction

(138S) *Han var [*sin hustru*] trogen [_PP_ *mot* t]
he   was his wife   faithful   to

Before I sum up the results of our data presentation in a survey, I want to present two additional properties that all four of the free word order structures have in common. First, all constructions allow multiple movement where possible; that is, it is possible that a construction involves movement of two constituents at once:

5.3.6 More Than One Element Can Undergo the Movement

5.3.6.1 Scrambling

In example 139 both the indirect object and the direct object have moved around the sentence adverb.

(139G) weil Peter [dem Jungen] [das Buch] nicht t t gab
        bec. Peter the boy   the book not   gave

5.3.6.2 HNPS

HNPS can also take two heavy constituents to the end of a sentence:

(140E) John told t t yesterday [a most incredible story]
        [to practically everyone who was still willing to listen]

5.3.6.3 Object Shift

It is also possible for both the indirect and the direct objects of a verb to undergo Object Shift at the same time.

(141S) Jag gav [henne] [den] inte t t
        I   gave her   it   not

5.3.6.4 AP-Adjunction

And, finally, two complements of an adjective can adjoin to AP.

(142G) weil wir [ihm] [das] schuldig t t sind
        bec. we him   that indebted   are
        'We owe him that'

The second property that I want to check the four constructions for is whether the moved element can pied-pipe its mother constituent.

5.3.7 The Moved Element Can Pied-Pipe Its Mother Constituent

We derived a theorem in Chapter 4 that said that moved arguments should not be pied pipers.

(143) The antecedent of a constituent in a θ-position is not a pied piper.

We can put this prediction to the test now, although it will not tell us anything about argument chains vs. operator chains, since neither head should be a pied piper. Nevertheless it is of some interest to test whether our assumptions in this chapter are consistent with those in Chapter 4.

5.3.7.1 Scrambling

With respect to Scrambling, the prediction is correct. The following sentence proves a scrambled element to be incapable of pied-piping the constituent to which it is adjoined.

(144G) *[*Was* gestern   gelesen] hat Hans
          what yesterday read   has Hans

5.3.7.2 Heavy-NP Shift

We get the same outcome if we construct the relevant structure on the basis of Heavy-NP Shift.

(145E)   *[Given to the girl *which interesting book you mentioned*] has John?

5.3.7.3 Object Shift

Shifted objects also behave as expected; that is, they are never pied pipers.[13]

(146I) *[$_{VP}$ *Hverju* ekki] tyndi Jón t ?
          what   not   lost   John
        'What did John not lose'

5.3.7.4 AP-Adjunction

AP-adjunction also confirms 143: an AP-adjoined phrase is not a pied piper:

(147G) *[*Wem* treu]   ist Hans?
          who faithful is Hans

Let us now collect the results of our investigation in two surveys, one that shows the properties of operator chains and one with the properties of argument chains.

(148)

	Operator chains		
	WH-mvt	Scrambling	HNPS
1. Movement constraints	+	+	+
2. Moves DP	+	+	+
3. Moves PP	+	+	+
4. Mover lacks Case	+	+	+
5. Licenses parasitic gaps	+	+	+
6. Strands prepositions	+	+	–
7. Multiple movement		+	+
8. Pied Piping		–	–

13. Examples of this sort may of course also be ungrammatical for the additional reason that we have moved a constituent whose head has been extracted. Be that as it may, they are at least ungrammatical for the reason that a moved argument cannot be a pied piper.

(149)

	Argument chains		
	DP-mvt	Object shift	APA
1. Movement constraints	+	+	+
2. Moves DP	+	+	+
3. Moves PP	−	−	−
4. Mover lacks Case	−	−	−
5. Licenses parasitic gaps	−	−	−
6. Strands prepositions	−	−	−
7. Multiple movement		+	+
8. Pied Piping		−	−

I have taken the freedom to fill in a suitable value for those properties that were not testable for one reason or another so that the entries in the surveys are licensed by the absence of evidence against them rather than by the existence of evidence in their favor.

With the exception of the preposition stranding behavior of HNPS, our data allow us to state that the properties of Scrambling and HNPS precisely mirror those of WH-movement (where testable) and that the properties of Object Shift and AP-Adjunction mirror those of DP-movement (where testable). We thus arrive at the conclusion in 150.

(150) *Generalization Concerning Free Word Order in Germanic*
    a. Scrambling and Heavy-NP Shift form Operator chains.
    b. Object Shift and AP-Adjunction form DP-chains.

It is clear that, should we succeed in deriving this generalization, we can predict most of the syntactic properties of the four free word order constructions of Germanic that we set out to examine in this chapter. In the next section I will try to convince the reader that 150 is indeed derivable from independent properties of the free word order structures, in particular, properties that can be assigned by parameters that are in full compliance with the restrictions imposed by the Saturation Condition.

5.4 Deriving the Chain Type Difference

5.4.1 Operator and Argument Features

The preceding sections of this chapter have demonstrated (1) that the conceptually most satisfactory treatment of the free word order structures is indeed the one that is called for independently by the empirical observation that scrambling structures obey all constraints on movement, at least in German; and (2) that the major free word order structures of German and English form operator chains, whereas those of Scandinavian form argument chains.

With the above facts established, we are very close to an appealing overall theory of free word order that can be expressed with the tools available in the Principles and Parameters approach for other constructions. So far in our analysis of free word order we have made use of the concepts "chain" and "modifier"; the first mechanism is independently needed for the description of such constructions as passive and raising (i.e. argument movement), and WH-movement and topicalization (i.e. operator movement). The concept "modifier" is required for a correct analysis of adjuncts such as relative clauses/adverbs and is used in the theory of pied piping.

To be able to derive all the correct predictions of our theory of free word order from the established modular framework, we need to find only one more link between our analysis and the concept of "chain," namely we have to answer the questions in 151.

(151) a. Why can scrambled/HNP-shifted elements head operator chains?
b. Why can O-shifted and AP-adjoined elements head argument chains?

A comparison with DP- and WH-movement will allow the reader to see why the answers to 151 would complete our analysis. We remember, for instance, that WH-movement is analyzed as follows:

(152) *The Analytic Tools of Operator Movement*
a. WH-phrases are identified by a morpho-syntactic feature ([+ WH]);
b. [+ WH]-phrases can head operator chains;
c. [+ WH]-phrases specify C′ (in English).

These assumptions interact with other principles of the grammar; for example, X-bar theory allows the operator feature to percolate in well-defined ways, and the relevant constraints on chain formation account for the movement conditions to which WH-sentences are subject. DP-movement is analyzed in a similar fashion, except that the chain type and the morphosyntactic feature relevant for the head are different.

(153) *The Analytic Tools of Argument Movement*
a. DPs are identified by a morpho-syntactic feature ([+ Case]);
b. [+ Case]-phrases can head argument chains;
c. [+ Case]-phrases specify I′.

Note that 153 already answers 151b. As was shown earlier, only DPs undergo Object Shift and AP-adjunction, and the moved DP has to land within the Case-marking domain of its head if it needs structural Case. Consequently, we can identify the elements undergoing these processes in the Germanic languages by referring to the morphosyntactic feature "Case," just as the moved elements would be characterized in passive and raising structures. We automatically predict that Object Shift and AP-adjunction form argument chains, since a Case-marked DP can only form argument chains (cf. 153b). All we have to add, now, is information about the landing site of the moved elements, e.g. in the case of AP-adjunction that Case-marked elements can stand in a modification relation to expressions of category AP, as is shown by the fact that more than one element can AP-adjoin per sentence, in conformity with our assumption that modification is recursive.

This information is easy to incorporate into a local parameter in the IPF-model.

(154) Expressions with the feature [+ Case] can modify APs.

The major properties of the AP-adjunction construction follow from the one simple local statement 154 that qualifies as a possible parameter of natural language in the IPF theory, since it obeys the Saturation Condition and all other constraints on parameters developed in Chapter 1. Only DPs can undergo AP-adjunction, the moved argument must be separated from its head adjective by the specifier (if there is one), but otherwise the movement is local, and the movement process displays none of the properties of operator chains. Furthermore, more than one element can undergo AP-adjunction within one sentence, for the reason just mentioned.[14]

14. One property that I have not built into the current presentation for ease of exposition is direction of Case-marking. Thus, there is a difference between German, Dutch, and Danish on the one hand, and Swedish, Norwegian, and Icelandic on the other in that AP-adjunction is obligatory in the first group and optional in the second. The following examples quoted from Vikner (1987) illustrate the difference between Swedish and Danish:

   (iS)   Peter var överlägsen *Martin*
          Peter was superior   Martin

   (iiS) Peter var *Martin* överlägsen t
          Peter was Martin superior

   (iiiDa) * Peter var overlegen *Martin*
             Peter was superior   Martin

   (ivDa)   Peter var *Martin* overlegen t
             Peter was Martin superior

We can account for these differences by restricting Case-marking by adjectives to the left in German, Dutch, and Danish, while allowing bidirectional Case-marking in the other languages. Our theory inherits this proposal from Koopman (1984). If θ-marking is to the right in all six languages, this predicts that PP-complements will always occur on the right, DP-complements occur to the left in German, Dutch, Danish, and on either side in Swedish, Norwegian, and Icelandic. This seems to be correct.

To derive the major properties of Object Shift in Scandinavian, we have to formulate one parameter each for MLS and Icelandic, since the constructions have slightly different properties in the two language groups. In the former, only pronouns can undergo the process, and the landing site is I', whereas in Icelandic all DPs move, and the landing site is VP. These differences are encodable in parameters that are well formed according to the theory of language proposed here.[15]

(155) *Object Shift in Scandinavian*
     a. Pronouns with the feature [+ Case] can modify I's.   (MLS)
     b. Expressions with the feature [+ Case] can modify VPs.

                                            (Icelandic)

All the above-mentioned properties of Object Shift that the two language groups share can now be derived—e.g. that only nominal elements can undergo Object Shift, that this process does not license parasitic gaps, that the shifted object has to land within the c-command domain of its Case-marker.

Having demonstrated that the major properties of AP-adjunction and Object Shift can be deduced from the IPF-compatible parameters in 154–155 and their interaction with other components of the theory, we now turn to

15. The theory presented here is in my view superior to that presented in Holmberg (1986) in unifying the four free word order constructions discussed in one precise chain theory that falls within the range of parametrization argued for independently on the basis of pro-drop, WH-movement, and directionality. However, this improvement would not have been possible without Holmberg's prior thorough investigation of the Object Shift construction, and his analysis still covers a number of aspects of this construction that my proposal glosses over.

Thus, Holmberg notes that the different domains of application of Object Shift in MLS and Icelandic, that is, in the former only pronouns can move, while in Icelandic there is no such restriction, correlate with another difference between these two language groups. While in MLS only pronouns show overt morphological case distinctions, in Icelandic all DPs do so. Consequently, Holmberg argues, the optimal descriptive generalization concerning Object Shift is that all and only M(orphologically)-Cased DPs can undergo Object Shift. If one allows reference in the grammar to a feature [+ MCase], then the two parameters for MLS and Icelandic would turn out to be even more similar, in fact, they would only differ in the adjunction site of the shifted object. My concern in this chapter was only to show that the four free word order constructions discussed can be captured with parameters of the sort motivated for the other grammatical phenomena mentioned above. The two Object Shift parameters formulated in the text satisfy these conditions, but do not yet express the largest possible generalization of this phenomenon. In a context that would not focus that strongly on the expressive power of Universal Grammar, I would of course follow Holmberg in trying to capture the most elegant generalization, even to the point that it can be avoided to stipulate different landing sites for MLS and Icelandic.

Holmberg's theory is empirically superior to mine in still another respect. His theory, but not mine, correctly predicts that Object Shift is blocked if the object has to cross over a verb particle or an unmoved indirect object. To account for these restrictions, Holmberg invokes Case-theoretic assumptions that would have to be added to my theory in one form or another.

Scrambling and HNPS. If we can similarly motivate the existence of a morphosyntactic feature in these constructions that can be made responsible for the operator characteristics of the moved phrases, then we have a complete and formalizable account of the free word order phenomena studied here. To this end we discuss HNPS and Scrambling once more, but now from a point of view that we have thus far ignored.

5.4.2 Characterization of Heavy-NP Shift

Is there any property of the HNPS construction that might explain that it forms operator chains rather than argument chains? I suggest that the answer to this question lies in the following characterization of HNPS from Rochement (1978) (emphasis added):

> I wish next to discuss a construction to which much attention has been given in the literature, but for which little in the way of a substantive analysis has been offered. This construction has traditionally been referred to as resulting from the application of the rule of Complex (or Heavy) NP Shift, but, as (69 d,e) show, heavy stress on the postponed NP obviates the requirement of "heaviness" [fn omitted]. *We will henceforth refer to this rule as FOCUS NP SHIFT (FNPS).* (Rochement 1978, 33)

Rochement notes that a necessary condition for HNPS is that the moved element be focused. We can illustrate this with the nice minimal pair 156 and 157.

(156E) * I introduced t to Mary [HIM]

(157E)   I introduced t to Mary [only HIM]

As 156 shows, pronouns cannot be HNP-shifted in English. Even focusing the pronoun alone does not make it focal enough to count as a grammatical Heavy-NP shifter. However, once we add a focus particle to the pronoun as in 157, all native informants agree that the sentence becomes grammatical. Since the difference in heaviness between *him* and *only him* is so small, it can be concluded that it is the focal strength of a constituent that decides its shiftability; that is, *the more focused an element is, the easier it is to Heavy-NP shift it.*

In analogy with the standard treatment of WH-phrases, it is natural to assume that the distribution of necessarily focused elements is also determined by a morphosyntactic feature; that is, we will assume that beyond the operator feature [+ WH] there is an operator feature [+ F] that has the function of licensing necessarily focused constituents. To fill the gap between the concept of operator chain and the requirement that HNP-shifted elements in

English must be focused, we merely add the following universal condition on operator chains:

(158) *The Universal Focus Constraint (First Version)*
       The head of a sentence-internal operator chain has to be necessarily focused, i.e. has to carry the feature [+ F]

With 158, it becomes possible to identify the phrases that can undergo HNPS (all [+ F] elements), and through its interaction with the properties of operator chains to derive the facts about HNPS structures mentioned in earlier sections. At the same time, our theory allows us to account for the discourse-pragmatic requirements to which the availability of HNPS is subject. The parameter licensing HNPS satisfies all constraints on parameters imposed by our theory.

(159) Nonverbal expressions with the feature [+ F] can modify VPs.

In the next section the examination of the focus behavior of Scrambling structures will guide us to the final formulation of the Focus Constraint, which will be interpreted as the unified explanation of the syntactic and discourse-pragmatic properties of the free word order structures involving HNPS or Scrambling.

5.4.3 Characterization of Scrambling

Our analysis of HNPS decomposes this phenomenon into the distribution and well-formedness conditions of the morphosyntactic feature [+ F] and the other modules of the Principles and Parameters system. We now turn back to Scrambling structures to motivate a similar account.

What I will demonstrate is that Scrambling, like HNPS, is subject to a focusation constraint, in this case the constraint that *the scrambled element must necessarily be unfocused*—i.e. that it has to carry the feature [− F], which will also be interpreted as an operator feature. As in the case of HNPS, all the syntactic properties of free word order structures in German will then be derivable from the interaction of the elements marked [− F] and the properties of operator chains.

To show that scrambled elements must necessarily be unfocused, we will rely heavily on the results of a study on the focus properties of different sentence types in German presented in Lenerz (1977). Thus, take the following sentences from the work just quoted which we assume to be base-generable:

(160G) Ich habe dem KASSIERER das Geld   gegeben
        I   have the   cashier   the money given

(161G) Ich habe dem Kassierer   das GELD gegeben
        I   have the cashier   the money given

Lenerz gives these data to demonstrate that in the base-generable order there
are no focus constraints on either the indirect or the direct object. Note, however, the effect Lenerz discovered when the direct object is scrambled around
the indirect object:[16]

(162G)   Ich habe *das Geld*   dem KASSIERER *t* gegeben
         I   have the money the   cashier   given

(163G) * Ich habe *das GELD* dem Kassierer   *t* gegeben
          I   have the money the   cashier   given

In the scrambled order we find a focus constraint. The scrambled direct object
has to be unfocused, while there is no such constraint on the indirect object
that is in situ.[17]

16. Lenerz' work stands in the tradition of such important contributions to German grammar
as Behagel (1892, 1929, 1930, and 1932). Throughout Behagel's work it is stressed that the order
of words in German is determined to a large extent by the relevance of the various constituents.
See also Boost (1955).

17. The statement needs some further interpretation, however, as Lenerz himself showed. Thus,
there are some well-defined environments in which the scrambled phrase *can* be focused. The
following sentence contains one such environment:

(iG) Ich habe *das GELD* dem KASSIERER *t* gegeben
     I   have the money the   cashier   given

What distinguishes (i) from the ungrammatical 163 is that the scrambled focused element here
has moved around a phrase that is itself focused.

The constraint on focusing scrambled elements is thus a relational one in that a scrambled
phrase must not be more focused than a phrase that it governs. That the constraint is to be formulated in such a way rather than as "a scrambled phrase has to be unfocused" is not surprising
when one takes into account that focus is a relational concept; that is, it does not make sense to
say that a phrase is focused or unfocused in isolation. Rather, one needs to state that a phrase is
focused relative to the elements in its environment. In this respect semantic focus does not behave
differently from phonological prominence. Thus, Liberman/Prince (1977) also argue that it does
not make sense to attribute "main stress" to a constituent in isolation. Rather, an element is more
prominent metrically than all other elements within a certain domain.

Even when one takes into account that focus has to be construed as a relational concept, our
focus constraint as stated is still slightly oversimplified in that it is not completely accurate empirically. Thus, Lenerz presents significant evidence for the claim that the focus constraint holds
between two constituents α and β in a government relation only if α (the governor) is more closely
related semantically to a predicate than β. Thus, the focus constraint holds in 163, because the
inverted patient argument is more closely related to the verb than the goal argument it comes to
govern after movement. Independent evidence that the patient argument is more closely related
to the verb than the goal comes from a number of sources, for instance idioms and compounds.

Thus, there are tens of idioms with ditransitive verbs in which the theme argument is idiomatic but the goal argument is free. Here are a few:

(iiG) jemandem den Kopf waschen
       somebody the head wash
       'to set someone straight'

(iiiG) jemandem die Suppe versalzen
       somebody the soup   make-salty
       'to spoil things for someone'

(ivG) jemandem einen Korb geben
       somebody a   basket give
       'to turn someone down'

(vG)   jemandem den Rücken stärken
       somebody the back   strengthen
       'to give someone encouragement'

However, there are few if any idioms in which the goal argument is fixed and the patient argument free. I have not been able to find any such examples.

Since the patient argument and the verb can form a constituent that can be assigned a noncompositional meaning so much more easily than a goal–verb combination, we can conclude that the patient argument is more closely related to the verb semantically.

We arrive at the same conclusion when we examine whether it is the goal or the patient argument that can be incorporated into a word with the verb through compounding. Thus note that all the ditransivtive verbs *schreiben* (write), *geben* (give), *verkaufen* (sell) can be compounded with their patient argument but not with their goal argument:

(viG) Briefe-schreiber   *Leute- schreiber
      letter writer   people writer

      Geld- geber   *Kinder- geber
      money giver   children giver

      Auto-verkäufer   *Leute- verkäufer
      car seller   people seller

To return to the focus constraint, Lenerz has found that if there is independent evidence that a scrambled phrase moves around an element that is more closely related to the verb semantically, then the scrambled element can be focused. The crucial examples involve psych-verbs with an external patient argument and an internal goal argument (cf. Grewendorf [1988] for good evidence that this is the argument structure of verbs like *gefallen*).

(viiG) weil [dem JUNGEN] das Buch [$_{VP}$ t gefallen hat]
       bec. the boy   the book   pleased has

Evidence that the patient argument—though external to the VP as shown by syntactic tests—is more closely related to the verb than the internal goal comes again from idioms involving the relevant verbs. Thus, it is typically the case that verbs of this kind form idioms with the external patient rather than the internal goal.

(viiiG) jemandem hat der Kopf geraucht
        somebody has the head smoked
        'somebody is mentally exhausted'

As Lenerz demonstrates, we also systematically find a focus constraint when an internal argument has scrambled around a VP-external adverb. This is shown by examples like the following:

(164G) weil er wohl das BUCH gelesen hat
        bec. he well the book read has
        'because he has probably read the book'

(165G) *weil er *das BUCH* wohl [$_{VP}$ t gelesen hat]
        bec. he the book well read has
        'because he has probably read the book'

The focus constraint on inverted orders can also be demonstrated with distributional differences between semantically definite and indefinite expressions. Thus, note that a definite DP can appear on either side of a sentence adverb like *wohl* (probably):

(166G) weil er wohl   das Buch gelesen hat
        bec. he probably the book read has
        'because he has probably read the book'

(167G) weil er *das Buch* wohl [$_{VP}$ t gelesen hat]
        bec. he the book probably read has
        'because he has probably read the book'

An indefinite direct object can only appear to the right of *wohl,* however— i.e. in its base-generated position.

(168G) weil er wohl   ein Buch gelesen hat
        bec. he probably a book read has
        'because he has probably read a book'

(ixG)   jemandem stehen die Haare zu Berge
        somebody stand the hair to mountains
        'someone's hair stands on end'

(xG)   jemandem steht das Wasser bis zum Hals
        somebody stands the water up to the neck
        'someone's up to his neck in it'

Thus, an empirically fully adequate focus constraint would have to be formulated so as to exclude a focused constituent from governing an unfocused constituent that is less closely related to the verb than the governee.

For purely expository reasons, the main text will abstract away from this more complex version of the focus constraint, since for the purposes of an explanatory theory of syntax it is sufficient to state that only elements marked [− F] are subject to the focus constraint whatever its exact formulation in a theory of discourse-pragmatics. We will thus continue to write that scrambled elements in German must be unfocused, relying on the reader's awareness that "unfocused" must be interpreted as laid out in this note.

(169G) *weil er *ein Buch* wohl [$_{VP}$ t gelesen hat]
        bec. he a   book probably read   has
        'because he has probably read a book'

Assuming that an unspecific indefinite phrase is inherently focused, the grammaticality judgments of the sentences in 166–169 follow automatically from
the constraint that an inverted element must be unfocused. Moreover, this
theory predicts that if an indefinite DP can get a specific reading—i.e. one in
which it would not have to count as focused—then it should be invertible.
Examples of this kind can indeed be constructed (cf. Lenerz [1977] again) and
show that the expectation is borne out. Thus, if we change the tense-mood in
169 to allow the indefinite DP to adopt a generic—i.e. a specific reading—
then the sentence becomes grammatical.

(170G) weil er *ein Buch* wohl [$_{VP}$ t lesen würde]
        bec. he a   book probably read would
        'because he would probably read a book'

The same effect appears strongly when we scramble a direct object around an
indirect object. The sentence in example 171, with an indefinite plural scrambled around an indirect object in a nongeneric tense environment, is sharply
ungrammatical.

(171G) *weil er *Blumen* [$_{VP}$ der Frau t gab]
        bec. he flowers   the woman gave
        'because he gave flowers to the woman'

If we change 171 into a generic present tense supported by a proper adverb
and by making the subject generic, the inverted indefinite direct object can
be interpreted as generic itself, and the sentence becomes fully grammatical.

(172G) weil man *Blumen* immer [$_{VP}$ der Frau t gibt]
        bec. one flowers always   the woman gives
        'because one always gives flowers to the woman (rather than the
        man)'

A final piece of evidence for the focus constraint comes from its effects on
relative frequencies of different word orders. Hoberg (1981) reports a statistical study on word order preferences in German. The survey presented in
173 is an excerpt from her results. As can be seen, the base-generable word
orders on the left are invariably more frequent than those in the same row on
the right, which would have to be derived by the scrambling process that is
focally constrained. Moreover, the survey documents the strong tendency to
prohibit indefinite DPs from inverting. Thus, although a definite dative precedes a definite nominative 18% of the time, an indefinite dative never pre-

cedes a definite nominative according to Hoberg's data, although—as a comparison shows—a base-generated indefinite nominative precedes a definite dative 57% of the time.

(173)

	Unscrambled		Scrambled
def Nom − def Dat:	82	def Dat − def Nom:	18
def Nom − def Acc:	99	def Acc − def Nom:	1
def Dat − def Acc:	60	def Acc − def Dat:	40
indef Nom − def Dat:	57	indef Dat − def Nom:	0
indef Nom − def Acc:	98	indef Acc − def Nom:	0
indef Dat − def Acc:	84	indef Acc − def Dat:	0
IP-Adv − def Acc:	73	def Acc − IP-Adv:	27
IP-Adv − indef Acc:	97	indef Acc − IP-Adv:	3

Hoberg's data thus provide additional support for Lenerz' insight that inverted orders (in the sense of note 17) are subject to a focus constraint, whereas noninverted orders are focally unrestricted.

These insights, combined with Rochement's observation concerning HNPS, allow us to unify the licensing conditions for the free word order phenomenon in the final version of the Focus constraint.

(174) *The Universal Focus Constraint (Final Version)*
The head of a sentence-internal operator chain must necessarily be focused ($[+ F]$) or unfocused ($[- F]$).

To capture the word order properties of arguments discussed earlier, the following IPF-compatible parameter is sufficient:

(175) *Scrambling in German and Dutch*[18]
Nonverbal expressions with the feature $[- F]$ can modify verbal expressions with the feature $[- Comp]$.

---

18. The word order facts of Dutch are similar to German with a few differences, cf. de Haan (1979), Hoekstra (1984), and Broekhuis (1988). Objects can in principle be moved around adverbs and other arguments, but it is harder to move direct objects around indirect ones, probably because Dutch, unlike German, does not have morphological case on full DPs to disambiguate different word orders functionally. The other major difference is that Dutch does not allow scrambling over an external argument that is highly topical, i.e. one that bears an agent θ-role. Psych-verb subjects can be crossed, since they typically bear the θ-role theme. It thus seems correct to me to allow syntactic adjunction to IP in Dutch also, and to make the pragmatic well-formedness conditions on the distribution of the $[- F]$ feature the reason why it is not allowed to scramble over an agentive subject. Supporting evidence for this view comes from German, where, though possible, it is also harder to scramble over an agentive subject than over an object or a nonagentive subject. This is exactly one of the points made in Lenerz (1977).

The parameter allows necessarily unfocused DP and PP arguments to appear in a modification relation with verbal, adjectival, and inflectional projections (e.g. the configuration under the top node of the tree diagram in 6). In conjunction with the modules of our theory, it predicts that more than one element can scramble per sentence (because the modification relation is recursive) and that the scrambled element cannot pied-pipe its mother node. Moreover, the analysis predicts that scrambling chains should share the major properties of other operator chains; that is, they should license parasitic gaps, should obey all movement constraints on operator chains, etc. It was shown earlier that these predictions are correct.

The previous discussion, especially the final version of the Universal Focus Constraint, completes our syntactic analysis of free word order structures by answering the question posed in 151a. Sentence-internally displaced elements that move out of the Case-assignment domain of their heads have to carry a morphosyntactic feature $[\pm F]$ that determines not only their *syntactic* but also their *discourse-pragmatic* properties. HNP-shifted elements must be $[+ F]$ and therefore (i) have to satisfy all movement constraints, (ii) can license parasitic gaps, can move categories other than DP; they are pragmatically identified as focused phrases, as analyzed in a proper theory of this kind. Turning to scrambled elements, they share all the syntactic properties with HNP-shifted constituents—that is they have all the properties of operator chains; moreover, relative to their environment they are pragmatically identified as unfocused constituents in the sense of note 17, again, as analyzed in a proper theory of such objects.

Before proceeding to discuss some further properties of free word order constructions, we emphasize once more the theoretical property that crucially sets our theory apart from other theories of free word order phenomena, i.e. its *compatibility with the Saturation Condition*. This is best illustrated by comparing the language-particular statements that we have made to capture the free word order phenomenon of German and English with the type of parameter postulated to be responsible for WH-movement phenomena in Chapter 1.

> (176) a. Nonverbal expressions with the feature $[- F]$
>   can modify verbal expressions with the feature $[- Comp]$.
>   (Scrambling)
>   b. Nonverbal expressions with the feature $[+ F]$
>   can modify VPs.   (HNPS)
>   c. Expressions with the feature $[+ WH]$ must specify C'.
>   (WH-movement)

When the format of relational parameters was motivated in Chapter 1 as obeying the Saturation Condition, this was done to restrict the range of parametrization of pro-drop, WH-movement, and directionality phenomena; free word order structures were not taken into account at that point at all. This chapter has shown that the constraints on relational parameters that the Saturation Condition embodies (i.e. that all such parameters assign a local relational property to a categorial property), constitute an even larger generalization, since they also restrict the free word order options of natural language to a domain that fully includes at least the pertinent Germanic phenomena, and hopefully also those of other free word order languages.

The Saturation Condition has thus emerged as a principle that on the one hand is conceptually well-motivated, and on the other hand is empirically highly explanatory in that it successfully limits, in a unified manner, the range of parametrization of such different facets of human language as pro-drop, WH-movement, directionality, and free word order.

If the phenomena mentioned above are at all representative of the general form-al structure of natural language (and, it seems to me, nature would have to be a perverse Cartesian deceiver to present us with a fragment of data in which these generalizations hold, but outside of which they break down completely), then they are crucial direct evidence against theories of grammar that do not contain a unified constraint on the range of parametrization of pro-drop, WH-movement, directionality, and free word order.

5.5 Other Free Word Order Languages

Our theoretical assumptions in connection with free word order phenomena in Germanic lead to the following typology of sentence-internal chains illustrated in 177.

(177)

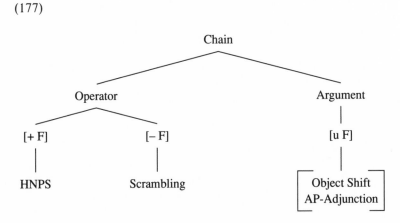

Sentence-internally, two types of chains can be formed: operator or argument chains; the head of an operator chain is either focused, leading to constructions like HNPS, or topical, leading to constructions like Scrambling. If the moved element is focally inert, then it can only form argument chains, with the consequence that only DPs can move and the movement is very local, since the head of a DP-chain has to be Case-marked. Given this system, we arrive at the following two expectations: if our system incorporates all mechanisms that Universal Grammar contains to license free word order structures, then these structures should obey all syntactic constraints on movement transformations where testable. To my knowledge, this prediction has only been tested thoroughly with respect to German in Webelhuth (1987, 1990, and the present work), and with respect to Bangla in Sengupta (1990). Saito/Hoji (1983), Saito (1985), and Hoji (1987) present important evidence from binding for the movement theory in Japanese, and de Haan (1979) and consequent work on Dutch leads to the same conclusion. The second prediction that our theory makes is that truly free word order languages—i.e. languages where both DPs and PPs (and maybe other categories) can move and where movement can lead out of the c-command domain of the mover's Case marker—should always be characterized by focus constraints on the individual word orders derived by movement, since the only way Universal Grammar allows to bring about an inverted order is through movement of a focally active element. On this prediction there is a substantial amount of data available from which I have drawn some excerpts for the presentation that follows (emphasis added throughout).

5.5.1 Dutch

> ... adverbials with scope over the whole clause can be freely scrambled with both direct and indirect object. ... Also other constituents can be scrambled, for instance direct and indirect object. ... What, then, is the parameter that gives Dutch a *relatively free word order* compared to English? (Koster 1987b, 5)

> NP-Placement [i.e. Scrambling; G.W.] has a *focus changing effect:* application of this rule reduces the number of possible foci. This can be demonstrated in quite a range of cases. (de Haan, 1979, 68)

5.5.2 Czech/Russian (Slavic)

> The former point is brought about by the *free character of the Czech word order.* (Sgall et al. 1973, 52)

> The properties of Czech word order (and to a somewhat lower degree, those of Russian) permit us to regard tentatively the order of symbols on the tectogram-

matical level as corresponding to the order of lexemic units with regard to their degree of *"communicative dynamism"*, . . . , that is to say, each lexical sememe has a higher degree of communicative dynamism than those standing to the left of it. (Sgall et al. 1973, 67)

5.5.3 Hungarian (Finno-Ugric)

Since in a large set of Hungarian sentences any permutation of the major constituents is grammatical, the conclusion of theoretically nonbiased traditional linguists has been that Hungarian *word order on the sentence level is basically free;* i.e. it is not rule governed. (Kiss 1987, 17)

Terminology of Hungarian Sentence Structure:

$$[_S \underline{\hspace{5cm}} \quad \underline{\hspace{5cm}}]$$
$$\text{inchoativum} \qquad\qquad \text{bulk}$$

In the Hungarian sentence, the inchoativum can consist of any, and any number of V complements. They are *always unstressed.* The bulk begins with the *most emphatic* complement of the V, which, if the sentence were an answer to a WH-question, would reply to the WH-phrase. (Kiss 1987, 36)

5.5.4 Tagalog (Austronesian)

Tagalog is basically a verb-initial language, but *word order among the full NPs following the verb is quite free.* There is a further constraint in the Tagalog clause in that one of the arguments of the verb must be put in focus. (Foley/van Valin 1984, 63)

Free permutation of the NPs is possible although there are some preferences . . . the NP in *focus* most commonly occurs in the clause-final position, and a *non-focused* actor in the immediately post-verbal position. . . . (Foley/van Valin 1984, 63f)

5.5.5 Warlpiri (Australian)

. . . Warlpiri exhibits *very free word order* on the clause level, and thus a sentence consisting of subject-object-verb-instrument-time constituents could result theoretically in 120 different combinations. (Swartz 1985, 1)

. . . the choice of a particular word order is determined by . . . *what has been talked about,* and by what if anything [the speaker] wishes to *emphasize.* (Swartz 1985, 15)

VO orderings seem to be called for in situations where . . . *the object is peripheral or is of relative insignificance* in terms either of the development of the story or in comparison with other participants. . . .

The order OV occurs in instances where . . . there is *contrastive focusing* of objects. . . . (Swartz 1987, 62,63)

5.5.6 Japanese (Altaic)

In Japanese, there is an *extensive scrambling rule*. . . . (Kuno 1972, 288)

. . . the distinction among theme, contrast, exhaustive listing, and neutral description . . . and the distinction, between *old, predictable information* and *new, unpredictable information,* which I showed to play a decisive role in Japanese syntax. . . . (Kuno 1972, 319)

5.5.7 Haya (Niger-Kordofanian)

Haya is a Lake Bantu language with basic SVO order. Definite objects (both direct and indirect) are distinguished from indefinite objects by the presence of an object agreement clitic in the verbal complex. Definite objects have them; indefinite objects do not. There is a left-dislocation rule which can *move object NPs to the pre-verbal position.* The NPs so moved must be *definite;* that is, there must be an object agreement clitic in the verbal complex. . . . Givón (1975) and (1976) report similar constraints in other Bantu languages, Rwanda and Swahili. Mould (1974) also reports this constraint for Luganda. Horton (1949) reports it for Luvale. (Tomlin 1986, 57f)

5.5.8 Quechua (Andean-Equatorial)

Quechua, like Hungarian, is basically an SOV language with *relatively free word order* in elicitation contexts. . . . Quechua differs from Hungarian in having a *topic*-marking suffix *-qa* and a suffix *-m(i)* that marks the *focused* constituent. . . . There is a strong tendency for the constituent marked with *-qa* to occur initially, even when it is a direct object; the constituent marked with *-m(i)* occurs in preverbal or postinitial position (as does the focus constituent in Hungarian). (Creider 1979, 16f)

5.5.9 Hindi

The word order in Hindi is however somewhat free. (Mahajan 1989, 4)

Special emphasis and context specification is required in some of the above variations. . . . (Mahajan 1989, 5)

Whereas the first prediction of our theory, the correlation between free word order structures and movement constraints, has not been seriously tested against most free word order languages, the second prediction seems fully vindicated, namely that free word order languages should typically show strong focus effects in their different word orders. To the extent that these data are representative, a theory of free word order like the one defended here is to be favored over theories that do not make such a prediction.

5.6 Scrambling and Binding Theory

The theory of Scrambling in German and Dutch that we have laid out in the previous sections makes the following predictions for the free word order structures in these languages:

(178)   Scrambling displays the same preposition stranding behavior as WH-movement contexts.
It obeys the Left-branch Condition.
It obeys the Specificity Constraint on extraction from DP.
It obeys the Coordinate Structure Constraint.
It obeys the Subject Condition.
Like WH-movement, it shows anti-crossover effects.
DPs can be scrambled.
PPs can be scrambled.
More than one element per sentence can be scrambled.
The scrambled element does not have to be c-commanded by a Case-marker.
Scrambling licenses parasitic gaps.
Scrambled phrases adjoin to verbal constituents.
A scrambled phrase is unfocused (in the sense of note 17).

In this section I discuss one final interesting property of scrambled elements, namely their binding-theoretic behavior. The data from German that I present will require a slight revision of the binding theory of Chomsky (1981), especially the typology of A and A-bar positions in this system.[19]

Taking as background the binding theory of Chomsky (1981), we face a paradox: scrambled phrases can enter both A-binding relations (a fact reported in Haider [1985] and inconsistent with my explicit claim to the contrary in Webelhuth [1984]) and A-bar binding relations as noted in Felix (1985) and Bennis/Hoekstra (1985). The following sentences establish the A-binding capacity of scrambled elements. We assume, as above, that the order

---

19. The data in this section have already been published elsewhere (cf. Webelhuth, 1987), but the information seems interesting enough to me to warrant its inclusion in this more complete presentation of a unified theory of free word order.

of the indirect and direct objects in the sentence in 179 is the only base-generable one.

(179G) Er hat [$_{VP}$ dem Mädchen einen Mann vorgestellt]
        he has   the girl   a   man introduced-to
                     IO   DO
        'He introduced a man to the girl'

The following sentence in which the indirect object binds the direct object is ungrammatical:[20]

(180G) *Er hat den Gästen einander   vorgestellt
         he has the guests each other introduced-to

However, when the direct object precedes the indirect object, binding *is* possible.

(181G) Er hat *die Gäste* einander   t vorgestellt
        he has the guests each other   introduced-to

The same effect we find with bound variable readings of pronouns. Sentences like 182 are ungrammatical, as noted in Webelhuth (1984). A pronoun within an external argument cannot be interpreted as a variable bound by a quantifier within an internal argument.

(182G) *weil seine Eltern [$_{VP}$ jeden Schüler besuchten]
         bec. his   parents   every student visited

However, in the work cited, I overlooked that this binding *is* possible if the object is moved to a position c-commanding the external argument.

(183G) weil *jeden Schüler* seine Eltern [$_{VP}$ t besuchten]
        bec. every student his   parents   visited

Examples 181 and 183 thus require an analysis of scrambled phrases as occurring in a position from which A-binding in the sense of Chomsky (1981) is possible.

As demonstrated in great detail earlier, however, scrambled phrases show virtually all the properties of operators; that is, phrases other than DP can be scrambled, they do not need to move to Case-marked positions, etc. In addition it was mentioned that scrambled phrases also license parasitic gaps, a property that discriminates between A and A-bar binders. I give another relevant example (from Felix [1985]):

---

20. This is still an underived fact in need of explanation.

(184G) ? Hans hat *Maria*$_i$ [ohne t$_i$ anzuschauen] t$_i$ geküßt
Hans has Maria   without to-look-at   kissed

From English-type languages we know that parasitic gaps can only be licensed by phrases in A-bar positions. Note the following contrast between WH-movement and DP-movement:

(185E)   [Which article] did John file t [without reading e]

(186E)   *[The article] was filed t [without reading e]

Since 184 is a grammatical parasitic gap example, we have to assume that the position occupied by the scrambled phrase qualifies as an A-bar position in the sense of Chomsky (1981).

That the scrambled phrases in 181 and 183 have to occupy an A-position in order to bind anaphors and pronouns, whereas the one in 184 has to be in an A-bar position to license the parasitic gap leaves us with two possibilities: (a) we maintain the distinction in Chomsky (1981) between A and A-bar positions and give the scrambled phrase the choice to assume one of these positional characteristics; (b) we reject the typology of positions in Chomsky (1981) and replace it with one that is compatible with the Janus-faced binding-theoretic behavior of scrambled phrases.

I will now proceed to show that the latter hypothesis is correct, i.e. that the theory of positions in Chomsky (1981) indeed needs to be modified.

According to the first hypothesis, scrambled phrases "choose" whether they occur in an A or A-bar position. This means that in a specific sentence they ought to show one and only one type of behavior: either they behave like an A-binder or as an A-bar binder, but they should not be able to show both types of behavior in the same sentence. The example in 187, including both an A-binding and an A-bar binding constellation, shows that this prediction is false.

(187G) ? Peter hat *jeden* Gast$_i$ [ohne e$_i$ anzuschauen]
seinem$_i$ Nachbarn t$_i$ vorgestellt
Peter has every guest without to-look-at
his   neighbor   introduced
'Peter introduced every guest to his neighbor without looking at'

To my ear this sentence, containing a scrambled phrase that licenses a parasitic gap and binds a pronoun at the same time, is as good or as bad as parasitic gap structures are in German. I cannot find a significant contrast between it and 184 above, which contains only a parasitic gap but no additional A-binding relation. The same effect can be achieved with anaphoric binding. Take as a neutral control sentence the following example:

(188G) ? Peter hat *die Gäste* [ohne e   anzuschauen]dem Pfarrer t
            Peter has the guests without looking-at   the   priest
            vorgestellt
            introduced-to
            'Peter introduced the guests to the priest without looking at them'

Now we substitute a reciprocal pronoun for the indirect object in 188, forcing it to be bound by the only plural DP in the sentence, the scrambled direct object.

(189G) ? Peter hat *die Gäste* [ohne e   anzuschauen] einander t
            Peter has the guests without looking-at   each other
            vorgestellt
            introduced-to
            'Peter introduced the guests to each other without looking at them'

I cannot detect a sharp decrease in grammaticality or acceptability in the transition from 188 to 189. If this judgment is correct, then the first hypothesis concerning the Janus-faced binding-theoretic behavior of scrambled phrases is disproved: the partitioning of phrase-structure positions into A and A-bar positions in Chomsky (1981) is too coarse; there has to be at least one more type of position, one from which both A and A-bar binding is possible at the same time.

Since we have deliberately chosen to focus on saturation phenomena in this book, I will only give a sketch of a revision of the theory of positional types that will predict the above observations.

The binding theory in Chomsky (1981) is stated as a theory of A-binding; that is, it defines binding constraints between two argument positions. Since the notion of A-binding is basic in this system, it categorizes argument positions against all others, in particular, against both operator and adjoined positions.

As we have seen above, this classification of positions is too coarse, since it cannot express the correct generalization that argument and operator (i.e. [Spec, C']) positions are indeed opposed binding-theoretically, but that adjoined positions pattern with both. The latter fact went unnoticed probably because the relevant data in its support are only available in a language with more overt adjunction than English, the language Chomsky's binding theory was based on.

What I propose, then, is that we maintain Chomsky's assumption that what it means to be an argument position is that only A-binding is possible from this position; but, contrary to Chomsky's theory, we will assume that the binding theory is formulated on two basic types of positions, i.e. we define [Spec, C'] as an operator position and decree that what it means to be an operator position is that only O-binding is possible from this position.

The theory resulting from the two assumptions that we have just spelled out leaves room for another type of position, one that is neither an argument position (like the subject or complement positions) nor an operator position (like [Spec, C']). The third type of position is, of course, exactly what we need for adjoined elements, and the theory predicts that elements in such positions should not be restricted in their binding potential, because they are not subject to the restrictions on argument or operator positions.

The predictions of the binding theory of Chomsky (1981) for English carry over to the revised binding theory just presented. The latter is an improvement over the former in that it predicts that the scrambled element in 189, repeated for convenience in 190, can bind a parasitic gap and a lexical anaphor in the same sentence, because it occupies a position not subject to binding theoretic constraints.

(190G) ? Peter hat *die Gäste* [ohne e   anzuschauen] einander t
Peter has the guests   without looking-at   each other
vorgestellt
introduced-to
'Peter introduced the guests to each other without looking at them'

This concludes our discussion of binding theory and Scrambling.[21] We first provided a detailed argument that the free word order phenomenon should be analyzed in terms of movement. Then, we proposed a general theory of

21. In a reanalysis of the paradigm presented here Mahajan (1989 a,b) has recently proposed to capture the binding-theoretic properties of scrambled sentences in terms of a radically enriched theory of phrase structure. In the earlier paper it is proposed that only base-generated specifier positions are available as landing sites of scrambling. Presumably because this theory was unable to match our theory's prediction that scrambling can license parasitic gaps (see footnote 26 of Mahajan [1989a]), the later work assumes that both specifiers and modifiers are possible landing sites. A binding-theoretic stipulation (roughly the counterpart of our theory of positional types) ensures that IP-internal specifiers can only A-bind while [Spec, C'] and adjoined positions can A-bar bind. In this way the additional IP-internal A-binding positions that we showed to be necessary are provided in a manner different from our original proposal.

Such a gross enrichment of phrase structure is undesirable on many grounds, both conceptual and empirical. I will sketch the major conceptual problems here, leaving the empirical difficulties for some other forum. cf. Webelhuth (in preparation).

this movement, including a chain theory that allows us to state the distribution of these structures in a manner analogous to WH-movement. We showed how different types of free word order fall into natural classes centered on the concepts of argument and operator chains. Finally, we adjusted binding theory slightly to generalize it to cases that the standard version did not cover. Most important, however, our analysis is cast completely in terms of concepts afforded to individual grammars by the Saturation Condition. I believe this is by far the most important result, because it shows that free word order is not a freak phenomenon, but joins the ranks of such everyday constructions as pro-drop and WH-movement.

The postulation of a large number of functional projections, including tense phrase, subject agreement phrase, indirect object agreement phrase, direct object agreement phrase (and at least one that remains without a name), is not in the spirit of reducing the theoretical options available to the language learner, especially because the proposals are not embedded in a theory of allowable parameters like the one developed in this book. Even less desirable than the unprincipled proliferation of categories is the fact that the categories necessary for the account to work are often and in some cases *typically absent* in the world's languages. For instance, the Mainland Scandinavian languages do not have subject agreement and no Germanic language has object agreement. With respect to the latter property Germanic is apparently typical among the world's languages, as it appears that not even a third of them have object agreement.

Equally disappointing from a conceptual point of view is that the enriched phrase structure theory, unlike our enriched binding theory, is not capable of describing Scrambling as a *unified process* in languages like German, Japanese, Korean, Bangla, and Hindi, where both DPs and other categories can undergo the movement process. Our theory is designed to capture the relevant binding-theoretic properties of Scrambling in these languages while invoking only one type of movement process, namely adjunction of a maximal projection. The enriched phrase structure theory must postulate two movements, one substitution for a specifier (to account for the A-binding properties of Scrambling) and one adjunction operation (to account for the fact that categories other than DP can move and that they can license parasitic gaps). Since many Scrambling languages allow both DPs and categories other than DP to move, it is desirable for the theory of grammar to make one unified process available to individual languages from which all its properties follow. The phrase structure theory fails in that respect and should be rejected.

The *major* conceptual objection to the enriched phrase structure theory is that it is not embedded in a theory of parametrization that succeeds in demonstrating that the range of differences between Scrambling languages is structurally analogous to the range of differences between WH-movement or pro-drop languages. In other words, the theory is merely a theory of Scrambling and not a theory of Scrambling as a construction following the same parametric restrictions as such comparatively well-understood constructions as WH-movement, pro-drop, etc. In contrast, our theory of Scrambling was purposely designed as embeddable into a general analysis of syntactic constructions that keep recurring in the world's languages. By demonstrating that the properties of Scrambling languages can be derived from a parametric framework that is general enough to cover such constructions as Scrambling, WH-movement, and pro-drop, while restricting the language-particular parametric options to selection of a sister in a binary branching tree, we have shown that Scrambling is not a "freak" or "voodoo" phenomenon that can only be captured at the cost of postulating violations of the Projection Principle, stylistic rules, or the "phantom" categories invoked by an enriched phrase structure theory.

Epilogue

The major goal of this book has been conceptual and very abstract. By examining the logical and empirical structure of Principles and Parameters we tried to shed light on the question of what "safeguards" have to be put into Universal Grammar for the system to be rich enough to account for the attested cross-linguistic variation, while at the same time providing the language learners with concepts rich enough to analyze the data of sense that represent their linguistic experience. The empirical topics of the foregoing chapters were chosen not only for their inherent interest but also because of the evidence they could bring to bear on the testing of our most far-reaching theoretical proposal, the Saturation Condition:

(1) *The Saturation Condition*
   a. Any well-formedness condition on saturation mentions only properties of the two elements of the saturation process;
   b. any two elements in a saturation process form a constituent.

In Chapters 1 and 2 we tried to demonstrate in detail that the Saturation Condition is of considerable explanatory value in that it restricts the parametric options of (1) WH-movement, (2) pro-drop, and (3) directionality phenomena to those that every descriptively adequate Universal Grammar must make available to individual grammars. Its effect consists in preventing such grammatical statements as those given in 2–4 from counting as possible parameters of natural language.

(2) *WH-movement*
   *Overt WH-movement applies in subordinate clauses if the subject of the main clause is expletive, but not if the subject is an argument.

(3) *Pro-drop*
   *Pro-drop is allowed only in sentences with a stranded preposition/ sentences with separable particles.

(4) *Directionality*

*Verbs govern to the right in sentences with doubly-filled Comps; elsewhere they govern to the left.

The above statements all characterize grammatical dependencies that cannot be expressed in phrase markers obeying the Saturation Condition. Since there do not seem to exist languages that would require parameter values of this sort, the Saturation Condition is a crucial component in the explanatory analysis of these three phenomena.

Chapters 3–5 argued that the Saturation Condtion leaves its characteristic mark on three additional construction types which, though independent of one another and the first three, are frequently attested in the world's languages.

Chapter 3 showed that—as predicted by the Saturation Condition—the categorial status of subject and topic sentences is not open to head selection. In this, these clause types differ from complement sentences. Since subject and topic clauses must have some category, however, there has to be some mechanism responsible for its choice. A detailed examination of the relevant patterns led us to propose two principles that seemed to make the correct predictions and also seemed independently motivated, the External Argument Universal and the Sentence Trace Universal.

Chapter 4 argued that the pied-piping phenomenon can be decomposed into the effects of various modules of grammar, including the Bijection Principle, the θ-criterion, and again, the Saturation Condition. The latter thus contributes to the explanation of why only specifiers and complements are potential pied pipers.

Finally, Chapter 5 contained a long series of arguments that the Saturation Condition also plays a role in the free word order phenomena of the Germanic languages. It was shown that four free word order constructions can be described successfully by invoking the process of chain formation familiar from such constructions as passive and WH-movement. This is exactly what we expect to find in a grammar based on the Condition, since its locality conditions on saturation force nonlocally dependent elements to be heads of chains.

Example 5 sums up all the evidence we have presented in favor of the Saturation Condition:

(5) *Evidence for the Saturation Condition*

Construction	Effect of the Saturation Condition
1. Pro-drop	Predicts that apart from pro, the availability of pro-drop can depend at most on the properties of pro's *sister constituent;*

2. WH-movement	Predicts that the properties of WH-movement depend at most on what kind of *sister constituent* WH-elements allow;
3. Directionality	Predicts that all word order generalizations can be reduced to statements on which side syntactic selectors take their *sister constituent;*
4. Argument clauses	Predicts that subject and topic sentences are not subject to idiosyncratic categorial selection, since they are not the *sister constituent* of a syntactic selector;
5. Pied piping	Predicts that the pied piping options of an element depend on the feature status and the grammatical relation of its *sister constituent;*
6. Free word order	Predicts that those orders in which a selector and its saturator are not string-adjacent *sister constituents* involve chain formation.

The fact that the Saturation Condition can be shown to influence the grammaticality judgments of a number of overtly independent constructions makes it a truly explanatory concept. In this sense it joins the ranks of such modules of the Principles and Parameters approach as θ-theory and Case theory, among others, which also derive their explanatory character from their global—i.e. construction and language-independent—domain of application. As universal, unbreakable, laws of grammatical structure, they collectively remove a large number of potentially formulable grammatical statements from the pool of possible hypotheses that language learners might bring to bear on the acquisition of their language. The remaining parametric options still allow for a wide variety of surface language types, and we hope that all natural languages can be projected into that class. Viewed from this angle, we arrive at a conclusion that might come as a surprise to some: for linguistic theory to be successful, it may not be necessary—in fact it might not even be possible—to establish a positive unity of the natural languages. It is sufficient, although rarely easy, to demonstrate that however different two arbitrary natural languages may be on the surface, linguistic theory unites them by showing how their constructions can be analyzed in terms of grammatical statements that satisfy the requirements of the Principles and Parameters approach.

With this outlook we conclude our journey through the Saturation phenomena of the modern Germanic languages, but not without giving the word one more time to Wilhelm von Humboldt who so long ago so wisely foresaw the conclusion we just drew:[1]

> ... probably the real reason for the multiplicity of languages is the internal need of the human mind to produce a variety of intellectual forms, a variety which, for reasons we do not understand, is limited, just as the variety of the forms of life in nature is limited. If one wants to pursue this similarity further, then one could possibly also argue that new languages don't really come into existence any more; rather only new versions, like what we witness in physical nature which is in general far more constrained.

---

1. Here is the original:

> ... vermutlich ist der eigentliche Grund der Vielheit der Sprachen das innere Bedürfnis des menschlichen Geistes, eine Mannigfaltigkeit intellektueller Formen hervorzubringen, welche ihre Schranke auf uns gleich unbekannte Weise, als die Mannigfaltigkeit der belebten Natur-bildungen findet. Will man diese Ähnlichkeit weiter verfolgen, so läßt sich vielleicht auch behaupten, daß eigentlich neue Sprachen nicht mehr entstehen; allein Spielarten viel mehr als in der, überhaupt weit fester begrenzten physischen Natur. (Humboldt 1973, 13)

Bibliography

Abney, S. (1987) *The English Noun Phrase in Its Sentential Aspect.* Ph.D. Dissertation, MIT, Cambridge, MA.

Aoun, J. (1985) *A Grammar of Anaphora.* Cambridge, MA: MIT Press.

Bach, E. (1983) "On the Relationship between Word Grammar and Phrase Grammar." *Natural Language and Linguistic Theory* 1, 65–89.

Bach, E. (1988) "Categorial Grammars as Theories of Language." In R. Oehrle, E. Bach, and D. Wheeler, eds., *Categorial Grammars and Natural Language Structures.* Dordrecht, Netherlands: Reidel, 17–34.

Bach, E., and R. Cooper (1978) "The NP-S Analysis of Relative Clauses and Compositional Semantics." *Linguistics and Philosophy* 2, 145–150.

Baker, C. L. (1979) "Syntactic Theory and the Projection Problem." *Linguistic Inquiry* 10, 533–582.

Baker, M. (1988) *Incorporation: A Theory of Grammatical Function Changing.* Chicago: University of Chicago Press.

Behagel, O. (1892) "Zur deutschen Wortstellung." *Zeitschrift für Deutschen Unterricht* 6, 265–267.

Behagel, O. (1929) "Zur Stellung des Subjekts im Nebensatz des Deutschen." *Zeitschrift für deutsches Altertum und Literatur* 66, 203–207.

Behagel, O. (1930) "Von deutscher Wortstellung." *Zeitschrift für Deutschkunde* 44, 81–89.

Behagel, O. (1932) *Deutsche Syntax: Eine geschichtliche Darstellung.* Heidelberg: Carl Winters Universitätsbuchhandlung.

Bennis, H. (1986) *Gaps and Dummies.* Dordrecht, Netherlands: Foris.

Bennis, H., and T. Hoekstra (1985) "Gaps and Parasitic Gaps." *The Linguistic Review* 4, 29–87.

Berwick, R. (1985) *The Acquisition of Syntactic Knowledge.* Cambridge, MA: MIT Press.

den Besten, H. (1977) "On the Interaction of Root Transformations and Lexical Deletive Rules." In W. Abraham, ed., *On the Formal Syntax of the Westgermania.* Amsterdam: Benjamins, 47–131.

den Besten, H. (1985a) "Some Remarks on the Ergative Hypothesis." In W. Abraham, ed., (1985) *Erklärende Syntax des Deutschen.* Tübingen, Germany: Narr, 53–74.

den Besten, H. (1985b) "The Ergative Hypothesis and Free Word Order in Dutch and German." In J. Toman, ed., *Studies in German Grammar.* Dordrecht, Netherlands: Foris, 23–64.

den Besten, H., and C. Moed-van Walraven (1985) "The Syntax of Verbs in Yiddish." In Haider/Prinzhorn 1985, 111–135.

den Besten, H., and G. Webelhuth (1990) "Stranding." In G. Grewendorf, and W. Sternefeld, eds., *Scrambling and Barriers.* Amsterdam/Philadelphia: Academic Press, 77–92.

Bever, T. G., and D. T. Langendoen (1971) "A Dynamic Model of the Evolution of Language." *Linguistic Inquiry* 2, 433–464.

Boost, K. (1955) *Neue Untersuchungen zum Wesen und zur Struktur des deutschen Satzes.* Berlin: Akademie-Verlag.

Borer, H. (1984) *Parametric Syntax.* Dordrecht, Netherlands: Foris.

Borer, H. (1986) "I-Subjects." *Linguistic Inquiry* 17, 375–416.

Bowers, J. (1987) "Extended X-bar Theory, the ECP, and the Left Branch Condition." In M. Crowhurst, ed., *Proceedings of the West Coast Conference on Formal Linguistics,* 47–62. Stanford: Stanford Linguistics Association.

Broekhuis, H. (1988) *A- en A'-Binden in het Nederlands.* M.A. Thesis, University of Amsterdam.

Chomsky, N. (1965) *Aspects of the Theory of Syntax.* Cambridge, MA: MIT Press.

Chomsky, N. (1970) "Remarks on Nominalization." In R. A. Jacobs, and P. S. Rosenbaum, eds., *Readings in English Transformational Grammar.* Waltham, MA: Ginn, 184–221.

Chomsky, N. (1981) *Lectures on Government and Binding.* Dordrecht, Netherlands: Foris.

Chomsky, N. (1982a) "Principles and Parameters in Syntactic Theory." In N. Hornstein, and D. Lightfoot, eds. *Explanation in Linguistics.* London: Longman, 32–75.

Chomsky, N. (1982b) *Some Concepts and Consequences of the Theory of Government and Binding.* Cambridge, MA: MIT Press.

Chomsky, N. (1986a) *Knowledge of Language: Its Nature, Origin and Use.* New York: Praeger.

Chomsky, N. (1986b) *Barriers.* Cambridge, MA: MIT Press.

Chung, S. (1984) "Identifiability and Null Objects in Chamorro." In *Pro-*

ceedings of the Tenth Annual Meeting of the Berkeley Linguistic Society. University of California, Berkeley.

Cinque, G. (1982) "On the Theory of Relative Clauses and Markedness." *The Linguistic Review* 1, 247–294.

Clahsen, H. (1982) *Spracherwerb in der Kindheit: Eine Untersuchung zur Entwicklung der Syntax bei Kleinkindern.* Tübingen, Germany: Narr.

Creider, C. (1979) "On the Explanation of Transformations." In T. Givón, ed., *Syntax and Semantics: Discourse and Syntax.* New York: Academic Press, 3–21.

Diesing, M. (1990) "Verb Movement and the Subject Position in Yiddish." *Natural Language and Linguistic Theory* 8, 41–80.

Di Scuillo, A., and E. Williams (1987) *On the Definition of Word.* Cambridge, MA: MIT Press.

Drach, E. (1937) *Grundgedanken der deutschen Satzlehre.* Reprint (1963). Darmstadt, Germany: Wissenschaftliche Buchgesellschaft.

Eisenberg, P. (1986) *Grundriß der Deutschen Grammatik.* Stuttgart, Germany: Metzlersche Verlagsbuchhandlung.

Ejerhed, E. (1982) "The Processing of Unbounded Dependencies in Swedish." In Engdahl/Ejerhed (1982), 99–149.

Emonds, J. (1978) "The Verbal Complex V'–V in French." *Linguistic Inquiry* 9, 151–176.

Emonds, J. (1985) *A Unified Theory of Syntactic Categories.* Dordrecht, Netherlands: Foris.

Engdahl, E. (1980) "WH-constructions in Swedish and the Relevance of Subjacency." *Cahiers Linguistiques d'Ottawa* 9, 98–108.

Engdahl, E. (1983) "Parasitic Gaps." *Linguistics and Philosophy* 6, 5–34.

Engdahl, E. (1984) "Parasitic Gaps, Resumptive Pronouns, and Subject Extractions." *Linguistics* 23, 3–44.

Engdahl, E., and E. Ejerhed, eds., (1982) *Readings on Unbounded Dependencies in Scandinavian Languages.* Stockholm: Almqvist & Wiksell.

Fanselow, G. (1986) *Konfigurationalität.* Tübingen: Germany: Niemeyer.

Farmer, A. (1980) *On the Interaction of Morphology and Syntax.* Ph.D. Dissertation, MIT, Cambridge, MA.

Felix, S. (1985) "Parasitic Gaps in German." In W. Abraham, ed., *Erklärende Syntax des Deutschen.* Tübingen, Germany: Narr, 173–200.

Fiva, T. (1984) "NP-internal Chains in Norwegian." *Nordic Journal of Linguistics* 8, 25–47.

Foley, W., and R. van Valin (1984) *Functional Syntax and Universal Grammar.* Cambridge: Cambridge University Press.

Frege, G. (1984) *Collected Papers on Mathematics, Logic, and Philosophy.* Edited by B. McGuinness. Oxford: Basil Blackwell.

Gazdar, G., E. Klein, G. Pullum, and I. Sag (1985) *Generalized Phrase Structure Grammar.* Cambridge, MA: Harvard University Press.

Gold, E. (1967) "Language Identification in the Limit." *Information and Control* 10, 447–474.

Grewendorf, G. (1986) "Relativsätze im Deutschen: Die Rattenfänger-Konstruktion." *Linguistische Berichte* 105, 409–434.

Grewendorf, G. (1988) *Ergativity in German.* Dordrecht, Netherlands: Foris.

Grimshaw, J. (1979) "Complement Selection and the Lexicon." *Linguistic Inquiry* 10, 279–426.

Grimshaw, J. (1986) "Nouns, Arguments and Adjuncts." Unpublished Manuscript, Brandeis University, Waltham, MA.

de Haan, G. (1979) *Conditions on Rules.* Dordrecht, Netherlands: Foris.

Haider, H. (1981) "Dependenzen und Konfigurationen." *Groninger Arbeiten zur Germanistischen Linguistik* 21, 1–59.

Haider, H. (1984) "Der Rattenfängerei muß ein Ende gemacht werden." Unpublished Manuscript, University of Vienna.

Haider, H. (1985) "The Case of German." In J. Toman, ed., *Issues in German Grammar.* Dordrecht, Netherlands: Foris, 65–101.

Haider, H., and M. Prinzhorn, eds., (1985) *Verb Second Phenomena in Germanic Languages.* Dordrecht, Netherlands: Foris.

Hale, K. (1983) "Warlpiri and the Grammar of Nonconfigurational Languages." *Natural Language and Linguistic Theory* 1, 5–48.

Harbert, W. (1989) "Subjects of Prepositions." Unpublished Manuscript, Cornell University, Ithaca, NY.

Heim, I. (1982) *Semantics of Definite and Indefinite Noun Phrases.* Ph.D. Dissertation, University of Massachusetts, Amherst, MA.

Hellan, L. (1986) "The Headedness of NPs in Norwegian." In P. Muysken, and H. v. Riemsdijk, eds., *Features and Projections.* Dordrecht, Netherlands: Foris, 89–122.

Hellan, L., and K. Koch Christensen, eds., (1986) *Topics in Scandinavian Syntax.* Dordrecht, Netherlands: Reidel.

Hoberg, U. (1981) *Die Wortstellung in der geschriebenen deutschen Gegenwartssprache.* München: Hueber.

Hoekstra, T. (1984) *Transitivity: Grammatical Relations in Generative Grammar.* Dordrecht, Netherlands: Foris.

Höhle, T. (1982) "Explikation für 'normale Betonung' und 'normale Wortstellung'." In W. Abraham, ed., *Satzglieder im Deutschen.* Tübingen, Germany: Narr, 75–153.

Hoji, H. (1987) *Hierarchical Structures and LF Representations in Japanese.* Ph.D. Dissertation, University of Washington, Seattle, WA.

Holmberg, A. (1983) "The Finite Sentence in Swedish and English." *Work-*

ing Papers in Scandinavian Syntax 3, University of Trondheim, Norway.

Holmberg, A. (1986) *Word Order and Syntactic Features in the Scandinavian Languages and English.* Ph.D. Dissertation, University of Stockholm, Sweden.

Holmberg, A. (1988) "On Bare Infinitivals in Swedish." Unpublished Manuscript, University of Uppsala, Sweden.

Hornstein, N., and A. Weinberg (1981) "Case Theory and Preposition Stranding." *Linguistic Inquiry* 12, 55–92.

Huang, J. (1982) *Logical Relations in Chinese and the Theory of Grammar.* Ph.D. Dissertation, MIT, Cambridge, MA.

von Humboldt, W. (1904) *Gesammelte Schriften.* Berlin: Königlich Preußische Akademie der Wissenschaften.

von Humboldt, W. (1973) "Über den Dualis." In W. v. Humboldt, *Schriften zur Sprache.* Stuttgart, Germany: Reclam, 21–29.

Huybregts, M. (1987) "On ECP Asymmetries and Pied Piping." Handout from the NELS Conference in Toronto, Canada, November 1987.

Huybregts, R., and H. v. Riemsdijk (1985) "Parasitic Gaps and ATB." *Tilburg Papers in Language and Literature.* Tilburg University, The Netherlands.

Hyams, N. (1987) "The Theory of Parameters and Syntactic Development." In Roeper/Williams (1987), 1–22.

Jackendoff, R. (1972) *Semantic Interpretation in Generative Grammar.* Cambridge, MA: MIT Press.

Jelinek, E. (1984) "Empty Categories, Case, and Configurationality." *Natural Language and Linguistic Theory* 2.1, 39–76.

Jespersen, O. (1927) *A Modern English Grammar on Historical Principles.* Heidelberg: C. Winter.

Kamp, H. (1981) "A Theory of Truth and Semantic Representation." In J. Groenendijk, T. Janssen, and M. Stokhof, eds., *Truth, Interpretation and Information.* Dordrecht, Netherlands: Foris, 1–41.

Kayne, R. (1984) *Connectedness and Binary Branching.* Dordrecht, Netherlands: Foris.

Kayne, R. (1985) "Principles of Particle Constructions." In J. Guéron, H.-G. Obenauer, and J.-Y. Pollock, eds., *Grammatical Representation.* Dordrecht, Netherlands: Foris, 101–140.

Kiparsky, P. (1973) "Elsewhere in Phonology." In Anderson, S., and P. Kiparsky, eds., *A Festschrift for Morris Halle.* New York: Holt, Rinehart, and Winston, 93–106.

Kiss, K. (1987) *Configurationality in Hungarian.* Dordrecht, Netherlands: Foris.

Klima, E.S. and U. Bellugi (1966) "Syntactic Regularities in the Speech of Children." In J. Lyons and R. J. Wales, eds., *Psycholinguistic Papers.* Edinburgh: Edinburgh University Press.

Koopman, H. (1983) *The Syntax of Verbs.* Dordrecht, Netherlands: Foris.

Koopman, H. (1984) "On Deriving Deep and Surface Order." In C. Jones and P. Sells, eds., *Proceedings of NELS 14.* University of Massachusetts, Amherst, MA, 220–235.

Koopman, H., and D. Sportiche (1982) "Variables and the Bijection Principle." *The Linguistic Review* 2, 139–160.

Koster, J. (1975) "Dutch as an SOV Language." *Linguistic Analysis* 1, 111–136.

Koster, J. (1978) "Why Subject Sentences Don't Exist." In S. J. Keyser, ed., *Recent Transformational Studies in European Languages.* Cambridge, MA: MIT Press, 53–64.

Koster, J. (1987a) *Domains and Dynasties: The Radical Autonomy of Syntax.* Dordrecht, The Netherlands: Foris.

Koster, J. (1987b) "The Relation Between Pro-Drop, Scrambling, and Verb Movements." *Groningen Papers in Theoretical and Applied Linguistics* 1, University of Groningen, The Netherlands.

Koster, J., and R. May (1982) "On the Constituency of Infinitives." *Language* 58, 116–143.

Kuno, S. (1972) "Functional Sentence Perspective." *Linguistic Inquiry* 3, 269–320.

Lebeaux, D. (1986) "The Interpretation of Derived Nominals." In A. M. Farley, P. T. Farley, and K.-E. McCullough, eds., *Papers from the General Session at the Twenty-Second Regional Meeting of the Chicago Linguistics Society.* Chicago: Department of Linguistics, 231–247.

Lebeaux, D. (1989) *Language Acquisition and the Form of Grammar.* Ph.D. Dissertation, University of Massachusetts, Amherst, MA.

Lenerz, J. (1977) *Zur Abfolge Nominaler Satzglieder im Deutschen.* Tübingen, Germany: Narr.

Liberman, M., and A. Prince (1977) "On Stress and Lingusitic Rhythm." *Linguistic Inquiry* 8.2, 249–336.

Lieber, R. (1980) *On the Organization of the Lexicon.* Ph.D. Dissertation, MIT, Cambridge, MA.

Mahajan, A. (1989a) "On the A/A-bar Distinction: Scrambling, Weak Crossover, and Binding in Hindi." Unpublished Mansucript, MIT, Cambridge, MA.

Mahajan, A. (1989b) *The A/A-bar Distinction and Movement Theory.* Ph.D. Dissertation, MIT, Cambridge, MA.

Manzini, R., and K. Wexler (1987) "Parameters, Binding Theory and Learnability." *Linguistic Inquiry* 18, 413–444.

McConnell-Ginet, S. (1982) "Adverbs and Logical Form." *Language* 58.1, 144–184.

Mills, A. (1984) *The Acquisition of Gender in English and German.* Habilitationsschrift, University of Tübingen, Germany.

Montague, R. (1973) "The Proper Treatment of Quantification in Ordinary English." In R. H. Thomason, ed., *Formal Philosophy: Selected Papers of Richard Montague.* New Haven, CT: Yale University Press, 247–270.

Montalbetti, M. (1984) *After Binding.* Ph.D. Dissertation, MIT, Cambridge, MA.

Partee, B. (1973) "Some Transformational Extensions of Montague Grammar." *Journal of Philosophical Logic* 2, 509–534.

Pesetsky, D. (1982) *Paths and Categories.* Ph.D. Dissertation, MIT, Cambridge, MA.

Platzack, C. (1983) "Existential Sentences in English, German, Icelandic, and Swedish." In F. Karlsson, ed., *Papers from the Seventh Scandinavian Conference of Linguistics.* University of Helsinki Publications No. 9, 80–100.

Platzack, C. (1984) "Clausal Complements in the Scandinavian Languages." Unpublished Manuscript, University of Lund, Sweden.

Platzack, C. (1986) "Comp, Infl, and Germanic Word Order." In Hellan/Koch Christensen (1986), 185–234.

Pollard, C. and I. Sag (1987) *Information-Based Syntax and Semantics.* Stanford, CA: CSLI.

Pollock, J.-Y. (1988) "Verb Movement, Universal Grammar, and the Structure of IP." *Linguistic Inquiry* 20.3, 365–424.

Postal, P., and G. Pullum (1988) "Expletive Noun Phrases in Subcategorized Positions." *Linguistic Inquiry* 19.4, 635–670.

Reinhart, T. (1976) *The Syntactic Domain of Anaphora.* Ph.D. Dissertation, MIT, Cambridge, MA.

Reis, M. (1985) "Satzeinleitende Strukturen im Deutschen: über COMP, Haupt- und Nebensätze, W-Bewegung und die Doppelkopfanalyse." In W. Abraham, ed., *Erklärende Syntax des Deutschen.* Tübingen, Germany: Narr, 271–311.

v. Riemsdijk, H. (1978) *A Case Study in Syntactic Markedness.* Dordrecht, Netherlands: Foris.

v. Riemsdijk, H. (1985) "Zum Rattenfängereffekt bei Infinitiven in deutschen Relativsätzen." In W. Abraham, ed., *Erklärende Syntax des Deutschen.* Tübingen, Germany: Narr, 75–98.

Rizzi, L. (1982) *Issues in Italian Syntax.* Dordrecht, Netherlands: Foris.

Rochement, M. (1978) *A Theory of Stylistic Rules in English.* Ph.D. Dissertation, University of Massachusetts, Amherst, MA.

Ross, J. R. (1967) *Constraints on Variables in Syntax.* Ph.D. Dissertation, MIT, Cambridge, MA.

Safir, K. (1982) *Syntactic Chains and the Definiteness Effect.* Ph.D. Dissertation, MIT, Cambridge, MA.

Safir, K. (1985) *Syntactic Chains.* Cambridge: Cambridge University Press.

Safir, K. (1987) "Comments on Wexler and Manzini." In Roeper/Williams (1987), 77–89.

Saito, M. (1985) *Some Asymmetries in Japanese and Their Theoretical Interpretation.* Ph.D. Dissertation, MIT, Cambridge, MA.

Saito, M. (1990) "Long Distance Scrambling in Japanese." Unpublished Manuscript, University of Connecticut, Storrs, CT.

Saito, M., and H. Hoji (1983) "Weak Crossover and Move Alpha in Japanese." *Natural Language and Linguistic Theory* 1, 245–259.

Scherpenisse, W. (1986) *The Connection between Base Structure and Linearization Restrictions in German and Dutch.* Frankfurt: Peter Lang.

Selkirk, E. (1982) *The Syntax of Words.* Cambridge, MA: MIT Press.

Sells, P. (1983) "Relative Clauses." Unpublished Manuscript, University of Massachusetts, Amherst, MA.

Sengupta, G. (1990) *Binding and Scrambling in Bangla.* Ph.D. Dissertation, University of Massachusetts, Amherst, MA.

Sgall, P., E. Hajicová, and E. Benesová (1973) *Topic, Focus and Generative Semantics.* Kronberg, Finland: Scriptor.

Steedman, M. (1985) "Dependency and Coordination in the Grammar of Dutch and English." *Language* 61, 523–568.

Stowell, T. (1981) *Origins of Phrase Structure.* Ph.D. Dissertation, MIT, Cambridge, MA.

Swartz, S. (1985) "Pragmatic Structure and Word Order in Warlpiri." Unpublished Manuscript, Summer Institute of Linguistics.

Swartz, S. (1987) *Measuring Naturalness in Translation by Means of a Statistical Analysis of Warlpiri Narrative Texts with Special Emphasis on Word Order Principles.* Preliminary Draft of M.A. Thesis, Pacific College of Graduate Studies.

Tappe, T. (1984) *Struktur und Restrukturierung: Eine Untersuchung zur Strukturkonzeption der Generativen Grammatik.* Ph.D. Dissertation, University of Göttingen, Germany.

Taraldsen, T. (1981) "The Theoretical Interpretation of a Class of Marked Extractions." In A. Belletti, L. Brandi, and L. Rizzi, eds., *Theory of Markedness in Generative Grammar: Proceedings of the 1979 GLOW Conference.* Scuola Normale Superiore, Pisa, Italy, 475–516.

Taraldsen, T. (1984) "Some Phrase-Structure Dependent Differences between Swedish and Norwegian." In *Working Papers in Scandinavian Syntax* 9, University of Trondheim, Norway.

Thiersch, C. (1978) *Topics in German Syntax.* Ph.D. Dissertation, MIT, Cambridge, MA.

Thiersch, C. (1982) "A Note on 'Scrambling' and the Existence of VP." *Wiener Linguistische Gazette* 27/28, 83–95.

Thráinsson, H. (1979). *On Complementation in Icelandic.* New York: Garland.

Tomlin, R. (1986) *Basic Word Order: Functional Principles.* London: Croom Helm.

Travis, L. (1984) *Parameters and Effects of Word Order Variations.* Ph.D. Dissertation, MIT, Cambridge, MA.

Vater, H. (1973) *Dänische Subjekt- und Objektsätze: Ein Beitrag zur Generativen Dependenzgrammatik.* Tübingen, Germany: Niemeyer.

Velde, M. van de (1977) "Der Nebensatztyp 'Ein Umstand, den zu berücksichtigen er vergißt' im Deutschen und im Niederländischen." *Studia Germanica Gandensia* 18, 73–118.

Vikner, S. (1987) "Case Assignment Differences Between Danish and Swedish." In R. Allan and M. Barnes, eds., *Proceedings of the Seventh Conference of Scandinavian Studies in Great Britain.* London: University College London, 262–281.

Webelhuth, G. (1984) "German is Configurational." *The Linguistic Review* 4, 203–246.

Webelhuth, G. (1986) "Some Data on the Verb-Object Relation in German." *Linguistic Inquiry* 17, 772–776.

Webelhuth, G. (1987) "A Universal Theory of Scrambling." In *Proceedings of the 10th Conference on Scandinavian Linguistics.* Bergen, Norway: Department of Linguistics, University of Bergen, 284–298.

Webelhuth, G. (1989) *Syntactic Saturation Phenomena and the Modern Germanic Languages.* Ph.D. Dissertation, University of Massachusetts, Amherst, MA.

Webelhuth, G. (1990) "Diagnostics for Structure." In G. Grewendorf and W. Sternefeld, eds., *Scrambling and Barriers.* Amsterdam/Philadelphia: Academic Press, 41–75.

Webelhuth, G. (forthcoming) "Binding Theory Parameters: A Reply to Manzini and Wexler." Unpublished Manuscript, University of Maryland, College Park, MD.

Webelhuth, G., (in preparation) "Scrambling without Functional Heads." Unpublished Manuscript, University of North Carolina.

Webelhuth, G., and H. den Besten (in prep.) "Remnant Topicalization and the Constituent Structure of the Germanic SOV-languages." Written Version of the GLOW Presentation, Venice, Italy, 1987.

Wexler, K., and R. Manzini (1987) "Parameters and Learnability in Binding Theory." In Roeper/Williams (1987), 41–89.

Williams, E. (1975) "Small Clauses in English." In J. Kimball, ed., *Syntax and Semantics: Volume 4.* New York: Academic Press, 249–273.

Williams, E. (1980) "Predication." *Linguistic Inquiry* 11, 203–238.

Williams, E. (1981) "Argument Structure and Morphology." *The Linguistic Review* 1, 81–114.

Williams, E. (1982) "The NP Cycle." *Linguistic Inquiry* 13.2, 277–295.

Zaenen, A. (1980) *Extraction Rules in Icelandic.* New York: Garland.

Index

A (= Argument)-chain, 157f, 159–214
A (= Argument)-position, 135, 205–10
A-bar. *See* Operator
Abney, S., 68*n*, 215
Accessibility, 8, 52*n*, 130, 132, 209*n*, 210*n*
ACI, 102
Adjective, 24*n*, 56–59, 70, 75, 82, 98f, 111, 122, 138*n*, 155, 165f, 174, 177*n*, 184, 191, 200
Adjective phrase (AP), 57, 78, 90, 99, 121, 128
  adjunction, *see* AP-adjunction
  and free word order, 159–214
Adjunct, 110ff, 175, 190
Adjunction, *see also* Scrambling; 110f, 126, 175, 177*n*, 182, 188, 192, 199*n*, 205
Adposition, 49*n*, 55*n*, 75f, 137, 140
Adverb, 22ff, 29, 70f, 126, 137*n*, 140, 145f, 160, 162f, 164, 167f, 175f, 187, 190, 197f, 199*n*
Adverbial, 54, 119, 121, 123f, 125, 177, 202
Affix(ation), *see also* Morphology; 55–64, 137–42
Agent (-of-Action), 134, 165*n*, 199*n*, 203
Agreement, 102f
Analogy, 131
Anaphor,
  and binding, 205–10
Antecedent, 93*n*, 94, 157f, 187
Anti-crossover effect, 172–74, 176, 178, 205
Aoun, J., 180, 215

AP-adjunction, 159–214
Argument (A),
  chain, 157f, 159–214
  clause, 66, 83–114
  feature, 189–201
  non-argument. *See* Operator
  position. *See* A-position
  structure. *See also* Theta; 56
Atomization,
  problem of, 47, 49, 55
Auxiliary, 184

Bach, E., 11, 77*n*, 215
Baker, C. L., 17, 215
Baker, M., 163*n*, 215
Bangla (= Bengali), 202, 209*n*, 210*n*
Barrier, 92*n*, 108
Base generated word order. *See Basic word order, Word order*
Base generation hypothesis, 160f, 164f, 179
Basic word order, 8, 67–82, 108ff, 140f
Behagel, O., 195*n*, 215
Bellugi, U., 68*n*, 220
Benesová, E., 222
Bennis, H., 76*n*, 101*n*, 175, 205, 215
Berwick, R., 17, 215
Besten, H. den, 76*n*, 88*n*, 91, 163*n*, 171*n*, 179*n*, 183, 215, 216, 223
Bever, T., 87*n*, 216
Bijection principle, 142, 143–58, 212
Binary branching, 11, 17*n*, 45, 209*n*, 210*n*
Binding, 12f, 17*n*, 39, 42, 43, 45, 103, 157, 169, 170–74, 205–10
  A-binding, 205–10